for Sandy –

~ yves –

Rachel

Oct. 2014

In the Illuminated Dark

In the Illuminated Dark

Selected Poems of Tuvia Ruebner

TRANSLATED & INTRODUCED
by Rachel Tzvia Back

Rachel Tzvia Back

HEBREW UNION COLLEGE PRESS
UNIVERSITY OF PITTSBURGH PRESS

Published by the University of Pittsburgh Press, Pittsburgh, PA, 15260,
and the Hebrew Union College Press, Cincinnati, OH, 45220

Library of Congress Cataloging-in-Publication Data
Ruebner, Tuvia, 1924–
  [Poems. Selections]
  In the illuminated dark : selected poems of Tuvia Ruebner / Tuvia Ruebner ;
translated and introduced by Rachel Tzvia Back.
    pages cm
  Includes bibliographical references and index.
  ISBN 978-0-87820-255-3
1. Ruebner, Tuvia, 1924---Translations into English. I. Back, Rachel Tzvia, 1960–
translator. II. Ruebner, Tuvia, 1924– Poems. Selections. III. Ruebner, Tuvia, 1924–
Poems. Selections. English. IV. Title.
  PJ5054.R49A2 2014
  892.41'6--dc23
                                2013042361
Book design by Raphaël Freeman
Cover design by Paul Neff

Permission has been granted for poems previously published by the following publishing houses:
Sifriyat Poalim; Even Hoshen; Keshev.

For Alice (Litzi) Ruebner

(1929–1942)

little sister

Between one voice and the next
suddenly she's

here, fleet-footed gazelle, quiet

as a shadow falling
over my open eyes

a figure lighter than fire

toying with me
with her games

"my father is dew
my mother the star's spire"

I'm still here and she's
gone.

CONTENTS

ACKNOWLEDGMENTS

This volume, born of devotion to Tuvia Ruebner's poetry, would have been impossible without the support and aid of many. It is a pleasure to now acknowledge and thank all those whose contributions to this project made all the difference.

Many thanks to the editors of the following journals and publications where earlier versions of translations first appeared: *Modern Poetry in Translation, Exchanges: A Journal of Literary Translation, Two Lines Online* (of The Center for the Art of Translation), and *Haaretz* English edition. I want to acknowledge in particular Sasha Dugdale of MPT and Vivian Eden of *Haaretz* whose enthusiasm for my renderings of Ruebner's poetry encouraged me greatly.

For their keen critical input and open-hearted support of this work, I am deeply grateful to Yiftach Reicher Atir, Aaron Back, Giddon Ticotsky, and Jeff Weinstock. I am wholly and happily indebted to John Linder, for his great faith in this book and for opening the right doors at just the right moment.

To David H. Aaron, I am profoundly grateful for his embrace of this collection and for the countless ways he has made this work inestimably better. His erudition, scholarly rigor and artistic spirit inform all parts of this volume. Many thanks to Sonja Rethy, for the incomparable care and intelligence of her editing, and for ushering this book through production with grace, professionalism and patience. My thanks also to Angela Erisman for the care and expert attention she has devoted to bringing this book into the public eye.

Many thanks to Meital Klachuk, for her help at every stage and for being the kind of research assistant everyone dreams of. I want to thank also Rafi Weichert, Ruebner's Hebrew editor, for his own devotion to Ruebner's work, which has resulted in poetry volumes that have enriched us all. Many thanks also to Norman Finkelstein for his generous and invaluable input.

I am deeply grateful to the Brown Foundation Fellows Program at the Dora Maar House, which provided me with the place and time to work intensively on these translations. It was during this month-long residency that a significant portion of the translation work was accomplished. I am particularly grateful to Gwen Strauss, resident director of the program, for her flawless facilitation of the fellowship, for her hospitality and kindness, and for all the ways she helped make that month as productive and peaceful as it was.

Many thanks also to Mishkenot Sha'ananim for hosting me at a crucial stage of my writing.

The Yehoshua Rabinowitz Foundation for the Arts also provided support for the project, and I would like to thank all those involved in awarding that grant.

Finally, to Talya, Ariel, Daniel and Yoni – deepest gratitude for accompanying me in this project these last three years, for listening to my endless deliberations about specific words and titles, for allowing this poetry to become part of our family life, and for contributing in real ways to making this work, truly, a labor of love.

Rachel Tzvia Back
December 2013

INTRODUCTION

I exist in order to say

these are the crossbeams and chronicles
of my parents, coal,
ash, wind
of my sister in my hair blowing
back and back...

I CHILDHOOD

Loss defines the "crossbeams and chronicles" of Tuvia Ruebner's life. Born in 1924 into a semi-secular Jewish family in Slovakia, Ruebner was also born into the catastrophe that would follow – the extermination of European Jewry and of his own family in the Holocaust. While his earliest childhood in the ancient town of Pressburg-Bratislava, situated along the banks of the Danube at the edges of the Carpathian slopes, gave no sign of what was to follow, Ruebner notes (on the very first page of his memoir *A Short Long Life*) the cursed coincidence of Adolph Hitler becoming Chancellor of Germany on January 30th, 1933 – Ruebner's ninth birthday. Six years later, in 1939, the race-laws enacted also in Slovakia banned all Jewish students from school; with the completion of ninth grade, Ruebner's formal education was ended.

His father, Manfred Moritz Ruebner (b. 1885), was a well-off, well-educated businessman; his mother, Elisabet née Ehrenreich-Grunwald (b. 1899), came from the more rural environs of Shastin, where her parents continued to reside. Ruebner's sister Alice, nicknamed Litzi, was born in 1929. With the horrors of Nazism spreading across Europe, Ruebner's father made preliminary plans to immigrate with the small family to Mandate Palestine; in 1938, he met with a representative of the Jewish Agency travelling through Europe and discussed buying land in the northern village of Shavei Tzion. The representative said he would return the following year – a return prevented by the onset of war; thus, the family's immigration plans were quashed. Meanwhile, the teenage Ruebner became more involved in the activities of Hashomer Hatzair, the Socialist-Zionist youth movement that Ruebner describes in his memoir as giving him and his peers "a feeling of self-worth in those days of constant Jewish humiliation" (48).[1] In 1941, permission papers to leave Slovakia were purchased for Ruebner and eight other youths by their families – papers that also stipulated they could never return to their native land. On April 28th, Ruebner bid farewell to his parents and little sister in the Pressburg-Bratislava train station – a farewell that Ruebner describes as "still weighing on my bones" decades later. From Bratislava to Budapest (where certificates permitting entrance into British-controlled Palestine awaited them), via the Black Sea to Istanbul, through southern Turkey to Aleppo in Syria, from there to Beirut and southward, the nine journeyed for weeks until finally crossing the border, at Rosh Hanikra, into Palestine.

Ruebner was settled in the Emek Yizrael (Jezreel Valley) kibbutz of Merchavia, where he worked as a shepherd, in the fields and kitchen, and in other branches of the communal economy; in the afternoons he and the other members of his group studied, primarily Hebrew and Bible. During his first six months in Palestine Ruebner still managed to exchange isolated letters with his parents and sister in Slovakia (and by then residing with the maternal grandparents in Shastin) – tiny missives of no more than twenty-five words, conveyed into occupied Europe via the International Red Cross. In January of 1942 Ruebner received what would be the last personal letter from his father: "Dear one, we've heard nothing from you since September. We hope you are well. We are all fine. Write every month. We think of you all the time. Loving kisses, your parents and everyone." Ruebner continued writing anxious and unanswered letters into the void. Only years later was his family's exact fate made known to him: in June 1942 his parents and sister were deported on Transport 46 from Shastin to Auschwitz-Birkenau, where they were murdered.

II 1943–1983

In 1944 Ruebner married Ada Klein, a fellow Slovakian immigrant. In 1945 World War II ended, the concentration camps were liberated, and records of the genocide slowly emerged. Israel's War of Independence broke out in 1948, and in 1949 Ruebner's daughter was born. A few months later, Ruebner and his wife Ada were involved in a bus accident; Ada was killed on impact and Ruebner was seriously wounded. After a lengthy hospital stay, Ruebner returned to the kibbutz and to his infant daughter, and, no longer able to do outside labor because of his burns and injuries, was appointed kibbutz librarian and high school literature teacher. Over the years, he became known in the still-fledgling intellectual and academic communities of Israel as a poet and man of letters, meeting with and befriending other immigrant writers such as Ludwig Strauss, Werner Kraft, Lea Goldberg and Dan Pagis. All of these figures shared the bifurcated identities of the Jewish European immigrant-refugee-survivor. In 1966, Ruebner was asked to join the faculty of Oranim College, and in 1972 he was invited to teach at Tel Aviv University and Haifa University. Eventually Ruebner devoted himself fully to Haifa University where, with only a ninth-grade education, he went on to become an esteemed and internationally known professor of German and comparative literatures.

Three years after the death of his first wife Ruebner married Galila Jizreeli, a pianist from Kibbutz Ein Harod, and two sons were born: Idan in 1956 and

Moran in 1960.[2] The wars in Israel marked the passage of time, and in early 1983, shortly after participating as a reservist soldier in the First Lebanon War, Ruebner's youngest son Moran left Israel to recover far from the battered and battering land. He stopped first in Boston to visit his parents (on sabbatical at Harvard), then journeyed on to South America. The few letters from the young man are full of detailed descriptions of the local landscapes and sites – and a starkly-stated desire to distance himself from the bloody Israeli reality. In a letter from mid-February, Moran asks after his father's new book, his mother's return to piano-playing, and then writes: "Don't write about what's happening in Israel, I don't want to know." The passage is underlined. Shortly after, the letters stopped. From that moment, all trace of Moran was lost, never to be found. "I see him every day before me," writes Ruebner in his memoir, "just as he looked [all those years ago] …. If only I could embrace him as I did then at the airport, I would be endlessly happy…" (153).

From a train station farewell in Pressburg-Bratislava to an airport farewell in Boston. From the anxious letters he sent to Europe in 1943 (12/5/1943: "My beloveds, no word, write! Has anyone heard from my parents? And Litzi, Litzi?"), to the desperate and unsuccessful search in 1983 for signs of the lost son. "Our dead live among us," writes Ruebner, "if we don't hide from them. Sometimes it seems to me I see them in the shadows of the air, more and more in the last years. No, I don't see them – I feel them" (33–34). The lost son and, above all, the lost little sister wander unceasingly through Ruebner's poems. Time does not distance their images or lighten the weight of their absence. "[Litzi] is closer to me now than she has ever been," writes Ruebner in 2006, sixty-five years after he said farewell to his little sister. "She has been for me the essence of grief and agony. When our lost son was added to her, one abyss did not cover the other" (79).

III 1983 AND ONWARD: LATE ACCLAIM

For many years, Ruebner's work was situated at the margins of the Israeli literary mainstream. One may surmise that various factors contributed to this position, from his rural locale (away from the Tel Aviv and Jerusalem literary centers), to his refusal to identify fully with the new Israeli culture and his continued focus on the lost European world. Ironically, his poetry, prose and translations all were lauded and celebrated in Germany long before they were recognized by the Israeli literary establishment. As early as 1955, Ruebner began receiving European literary awards, awards that later included the D. Steinberg Prize (Zurich, 1981), the Christian Wagner Prize (Germany, 1994), the Jeanette Schocken Prize (Germany, 1999), the Theodor Kramer Prize (Austria, 2008) and most recently the Konrad-Adenauer Prize (Austria, 2012).

At the very end of the twentieth century, Ruebner's work enjoyed a certain renaissance, and the demands of the literary establishment shifted as well; as a result, Ruebner's books began to garner in Israel greater critical and popular attention and acclaim. This acclaim and acknowledgment of Ruebner's distinctive poetic voice and significant contribution to Hebrew letters has resulted in his poetry receiving, in the last fifteen years, every major Israeli literary award, including the Jerusalem Prize, the Prime Minister's Prize for Hebrew Writers (twice) and the most prestigious Israel Prize (in 2008). This "Elder of the Tribe" (as he's been named), at ninety, having outlived by many years most of the Hebrew poets of his generation (for example, Yehuda Amichai, Dan Pagis, T. Carmi), continues writing in his kibbutz home, ever examining the world that was, the world that is, and the fleeting redemptions offered through poetic expression.[3]

IV THE POEMS

What language?

To date, Tuvia Ruebner has published fifteen poetry collections in Hebrew, from his 1957 collection, *The Fire in the Stone,* to his 2013 collection, *Last Ones.* The number is considerable, all the more so when one factors in that Ruebner wrote exclusively in German for the first twelve years of his life in Palestine/ Israel. Ruebner's adherence to his native tongue was an anomaly in the literary landscape of the day, where immigrant writers more commonly adopted the newly reborn Hebrew – a choice that was often charged with ideological and nationalistic fervor. Ruminating aloud in a video documentary on his life as to why he continued composing in German for so long, Ruebner suggests a twofold reason: German was the language in which he spoke to his lost beloveds, and German served as a protection from the overwhelming strangeness of his new land and life.[4] Indeed, German was the language of the literature he read and loved (Kafka, Hoelderlin, Rilke), and the language in which he had written, primarily short stories, already from primary school. German was his home and his childhood.

However, in 1953, Ruebner began composing poems in Hebrew – a Hebrew he had learned "from the new Hebrew, the Bible and Agnon" (94) – and from then on he wrote his poetry exclusively in Hebrew.[5] Ruebner's literary mentors, Ludwig Strauss and Werner Kraft, were instrumental in effecting this significant change, encouraging him to compose his poems in the language in which he lived and spoke. In addition, Ruebner's marriage that same year to Galila Jizreeli contributed to the shift in languages, as his new wife and love did not read or understand German. In his poem "Hebrew, My Love," Ruebner describes his relationship with Hebrew as fraught and complex: "I turned my back on you / You turned your back on me / though still we pulled toward each other like magnets to the pole." The inevitability of the attraction did not guarantee ease of expression: "I stuttered, became silent, I begged and I whispered," continues Ruebner in the same poem. The motifs of the stutterer and of an ever-encroaching silence are repeated in many Ruebner poems. The stutterer reference unavoidably evokes the biblical Moses who was, by his own account, "heavy of mouth and heavy of tongue" (Exodus 4:10). Midrashic interpretations attribute this "heavy tongue" – traditionally read as a stutter – to his having burned his tongue on hot coals as an infant. The hot coals of the midrashic story become in Ruebner's life the burning coals of the Holocaust.[6] Thus, the "foreign tongue" flailing about in the poet's mouth becomes the literal and figurative expression of the difficulty, and often impossibility, of speech before the devastation of the twentieth century: "To these too many bones you sent me, Lord / me, the stutterer... / ... / I fall mute upon the bones" ("Oblivion").

An Evolving Poetics

"If we only knew how to privilege the poem over our emotions and our thoughts, the poem would not betray us," wrote the well-known Czechoslovakian surrealist poet Vítězslav Nezval, as an inscription in a poetry collection owned by one of Ruebner's childhood friends. Ruebner always remembered this statement – as a type of warning – and quotes it in his memoir as an early and central tenet of his own evolving poetics. The poetic craft itself, argues Ruebner – the attention to language, form and, above all, sound – will result in a true poem; the indulgence of emotion and thought will not. Indeed, Ruebner's poetry is characterized by a sparse and exacting lexis, by language creating meaning through sound connections across and within lines, and by a great formal restraint. Thus, in a short and untitled poem on his thirteen-year-old sister's death, Ruebner avoids any direct expression of what he *feels* on losing his sister; instead, he relies on anaphoric repetition, simple descriptions and similes, and phrases that are as though aborted at each line's end, to build the poetic effect:

> In the air that no longer flows
> in the air that clenches like a fist
> in the air that crumbles to dust
> and the dust to needles
> in the air of the fire blind
> in the air sweet-not-from-blossoms
> in the air thin as a cry
> in the air that tears at a thousand eyes

and every eye sees darkness
in the air that is dwindling between her lips
my little sister lives the last minute's
eternity.

Ruebner refuses an outburst of emotion, as one might have expected; in fact, the speaker himself is all but absent, alluding to himself only in the penultimate line and only through his relationship to the poem's subject, the lost little sister. The poet's control and devotion to the unfolding poetic creation, to its embedded truths and inevitabilities, create a suspense that carries the reader into the poem's final, quiet devastation. What remains at poem's end is a doubled horror (flawlessly conveyed through a single line-break): the unbearable, enjambed description of the little sister's "last minute's / eternity," and the closing line of a single word, the unqualified, unqualifiable "eternity" of this moment in the speaker's imagination.[7]

A second and related tenet of Ruebner's poetics is his insistence on the importance and centrality of poetic form. "Artistic creation is *about* form," he writes in his memoir. "Form grants the creation validity, gives it honor, worth and, I believe, form is about integrity too" (64). Formal choices and constraints are, for Ruebner, an expression of the poet's necessary restraint, and are instrumental in the poet's task of distilling from the everyday its poetic essence. "The distinction between poetic language and prosaic language is the distinction between the Sabbath and the secular," writes Ruebner in a 1988 single-page tract on poetics. "Just as the Sabbath is said to emit its aura over the everyday, so too should art serve as a type of radiating corrective over reality."[8] But what distinguishes the Sabbath from the everyday? It is, in fact, the jealously preserved *form* of the Sabbath – its predetermined framework, rituals and time-boundaries – that imbues it with its sacred essence, just as form imbues the poetic with its sacredness (in the broadest sense of the word). The forms that Ruebner chooses, however, are rarely predetermined, as "closed" and inherited forms are; for example, he does not write in sonnets or standard quatrains. Instead, each poetic foray dictates its own unique, no less exacting, formal choices – from the precise tercets of "Go, If You Can" to the single, full-page stanza of the "Postcards From" series (as though there is no interrupting the flow of the experience at each revisited site), from the impossibly short lines spilling from one page to the next in "All This Suffering" to the unforgiving, haiku-like quatrains of the "One Plague and Another" poems (to name only a few formal choices represented in this collection).

A third, inevitable tenet of Ruebner's poetics – not of his choosing, but unavoidable – is the influence of the Holocaust on post–World War II writing. The Holocaust influence extends beyond the personal loss of his family; for Ruebner, Auschwitz is, and must be recognized as, the central and definitive event of the twentieth century. It was Auschwitz, he argues, as reality and symbol both, that "…created a new human being, a person who is terror-stricken. With Auschwitz before his eyes, he sees clearly now what he is capable of…" (83–84). Ruebner wonders how the Holocaust is not more present in the writings of his fellow Hebrew poets – not as thematics but through the very form of the texts. In his own texts, the absent, the broken and the fragmented are ever-present. Poems and poetic lines break off in mid-thought, shift direction, mark what they do not say. For example, the last eight lines of the fourteen-line poem with the seemingly light-hearted title "A Family Song" unfold as follows:

> I live under the memories
> with you, my children, the birds and the dark
> from within me, from within my mother my father me
> I bring forth words,
> cloud, lament, you[9]
> in the quiet of my life, in a howl
> I live, no longer
> in me, in the other.

No single image is completed, almost every line is as though disrupted by the white-page silence, and the final two lines open to various, perhaps contradictory, readings. Is the speaker stating he no longer lives, or that he no longer lives in himself, only in and through the "other"? Or might the lines be read as the speaker stating he lives detached not only from himself but detached also from the enigmatic, though definite, "other"? Who is the unnamed "other" who lingers at poem's end? The poem abounds in figures, from the present and past alike; but perhaps "the other" is someone exterior to the text entirely? The questions remain open, and by poem's end this "family song" reveals itself to be a doubled song of (re)birth and death; a family song of the newly-formed family (wife and children), and of the lost family (murdered parents, sister and grandparents) alike. The lines' insistence on indeterminacy reflects the indeterminacy of a new life built in the shadows of a lost old one. Textual rupture and fragmentation reflect historical rupture and fragmentation. Thus, Ruebner has accomplished the all-but-impossible feat of writing a poem that is both an ode to new life and a lament.

A final tenet of Ruebner's poetics, which by all rights should have come first, is Ruebner's reiterated insistence on poetry as a sound-propelled art form. Rhythms, rhymes and other musical patterns are an essential and significant element in Ruebner's poetry; indeed, it is often this element that leads the poem forward. In his encounter with words, isolated and also as they form connections between and among themselves, Ruebner seems to be first listening to the sound of the word, only then assimilating its meaning.

Like a foreigner encountering a foreign language for the first time and hearing only the strange sounds it produces, Ruebner retains an awareness of his adopted language's strangeness, and its great musicality. Thus the overwhelming strangeness of his adopted land and language, a strangeness which he once resisted by producing German-language poems in his Jezreel Valley home, is transformed over the years into an important, defining and, finally, embraced element of his poetry and poetic self.

Ekphrasis

One of the paradoxes of Ruebner's poetics is that the emphasis placed on sound and music – the aural aspects of poetry – is countered by the pronounced visual focus of much of his work. "I am a very visual poet; I am a man of eyes," declares the poet, who is also a renowned photographer. In discussing his photography in a video-documentary on his work, and with more than a little whimsy in his voice, he asserts that "the great advantage of photography is that it doesn't need words." Photography, and, by extension, all visual art, do not *need* words; however, the poet gives words to the images nonetheless. Thus, one of Ruebner's favored rhetorical forms is the ekphrastic poem, the poem describing or commenting on a visual representation or work of art. Already in his early 1967 collection *As Long As* Ruebner offers an ekphrastic poem, the sparse and poignant "Rondanini Pietà," a poem composed after he first saw the unfinished sculpture during his years in Europe in the 1960s.[10] Ruebner describes his encounter with Michelangelo's unfinished masterpiece thus: "... [when] I entered the room with the Rondanini Pietà...everything else melted away. I stood before the unfinished sculpture and I couldn't move" (104). From that first poem and over the next five decades of poetic composition, Ruebner proceeded to write numerous ekphrastic texts on paintings, photographs, sculptures, tombstones and other artifacts, even devoting a complete poetry collection, *A Graven and A Molten Image* (1982), to the form. These poems are an expression of the poet's visual orientation, and of his great appreciation of what might be accomplished through the visual mediums.

However, his choice of artifacts and his perspectives on those artifacts make clear that Ruebner's ekphrastic poems are above all expressions of the poet's existential contemplations, and existential sorrow. Time and again, the relationship between life and death, and between the present and past, is queried through the encounter with the artwork. The canvases hang and the sculptures stand, with all their beauty and culturally imbued importance, in various European museums, and whether ancient, Renaissance or modern, they all seem to reflect, as seen through Ruebner's eyes, lost people and lost worlds. Great artworks of western Europe in particular attest to a cultural wealth and world that proved, with the rise of Nazism, utterly devoid of ethical worth.

The art seems to exist as though in a vacuum, as though in a resounding silence. In fact it is these works' very silence that draws Ruebner to them; it is a silence that "…answers no question [and] asks none" (from "Why" – a poem on the crystal skull artifacts in the British Museum), a silence that may be the truest expression of the twentieth century.

Silence, however, is ultimately antithetical to the poet who exists through the not-silence. Ruebner's delicate and complex verbal representations of the visual offer a cautiously generative response to the silence, and to the devastation all around. Through these representations, silence is given voice; stasis is given the motion of poetic rhythms. Above all, the generative element of these poems resides in Ruebner's repeated focus on the individual human encounter with the art. The personal, the local, the interpretive and associative all enter into these "descriptions" of masterpieces (and some lesser-known artworks too), and become part and parcel of their existence. Thus, in these many museum halls that he wanders through, Ruebner draws our attention as much to the gazing eyes as to what they are gazing at. For example, the poetic speaker in "Memory of a Woman in the Egyptian Wing" is less engaged by the artifacts around him than he is struck by, and compelled to find, a woman he saw among the Egyptian sarcophagi, describing her as

> foreign woman in a foreign crowd
> [….]
> …her eyes welling up with tears there she stood
> secretly crying on seeing the dead Egyptian man
> drawn on his casket cover
> her eyes as black as almonds
> she stood there gazing through tears
> at all that beauty

The emotion evoked by art, whether it is joy, despair, or an inexplicable longing, is ever the focus of Ruebner's ekphrastic poems.

V THE POLITICAL

The disasters of the twentieth century swept Ruebner from Europe to Israel, from German to Hebrew, from the familiar to the strange. Chance and seemingly insignificant choices were responsible for his survival.[11] The losses he suffered and the destruction he survived could have transformed him into a fervent ideologue; he took, instead, a different path. Ruebner is a devotee of no movement or ideology, stating clearly, in his memoir and in interviews alike, that he has "no talent for ideology." Ideology, he argues, "demands loyalty from its followers and I am capable of being loyal only to people."[12] In the ideology-propelled landscapes of the Middle East in general, and Israel specifically, where the nationalistic (and often religious) rhetoric of zealots on all sides of the conflict keeps cycles of violence ever in motion, Ruebner's poetry and prose cast a critical gaze on the country that saved him. "I live in a blood-drenched land" are the startling opening words of his 2006 memoir, and even as early as a 1970 poem, deceptively named "Summer," he writes of this "death-demented, blood-dreaming land."[13] A cult of death has taken hold of Israel, he argues, where "Moloch and the Gods of *Sheol* [the underworld]" are worshipped.[14] Death is romanticized and sanctified, and the living are left in its wake.

Indeed, in a fashion that may be considered by some blasphemous, Ruebner is critical of the very notion and reality of national identities and of statehood. "The [idea and reality of] 'State' in no way excites me. It is, after all, simply an organization of power. I see 'the State' as a necessary evil – nothing more" (17). Similarly, Ruebner interrogates the emotionally charged, often idealized and idolized, notion of "homeland": "Lea Goldberg wrote that there are [for her] two homelands [the one in which we are born and the one we choose].[15] I feel that I have two 'no-homelands.' I was uprooted twice. A person can have only one homeland: the place where he was born. Slovakia spewed me out and what is happening in Israel today has uprooted me again." Thus, Ruebner identifies himself as ever between homelands, drawn to both the light-drenched, verdant landscapes of his youth and to the once desert-like, now fertile landscapes of his adulthood, but finally belonging to neither. The single place of belonging becomes the literary: "Poetry became my homeland," he states simply.[16]

Ruebner's virulent critique of late twentieth-century Israel includes a fierce censure of Israel's ongoing occupation of the West Bank and, with this forty-six years of occupation, its oppression of two million Palestinians. This Holocaust-identified poet refuses that single categorization – refusing thus the self-righteousness and self-justification that Holocaust rhetoric has often spawned – and has written poems that gaze with an unflinching eye at the wrongdoings and crimes of the occupation. These poems protest the military violence directed at Palestinians, a violence that has stripped an entire people of their basic human rights and has resulted in the deaths of countless innocents. In his poem "Victim, Again," he writes

> In Khan Younis five children on their way to school stepped on something. In one second they became torn flesh, ragged flesh. A sixth child was shot there the same day, on the twenty-third of November 2001. The army...is checking... investigating...from that same spot... artillery fire was shot...expresses...deep...sorrow...

From the almost matter-of-fact reportage of the event to the unadorned (though repeated) description of "torn flesh, ragged flesh," and finally to the ludicrous military-speak ("...is investigating...," "...expresses...deep...sorrow") – with the ellipses marking the annihilating gaps intrinsic to this prevaricating discourse – this poem situates itself firmly in the tradition of poetic dissent. In other texts, such as the startling haiku-like series "One Plague and Another," Ruebner's voice adopts the tenor of the biblical prophets of rage, those who saw and named the crimes of their people, and knew that also their own doom was embedded in these deeds:

> The Heart is parched. The dirty blood shines.
> You, me, he.
> What we have done even God, Full of Compassion, will not forgive.
> And the panicked run wild through the City of Terrors.

The poet as witnessing prophet, testifying to what he has seen and beholden only to the truth, insists that there is no mitigating narrative that justifies oppression and violence; blood is blood, the innocent are innocent, and the deaths of these innocents is unforgiveable.

VI WONDER

A poem entitled "Wonder" from Ruebner's 2011 collection *Contradictory Poems*, written in the poet's ninth decade of life, reads as follows:

> If after everything that has happened
> you can still hear the blackbird,
> the tufted lark at dawn, the bulbul and the honey-bird –
> don't be surprised that happiness is watching the clouds being
>   wind-carried away,
> is drinking morning coffee, being able to execute all the body's needs
> is walking along the paths without a cane
> and seeing the burning colors of sunset.
>
> A human being can bear almost everything
> and no one knows when and where
> happiness will overcome him.

The wonder of Tuvia Ruebner is that after a lifetime of loss and tragedy he remains open to the possibility of happiness, listens for it as one listens to the songbirds at dawn and dusk. This open-heartedness accommodates the many paradoxes and conflicts of life, and infuses his poetry with an enduring compassion for the lost and for the living both. Thus, in the poems of his old age, from a poem describing in perfect detail the tensed-up backs of the red-bereted soldiers standing at the gravesite of a comrade-in-arms, to a poem remembering a childhood friend, dead 70 years, who "...had that fair look, seemed always illuminated / as if his golden heart shone outward," Ruebner continues to articulate with poetic precision the elusive world of the heart, his own and of others.

"The poet writes poems when he writes poems," Ruebner offers, in a characteristically tautological fashion. "[The poet] writes when his life becomes language. When the distant is near and the near is distant. When frost is fire and fire – frost. When words that were once strangers find each other, and are amazed they were not connected previously. When a word finds its sister...."[17] Poetry, Ruebner knows, has an ever-more marginal place and status in the modern world – and still one may very well be lost without it. Poetry's attention to the details of language, its unwavering distinction between the chaff and the wheat, its insistence on distilling, presenting and preserving life's essence, may, Ruebner suggests in his memoir, "strengthen the stand against the lies and the liars that have engulfed us, and may encourage the search for truths" (127). The truths of words finding their destined forms, and the testimony of an unfailing gaze toward what is and what was, propel Ruebner's poetry onward. In a tone of wonder, Ruebner notes that "after the complete destruction of World War II, everything that exists is a kind of miracle, and one can sing a song of praise in its honor" (14). To return to the poem that stands as epigraph to this introduction, Ruebner's poetry – existing in order to say what was and is no more – is a poetry that knows the abyss but does not surrender to it, a poetry that says "... *yes* / in the emptiness" ("Testimony"). In testimony, in truth-telling and in praise-songs, Tuvia Ruebner's poetic oeuvre offers us an exquisite and indispensable voice of the twentieth century.

TRANSLATING THE POETRY OF TUVIA RUEBNER:
A PRAXIS & POETICS OF PARADOX

"the same – different – the same attributes,
different yet the same as before."

~ H.D., *Tribute to Angels*[18]

Early in his memoir *A Short Long Life*, Tuvia Ruebner describes his move from writing poetry in German, his mother-tongue, to Hebrew, the language of his adopted homeland. At the relatively late age of twenty-nine, in a Hebrew he learned from "the new Hebrew poetry, the Bible and Agnon," Ruebner "...started trying to write in Hebrew" (the qualifying "trying" in his description emblematic of his characteristic modesty). The passage continues, but instead of elaborating on the struggles or joys of composing poetry in this new/ancient language, Ruebner unexpectedly shifts his attention to the issue of translation:

> Once I started [writing in Hebrew], I was addicted and I didn't want my poems translated into any other language. As a devoted student of Ludwig Strauss, I knew that sound plays a central role in the meaning of a poem, and aside from rare instances, we are unable to transfer sound from one language to another. (69)[19]

Thus, from the very start of his Hebrew writing career, which is the start of his poetic career, Ruebner is preoccupied by issues of translation, a preoccupation that undoubtedly emanates not only from the multilingual nature of his upbringing, but also from the violent translocations and dislocations he experienced in his young life. It seems as though the ancient and melodious Hebrew rhythms offered Ruebner a refuge of beauty and fashioned-wholeness in a ruptured world, and the early refusal to have his Hebrew poems translated into other languages speaks to a refusal to undergo additional loss – the inevitable loss that accompanies any transfer from language to language, as from land to land.

However, this resistance belies the fact that Ruebner's poetry and poetic sensibility occupied from the very beginning a place of being "always already in translation," a place of in-betweenness, doubleness and fragmentation, eschewing in content and form notions of poetic (and political) completion, perfection or redemption.[20] The seeming redemption offered in poetic music – the untranslatable sound of a poem that carries and conveys so much of the poem's meaning and essence – is fleeting and changing, and the ancient homeland-contours of Hebrew in no way counter the enduring exilic resonances of

Ruebner's work. Indeed, Ruebner's early and youthful resistance to transla-
tion ebbs, and he agrees to having his poetry translated; his poetry eventually
finds an avid reading public in other languages beyond the borders of Hebrew,
most pronouncedly in the German-speaking world.[21] In addition, the poet
himself becomes a renowned translator (from Hebrew to German, and Ger-
man to Hebrew), best-known for his translations of the work of S.Y. Agnon.

I offer this passage describing Ruebner's early resistance to poetry-in-trans-
lation, and the changes that resistance undergoes, as a portal into my own
evolving understanding of the translator's work. Doubtlessly, translation
of poetry is a daunting task, deemed by many as destined to fail, seemingly
impossible from the outset. Unlike prose that often has plot, character and
other elements to rest on, the primary world of the poem is its language – the
sounds and shapes of that language, the manner in which individual words
and entire phrases rest upon or push against each other. Extracted from the
original language and transplanted elsewhere, what can the poem still say?
How can the poem still evoke the affects it means to evoke? What, finally,
should the translator's objectives be? Theoreticians of verse translation often
find themselves engaged in debates regarding these questions (and others)
based on dichotomous positions: is the translator's goal to familiarize and
domesticate the poem-in-translation – that is, make the poem "at home" in
the translation, as though it were originally written in that language – or is
the translator's goal to "foreignize" the poem-in-translation, announcing
through syntactic and lexical choices its other language origins? Is fidelity
(which seems to mean literalness) to the original text paramount, or should
the translator enjoy freedom to depart from the original in the interest of pro-
ducing the "best" translation? Is the poem-in-translation meant to re-enact
the original poem in the foreign language, or is the poem-in-translation in fact
an independent artistic entity?

The debates are important and fruitful, and the temptation to adopt one
position over another is great; and yet, the most successful poetry translations
very well may emanate from resistance to singular and categorical positions.[22]
Thus, I offer the following as an articulation of how I see the verse translator's
responsibilities and aspirations: the translator of poetry must strive toward
loyalty to the original and must also exercise a significant degree of creative
freedom in order to convey in translation the poem *as a whole* in the best
fashion. The translator of poetry must immerse herself fully in the lexical, lin-
guistic, cultural and musical world of each poem she's translating, and must
also, at a certain point, separate herself from that world in order to hear the
translated text in its own literary and sound contexts. The translated poem is
beholden to and an extension of the original poetic text, just as the translated
poem must also stand on its own as a successful poetic entity. Of course these
objectives seem, and in many ways are, oppositional to each other; indeed,

the translator's craft and art is a confluence of paradoxes. The challenge to the translator is to negotiate these paradoxes without attempting to resolve them, for it is the very paradoxes of translating poetry that are the source not only of translation problems, and even failures, but also of generative possibilities in literary representation and cultural bridgings.

Locating my translation praxis and poetics within this arena of paradox, as the translator of Tuvia Ruebner's poems into English I am responsible for conveying as accurately as possible the *intention* of his poems and the *experience* of reading them from the Hebrew into the English language texts. Accurately, however, does not mean equivalently, and reading the translations for one-to-one equivalencies with the Hebrew (a great temptation in a bilingual edition) undermines the essence and purpose of the translated poem – which is, finally, to stand in its own right (though ever acknowledging its place of origin, the Hebrew original). As Ruebner's translator, I must attend religiously to the formal, lexical and syntactic choices he makes (from poem length, length of individual lines, stanzaic structure, to gendered discourses and addresses, inverted syntax, etc), and strive to be faithful to these elements in my translation choices. However, the issue of "faithfulness" to the origin is significantly complicated by the fact that the practical "kinship" between English and Hebrew is a distant one indeed, and the transfer from a highly inflected, gendered and syntactically more flexible language like Hebrew to a weakly inflected, ungendered and syntactically rigid language like English results in countless instances where deviations from the original are not only unavoidable but are in fact essential.[23] As Ruebner's translator, I must listen closely for the many allusions, primarily biblical and liturgical, that are often the "warp and woof" of his poems.[24] However, once the allusion is uncovered, the question of how to convey it – through direct insertion into the text, through notes, or not at all – remains to be answered and carries with it numerous considerations. As Ruebner's translator, I must follow the sound patterns of the Hebrew original and register their effect, then work to create in the English translation "a new music," a music that is true in the English even as it evokes, in Walter Benjamin's phrase, "the echo of the original" – though that "echo of the original" also marks what is, inevitably, lost.[25]

But that which is lost is hardly the last word on the translation project (contrary to oft-quoted axioms on the matter). For whatever is lost in the transfer, other attributes and elements are gained. Indeed, the art and act of translating poetry is, finally, an art and act of transformation; as Benjamin states, there is "a renewal of something living – the original undergoes a change."[26] Through that renewal, the original gains a new life it might not have had otherwise – a presence in the world that is, as the epigraph to this piece suggests, "...the same – different – the same attributes, / different yet the same as before" (H.D.). The language into which the poem is translated is, ideally, also transformed through its wrestling with the foreignness of the original language. In the best cases, the language-wrestling leaves an origin-telling mark on the target language – reminiscent, perhaps, of the mark left on Jacob's thigh after his own night of wrestling with an unnamed, intimate other.[27]

As previously stated, Ruebner's early resistance to having his poems translated dissolved and he eventually became an important translator in his own right. One of his most significant translation projects was the translation into German of the work of Nobel Prize winner S.Y. Agnon, work that played a part in Agnon achieving the world-wide recognition he did. "Gershom Scholem wrote," states Ruebner in his memoir, "…that it was my translation [of Agnon] that was before the eyes of the judges on the Nobel Prize committee. I am proud of that" (96). But a different effect of his translations seems to be of even greater importance to Ruebner and articulates most elegantly the power of the literary translation. After journeying to Agnon's home in the Talpiot neighborhood of Jerusalem, precious pages of his translation in hand (a journey that involved Ruebner getting drawn into an antiquarian bookstore beside his bus stop in Jerusalem's city center, getting distracted by forty-five volumes of Goethe in translation, then missing his bus and arriving in Talpiot late – to find Agnon himself waiting for him in the hot sun), Ruebner shares his translation of *Shevuat Emunim* (*The Oath*) with Agnon and remembers the moment thus:

> After I read for [Agnon] my translation, tears filled his eyes and he called out: "Estherlein, Estherlein, come and hear how beautiful!" I say the following not out of false modesty…but I know for certain that Agnon was referring to the story itself, which he had not engaged with in a while, and not to the translation. The fact that the translation revived for him the original is praise enough for me. (96)

Hence, Benjamin's aforementioned "renewal of something living" resonates and is expanded in Ruebner's vivid description of translation as a "reviving," a restoring of life to that which is already alive. This "revival" of the living text – for the author, the reader and the translator all – is as apt a way as any to describe the translator's paradoxical work.

Images are translated by time and by circumstances; across years, resemblances make the connections we seek. Thus, I conclude this brief consideration of the translator's work with an anecdote mirroring the image offered above. In spring 2013, the journal *Modern Poetry in Translation* published six of Ruebner's poems in my renderings. On the Shavuot holiday – the Festival of First Fruits – I travelled to Kibbutz Merchavia to visit with Tuvia and his wife Galila, and to give him a copy of the journal. I left the journal with him; the next day, I received the following email:

Rachel my dear,

Something very nice happened to me this morning. I was reading through the journal you left here yesterday, from right to left as is my fashion, when my eyes fell on a poem that ended with the words "A human being can bear almost everything / and no one knows when and where / happiness will overcome him." I thought to myself, now *that's* a very good poem, I wish I had written it; then I saw my name on the poem and realized, with pleasure, I *did* write it…

~ Tuvia

The art and act of poetry translation precipitates the unexpected across language borders; the translator of poetry is the privileged practitioner of the multiple, the unexpected, the paradoxical, and the ceaselessly coming into being.

POSTSCRIPT: ON ORIGINS AND GRATITUDE

I started my journey toward Tuvia Ruebner's poetry a decade ago. I was working on a collection of Lea Goldberg's poetry in English translation and, as Goldberg's literary executor and friend, Tuvia Ruebner was everywhere. He was the editor of her posthumously published exquisite final collection *The Remains of Life* and of Goldberg's three-volume collected poems, and he was the author of the single most important monograph on the poet, her life and work. While immersing myself in the work of Goldberg, I felt an intimacy with and tremendous gratitude toward Ruebner – whom I had yet to meet – for his careful and devoted editing of Goldberg's poetry, and for his gracious opening of countless doors into her work.

Four years later, while engaged in a translation project of a different sort, I encountered Ruebner again, this time through his own poems. I was editing and doing much of the translation work on an English version of an anthology of Hebrew protest poetry entitled *With an Iron Pen: Twenty Years of Hebrew Protest Poetry*; in the collection there were four haiku-like poems and one longer poem by Ruebner.[28] The haiku-like poems were devastating in their unforgiving brevity, their direct gaze on wrongdoings, and their fierce prophetic tone. The longer poem, entitled "Victim, Again," entwined newspaper reporting through a text of lyrical descriptions and longings, and became one of the most quoted poems from the English anthology once it was published. I translated the Ruebner poems and made contact with him for the first time, discovering him to be a very gentle gentleman, of European mannerisms and graciousness coupled with a Jewish whimsy and story-telling propensity. I began reading more of his work, picking up original editions of his out-of-print collections from the various second-hand bookstores I frequented, discovering as I read how this Hebrew poet so often associated with Holocaust poetry defied rigid categorization and was no less a poet of post-modern sensibilities and protest.

Finally, in the autumn of 2010, I travelled to an artists' residency in a tiny town at the southern tip of Italy, hoping to complete there the collection of elegies I had been working on for two years, the book that would become my poetry collection *A Messenger Comes*. I sent ahead a box of books and folders to accompany me during my month-long retreat. Among the books I packed, quite randomly, were various poetry collections I had on my shelf but had not yet had the chance to read; Ruebner's 1967 collection *Kol Od* (*As Long As*) was one of the books. And so I found myself sitting one late afternoon in the stone-silent plaza at town center, in the shade of the church steeple where bells chimed the hour every hour, reading from the slender, yellow-paged volume in hand Ruebner's poems of longing and loss. From "Go, If You Can" to "She Was" to "When the statues started moving," every poem seemed a type of elegy, deeply familiar to my heart and hauntingly at home in the solitude and stone alleyways where I walked.

I have always felt that translation projects announce themselves to the translator, telling her "this is the one you must do now." The translator needs only to listen and be receptive to the book or the poet that chooses her next. These are moments of self-recognition and revelation, finding oneself in the work of another, knowing one has the voice with which to bring that foreignness into one's own language and context. I also know that many steps and seemingly unrelated elements along the way (Goldberg, protest poetry, the purchase of a random second-hand poetry book) lead up to these singular moments of revelation. And so it was there, in the autumn of 2010, in a forgotten Italian town (that spoke a fair amount of Greek), at the southern edges of the continent, reading a collection of Hebrew poetry published over forty years earlier, I felt possessed by a poet I had yet to meet and filled with a sense of urgency that moved me to contact Ruebner at once, and set the translating work in motion.

That was three years ago. Over the last three years I have immersed myself in Ruebner's many collections, reading, studying, analyzing and listening as closely as possible, hoping also to hear even in the Hebrew reading the English rhythms the poem might produce. I have debated with myself (and with Ruebner) which poems to include (and which to exclude) in this volume which means to be representative of the poet's seven-decade poetic trajectory. The translator is not a sieve through which the original travels unchanged; the translator inevitably interprets as she works. The aspects of interpretation are multifold and operative (if not always evident and obvious) at every stage of the work – from which poems are translated and how the book is ordered to every individual translation choice. The anxieties a translator often experiences about misrepresenting or misinterpreting the original text, or simply making translation errors, have been significantly eased for me by the fact that I have been able to consult with the poet himself at every stage of the work. Indeed, working with Tuvia has been a great pleasure and an even greater privilege. And so I end this postscript with profound gratitude to the poet – for his ongoing support of the project, for his gracious embrace of my renderings, for his gentle corrections and elucidations, for his kindness and faith in me throughout and, above all, for his poetry that has kept me company these last years and has enriched my days and nights.

NOTES

1. *A Short Long Life*, 2006 [Hebrew]. Page references throughout are from this memoir. All passages from the memoir are my translations.
2. An accomplished pianist already from an early age, Jizreeli won the Israeli Chopin Prize in 1950 when she was only 18. Jizreeli traveled and performed with the Israeli Philharmonic Orchestra, and came to Kibbutz Merchavia with the Israeli Philharmonic Quartet to play the piano quintet by Brahms. Ruebner calls Brahms his "matchmaker."
3. Amichai, born the same year as Ruebner, passed away in 2000. Pagis (1930–1986) was an intimate friend and colleague of Ruebner. Carmi was born in 1925 and died in 1994. Ruebner continues to live in Kibbutz Merchavia with his wife of 60 years, Galila. His daughter Miriyami raised a family of her own in Iceland, where she resides until today. His older son Idan is a Buddhist monk in Nepal; both Miriyami and Idan have maintained close contact with their parents.
4. "Poetry from Deep in the Fields" ("שירה מעומק השדה") by Omri Lio. See www.docunet.co.il.
5. It is worth noting that the move to composing his poems in Hebrew did not end Ruebner's relationship with German. He began translating, from Hebrew into German (most notably, and to great acclaim, the works of Nobel Prize winner S.Y. Agnon), and from German into Hebrew. Ruebner also became a renowned researcher and scholar of German literature.
6. An additional element of relevance from the Moses story was the biblical leader's great reticence to be God's spokesperson; a similar reticence is expressed in Ruebner's poetic "I." His is a voice that struggles with speech and speaks for no one but itself.
7. The Hebrew original ends not with "eternity" but with "last minute." Rendered literally, the final two lines would read "lives my little sister the eternity / of the last moment." Thus, in Hebrew, the suspense is carried into the poem's final line.
8. *Iton 77*, issue 100. A Literary Monthly in collaboration with Beit Berl, Tel Aviv (May 1988) 75 [Hebrew]. All renderings in this introduction of critical sources from Hebrew are mine. It is worth noting that Ruebner is a secular Jew.
9. The "you" is female – את. The reference seems to be to wife and sister both.
10. Ruebner was General Director of the Jewish Agency in Zurich from 1963–1966. During those years, he lived in Zurich with his family and traveled extensively through Europe.
11. "I am alive," writes Ruebner in *A Short Long Life*, "because when I was twelve or thirteen I joined the Jewish swimming club BKB (Bar-Kokhvah Bratislava)…. My parents wanted me to learn how to swim" (48). Through the swimming club, Ruebner joined Hashomer Hatzair youth movement, which led to his fleeing Slovakia in time to be saved.
12. *Haaretz*, Interview with Dalia Karpel, July 29th, 2009.
13. Oddly, the wars in Israel have all erupted in summer and early autumn months.
14. The reference to Moloch evokes the death of children in particular, sacrificed by

their parents to appease the ancient Ammonite god. The death of the young, particularly young men, is a resonant motif in Ruebner's poetry

15. Ruebner is alluding in particular to the penultimate stanza of Goldberg's famous and often-quoted poem "Pine." The stanza reads as follows: "Perhaps only migrating birds know – / suspended as they are between earth and sky – / this heartache of two homelands." See *Lea Goldberg: Selected Poetry and Drama*, 91. Translated by Rachel Tzvia Back (New Milford, CT: The Toby Press, 2005).

16. *Haaretz*, Interview with Dalia Karpel, July 29th, 2009.

17. Interview with Sari Shragar and Hanan Rotem, "Post-mortem – Haifa University," January 26th 1972. Quoted in Hillel Barzel's "Poetry as Connection: An Investigation of the Poetics of Tuvia Ruebner," *Alei Siakh* 21–22 (1984) 49–63 [Hebrew].

18. Hilda Doolittle (1886–1961), American poet, novelist and memoirist. The pen name H.D., under which Doolittle published most of her writings, was given to her by Ezra Pound. *Tribute to Angels* is the second part of H.D.'s epic post–World War II series *Trilogy*, published between 1944–1946.

19. Ludwig Strauss (1892–1953), German/Israeli scholar and writer, was a mentor and close friend of Ruebner's.

20. I borrow the wonderfully evocative term of "always already in translation" from Phillip E. Lewis, in "The Measure of Translation Effects," as quoted by José María Rodríguez García in "Introduction: Literary into Cultural Translation," *Diacritics*, Volume 34, Number 3/4 (Fall–Winter 2004) 27.

21. To date, eight collections of Ruebner's poetry in German have been published. In his memoir, Ruebner epigraphically expresses some of his discomfort over Germany being the country that has embraced his work most avidly through the imagined response of his deceased friend and colleague Swiss playwright Friedrich Durrenmatt (1921–1990) to this popularity: "'Grotesque,' Durrenmatt would say, and he would be right" (69).

22. Offering an elegant and powerful argument for the importance of engaging not only in translation work but also in thinking about translation work, Esther Allen and Susan Bernofsky write the following: "Thinking about translation means thinking about the gaps in our literature and our ability to communicate…. It also means thinking about the gaps in our political and cultural discourses, asking ourselves what and who has been left out." "Introduction: A Culture of Translation," in *In Translation: Translators on Their Work and What It Means* (New York: Columbia University Press, 2013) xviii.

23. I am alluding here to Walter Benjamin's striking notion of "the kinship of languages," the notion that "…languages are not strangers to one another but are, a priori and apart from all historical relationships, interrelated in what they want to express." From "The Task of the Translator," 1923; translated by Harry Zohn, 1968. In Walter Benjamin's *Illuminations*, edited and with an introduction by Hannah Arendt (New York: Harcourt, Brace and World, 1968) 71–82.

24. See Robert Alter's discussion of the biblical and liturgical in modern Hebrew poetry and his argument that "…allusion is not an occasional or even frequent elective device but in many texts is the warp and woof of the poem.…" In Alter's

Hebrew and Modernity (Bloomington and Indiana: Indiana University Press, 1994) 10–11.

25. I have borrowed the phrase "a new music" from Eliot Weinberger, who develops this notion beautifully in the following passage: "... the primary task of a translator is not merely to get the dictionary meanings right – which is the easiest part – but rather to invent a new music for the text in the translation language, one that is mandated by the original." See Weinberger's "Anonymous Sources: On Translators and Translation," in *In Translation: Translators on Their Work and What It Means*, 24. Benjamin's phrase "the echo of the original" is from "The Task of the Translator," 77.

26. Benjamin, "The Task of the Translator," 74.

27. Of course, the mark on Jacob's thigh is only one sign of the ways the night wrestling changes him. At night's end, he is given a new name and Jacob is transformed – translated – into Israel. See Genesis 32:23–32.

28. The original Hebrew version of the anthology, entitled *Be'et Barzel*, was edited by Tal Nitzan and published by Xargol Press in 2005. I later learned that Ruebner's four haiku-like texts were part of a series of ten poems entitled "One Plague and Another," evoking and rewriting the ten plagues visited on the Egyptians before the Exodus. This series can be found in this volume on pages 194–197, and the longer poem ("Victim, Again") opens the section "How Do We End that Which Has No End," on pages 176–177.

29. Ruebner continues composing poetry; however, he has repeatedly declared that he will publish no additional book in his lifetime and that the poems he writes now are for his literary estate.

30. Section IV, composed of poems from Ruebner's 1982 collection *A Graven and A Molten Image*, closes with the poem "Memory of a Woman in the Egyptian Wing," from Ruebner's earlier collection *A Midnight Sun*. Section VII, composed of poems from Ruebner's 2002 collection *Almost a Conversation*, closes with the poem "Erase your traces," from his 1982 collection. Information regarding the source books of poems in each section is provided in this volume's endnotes.

A NOTE ON ORGANIZATION

In the Illuminated Dark: Selected Poems of Tuvia Ruebner covers the seven decades of Ruebner's poetic career, from his first poetry collection *The Fire in the Stone* published in 1957, to his last volume, titled *Last Ones*, published in 2013.[29] The ten sections of the book are representative of different periods and publications in Ruebner's poetic oeuvre and they proceed in a chronological trajectory. The opening section of the collection, "Testimony," includes poems from Ruebner's first two published collections, *The Fire in the Stone* (1957) and *Poems Seeking Time* (1961); seven of the sections that follow, sections 2, 4–5, and 7–10, include poems from a single poetry volume each.[30] The third section of this book, "The Battles of the Night Left Behind," assembles poems from four different Ruebner collections: *As Long As* (1967), *Unreturnable* (1970), *Midnight Sun* (1977) and *And Hasteneth to His Place* (1990). The poems in this section together touch upon Ruebner's vision of war-ravaged Israeli landscapes, and introduce his first poems of personal loss experienced in his new homeland. The sixth section of this book, "How Do We End That Which Is Has No End," congregates a selection of Ruebner's protest poems from 2002 and onward.

Various attributes and considerations governed the selection process of which poems to include in this collection, from a poem's beauty and innovativeness to the marked centrality of a text in Ruebner's unfolding oeuvre. Every attempt was made to include poems that reflect and represent the poet's range of thematic and formal concerns. The ordering of the poems in each section was determined on the basis of the poems' relationship to each other in their English renditions, with an eye and ear to the integrity of each section's emerging tale.

The book's endnotes serve several purposes. First, the notes elucidate the many biblical and liturgical allusions woven through Ruebner's texts by directing the reader toward the relevant source materials; the second purpose of the notes is to articulate significant aural elements at play in the Hebrew which have been lost or altered in the English. In addition, any pronounced deviations from the Hebrew original, whether in line and stanza length, or lexis changes, are addressed and explained in the endnotes. The notes also provide additional historical and biographic information when such information impacts directly on the reading of the poem.

The images with which Ruebner's ekphrastic poems are in conversation can be viewed at http://press.huc.edu/ekphrastic-poems-image-gallery/.

Finally, a note on Ruebner's untitled poems: in the Table of Contents, these untitled poems are identified by the poem's first line in brackets. However, the poems themselves are marked only by a diamond symbol at page's top, in order to recreate the opening spatial silence evoked by an absent title.

I

TESTIMONY

תעודה

אֲנִי קַיָּם כְּדֵי לוֹמַר

בַּיִת זֶה לֹא בַּיִת,
מִשְׁטַח חֲרָמִים, צְחִיחַ סֶלַע, פַּחַד
שָׁם לְיַד הַכְּפָר, אָמַרְתִּי כְּפָר?
צִיָּה מְרֻצֶּפֶת.

אֲנִי קַיָּם כְּדֵי לוֹמַר

דֶּרֶךְ זוֹ לֹא דֶרֶךְ,
יִלְפְּתוּ אָרְחוֹתֶיהָ, יַעֲלוּ בַּחֲלֻדַּת חֲלוֹם
מִן הַיַּעַר, הַר הַחוֹל
אֲנִי הוֹלֵךְ? שָׁם, מִי הוֹלֵךְ? שֶׁהָיִיתִי
הוֹלֵךְ בְּשַׁעֲלֵי יֶלֶד, בְּשֶׁמֶשׁ
חִדָּלוֹן, בְּפֶשֶׂט יָדַיִם, שׁוֹאֵל,
הוֹלֵךְ שׁוֹאֵל פְּנֵי אָבִי וְאִמִּי

אֲנִי קַיָּם כְּדֵי לוֹמַר

קוֹרוֹת אֲבוֹתַי, פֶּחָם,
אֵפֶר, רוּחַ
אָחוֹתִי בְּשַׁעֲרֵי הַנּוֹשֵׁב
אָחוֹר, אָחוֹר, רוּחַ לֵילִית

בְּיוֹמִי אֲנִי קַיָּם כְּדֵי לוֹמַר
לְקוֹלָם הַלֵּילִי כֵּן, כֵּן לִבְכָיָם, כֵּן
לְאוֹבֵד בְּבֵית אֵינוֹתָם, לַנּוֹפֵל מִצֵּל קִירוֹתָיו
עַל פַּחַד קוֹלִי לוֹמַר כֵּן
בַּשֶּׁטַח הָרֵיק.

TESTIMONY

I exist in order to say

this house is not a house,
place of confiscations, parched rock, fear
there by the central square, did I say central square?
Paved wilderness.

I exist in order to say

this road is not a road,
clung to by its travelers, ascending on dream's rust
from the forest, the sand mountain where
I walk, there, who is walking? There where I used to
walk, a child in the sun
of cessation, with outstretched arms, searching
and searching for my father's face my mother's

I exist in order to say

these are the crossbeams and chronicles
of my parents, coal,
ash, wind
of my sister in my hair blowing
back and back, a night wind

in my day I exist in order to say
to their nighttime voices *yes, yes* to their weeping, *yes*
to the lost in their house of abeyance, to the falling from its wall's shadows
on the fear in my voice saying *yes*
in the emptiness.

◆

כְּמוֹ קוֹל בְּלִי הֵד,
גֶּשֶׁם בְּלִי עָנָן
לִפֹּל, לִנְדֹּד
כְּמוֹ חוֹל בְּלִי חוֹף
לְהִתְפַּזֵּר
עַד הַגְּבוּל הָאַחֲרוֹן
וְאֵין גְּבוּל בָּאֹפֶק הָעוֹלֶה
כְּסֻלָּם בְּלִי חֲלוֹם,
כִּפְרִידָה בְּלִי נִפְרָד
הַרְחֵק אֶל הַשָּׁוְא
כְּמוֹ עֵץ אֶל כּוֹכַב שָׁרָשָׁיו.

◆

Like an echoless voice,
a cloudless rain
falling, wandering
like sand with no shore
scattering
to the final border
and there's no border on the horizon rising
like a dreamless ladder,
like a leave-taking with no one being left
far off toward the nothingness
like a tree toward its starred roots.

בֵּין אֵלֶּה הֶהָרִים

בֵּין אֵלֶּה הֶהָרִים וְאֵלֶּה הָרוּחוֹת,
בְּחוֹף הַיָּם הַזֶּה שְׂפָתַי הַמְּלוּחוֹת
תִּנְשֹׁמְנָה, פְּשׁוּקוֹת, רֵיחוֹ שֶׁל יַעַר
אָפֵל וָזָר בְּאֶלֶם-פְּלִיאוֹתָיו,
בְּיַרְקוּתוֹ אֶטְבֹּל בְּעֵינֵי-נַעַר
וְעַל מִצְחִי עוֹדוֹ חָרוּת הַתָּו
אֲשֶׁר יִפָּתַח בְּבוֹא הָעֵת הַשַּׁעַר,
שָׁם יַקִּירַי כֻּלָּם כְּנוּסִים יַחְדָּו.

AMONG THESE MOUNTAINS

Among these mountains and these winds,
at this sea-strand where my salt-covered lips
breathe the far fragrance of the forest
dark and strange in its silent wonders, I gaze
with a boy's eyes at its extravagant green,
on my forehead still etched the mark
that will one day open the gate
where all my beloveds are gathered, and wait.

♦

בָּאֲוִיר שֶׁאֵינֶנּוּ זוֹרֵם עוֹד
בָּאֲוִיר הַסּוֹגֵר כָּאֶגְרוֹף
בָּאֲוִיר הַמִּתְפָּרֵק לְעָפָר
וְהֶעָפָר לַמְּחָטִים
בָּאֲוִיר הָאֵשׁ הָעוֶּרֶת
בָּאֲוִיר הַמָּתוֹק לֹא מִפְּרִיחָה
בָּאֲוִיר הַדַּק כִּילָלָה
בָּאֲוִיר הַקּוֹרֵעַ אֶלֶף עֵינַיִם
וְכָל עַיִן רוֹאָה חֹשֶׁךְ
בָּאֲוִיר הַמִּתְגַּמֵּד בֵּין שָׂפָה לְשָׂפָה
חַיָּה אֲחוֹתִי הַקְּטַנָּה אֶת נֵצַח
הָרֶגַע הָאַחֲרוֹן.

◆

In the air that no longer flows
in the air that clenches like a fist
in the air that crumbles to dust
and the dust to needles
in the air of the fire blind
in the air sweet-not-from-blossoms
in the air thin as a cry
in the air that tears at a thousand eyes
and every eye sees darkness
in the air that is dwindling between her lips
my little sister lives the last minute's
eternity.

שכחה

לַעֲצָמוֹת רַבּוֹת כָּל־כָּךְ שָׁלַחְתָּ, אֲדֹנָי,
אוֹתִי, הַמְּגַמְגֵּם. הָיְתָה בִּי רוּחֲךָ.
עַתָּה אֲנִי עוֹמֵד בַּגַּיְא הָרַע
וּלְבָנוֹת וִיבֵשׁוֹת עֵינַי.
אֵלִי, וּמָה אֹמַר? הַשִּׁכְחָה
עוֹטָה דְּבָרֶיךָ... קוּמוּ! ... כְּמוֹ...
בְּפִי חוֹבֶטֶת לְשׁוֹנִי זָרָה.
כְּבֵדָה רוּחִי עָלַי כְּרוּחַ הַקָּדִים,
מַחֲרִיב, מַרְדִּים,
הָהּ, אֱלֹהִים הַמְּבַקֵּשׁ עַמּוֹ,
אֲנִי נוֹפֵל אִלֵּם עַל הַשְּׁלָדִים.

OBLIVION

To these too many bones you sent me, Lord,
me, the stutterer. Your spirit was within me.
Now I stand in the Valley of Evil
and my eyes are white and dry.
My God, what am I to say? Oblivion
veils your words... Arise!... As...
In my mouth my foreign tongue flails about.
My spirit is heavy upon me like an eastern wind,
ravaging, enslumbering.
Oh, God who desires and seeks out his people,
I fall mute upon the bones.

אחותי הקטנה

1

בַּהֲמוֹן הָרוּחַ הַבָּהוּל לְאָן
אֲחוֹתִי הָאִטִּית
לֹא מְצָאתִיהָ.

בֵּין הַזֵּיתִים בַּדֶּרֶךְ הָעוֹלָה
אֲחוֹתִי עָנָן
לֹא מְצָאתִיהָ.

הִיא מְתַעְתַּעָה בִּי, עָשָׁן לְפָנַי
אֲחוֹתִי הַקְּטַנָּה
בּוֹעֶרֶת בְּעֵינַי.

2

שֻׁלְחֲנוֹת־הַחַיִּים עֲרוּכִים:
כַּדֵּי־הָאוֹרָה קוֹרְאִים לָאוֹרְחִים
אֲחוֹתִי מֻטֶּלֶת בֵּין הַפְּרָחִים.

קוֹל הָאָבִיב נִשְׁמָע בְּאַרְצִי
בְּגַנֵּי הָרוּחוֹת יָרֹק הֶעָנָן.

פַּרְפְּרֵי־הַפְּרִיחָה לְעֵצִי
בִּמְעוּפוֹ שֶׁל רֵיחָם הַלָּבָן.
אֲחוֹתִי מֻטֶּלֶת בֵּין הַפְּרָחִים.

אַט עַל עֵינֵי־אֲחוֹתִי נוֹטְפִים
יֵינוֹת־הַשֶּׁמֶשׁ מִכַּדִּים שְׁקוּפִים.
אֲחוֹתִי מֻטֶּלֶת בֵּין הַפְּרָחִים.

3

אֲחוֹתִי הַקְּטַנָּה, לָהּ עֵינַיִם גְּדוֹלוֹת
בִּקְרָה בִּשְׁנָתִי.

MY LITTLE SISTER

1

In the roar of the wind rushing toward where
is my sister the slow-moving one
I could not find her.

Among the olive trees on the path ascending
is my sister a cloud
I could not find her.

She plays tricks on me, is smoke before me
my little sister
burning in my eyes.

2

Life's tables are set:
The jugs of light beckon the guests,
my sister is strewn among the flowers.

The sound of spring is heard in my country,
in the wind-gardens the clouds are green.

Butterflies of blossomings alight on my tree
with the flight of their white fragrance.
My sister is strewn among the flowers.

Sun-wines from clear vases slowly
drip over my sister's eyes.
My sister strewn among the flowers.

3

My little sister, she of the large eyes
visited me in my sleep.

נִכְנְסָה לְגוּפִי וְשָׁטָה דּוּמָם
בְּנַהֲרוֹת דָּמִי.

בָּאֹפֶל, בָּאֹפֶל
דַּג־זָהָב בְּדָמִי
אֲחוֹתִי הַקְּטַנָּה דּוּמָם בְּדָמִי
דּוּמָם.

אֲחוֹתִי הַקְּטַנָּה לְעֵץ הָיְתָה
לְעֵץ הָיְתָה אֲחוֹתִי הַקְּטַנָּה
וְשָׁלְחָה אֲמִירָהּ עַד גְּרוֹנִי.

אֲחוֹתִי הַקְּטַנָּה מֵהָעֵץ עָלְתָה
אֲחוֹתִי הַקְּטַנָּה צִפּוֹר שְׁחֹרָה
מֵהָעֵץ עָלְתָה עַד עֵינִי.
אֲחוֹתִי הַקְּטַנָּה, כְּנָפָהּ הַשְּׁחֹרָה
כְּנָפָהּ הַשְּׁחֹרָה עַל עֵינִי.

הַצִּפּוֹר הַשְּׁחֹרָה לְעָנָן הָיְתָה
אֲחוֹתִי הַקְּטַנָּה כְּעָנָן הָיְתָה.
הֶעָנָן מְכַסֶּה אֶת חַיַּי.

She entered my body and wandered
in the rivers of my blood silently.

In the gloom and the gloom,
a goldfish in my blood
my little sister, mute and hushed
in my blood.

My little sister became a tree
a tree she was
sending treetop words into my throat.

My little sister rose from the tree
my little sister a blackbird
rose from the tree toward my eyes.
My little sister, her black wings
black over my eyes.

The blackbird became a cloud
my little sister like a cloud become.
The cloud that covers my life.

קוֹלוֹת

אֲנִי הוֹלֵךְ. תָּמִיד אֲנִי הוֹלֵךְ. לְאָן
אֲנִי הוֹלֵךְ? אֵינֶנִּי כָּאן.

מֵאַיִן הָעֵצִים הָאֵלֶּה בְּיָדִי?
הָאֵשׁ הַזֹּאת? אֵינָם שֶׁלִּי. אֵינִי שֶׁלִּי. בִּכְדִי

– אֲנִי בְּעִקְבוֹתֶיךָ וְלַשָּׁוְא...

אֲנִי יוֹדֵעַ, בְּנִי, אֲנִי הָאָב.
אֲנִי מוֹלִיךְ אוֹתְךָ, שְׁנֵינוּ הוֹלְכִים יַחְדָּו.

– אֵינִי יָשֵׁן. אֵינֶנִּי עֵר.

אֲנִי יָשֵׁן. לִבִּי עֵר
אַיָּל אָחוּז בַּצַּלְעוֹת הַשְּׁחֹרוֹת

גִּמְגּוּם דּוֹמֵם מִתְאַלֵּם בֵּין פְּאָרוֹת
הַזְּמָן הַמִּסְתַּבֵּךְ בְּיוֹמוֹ וְלֵילוֹ...

כֵּן. הִנְנִי.

לֹא!

VOICES

I am walking. I am always walking. Where
am I walking? I am not here.

From where is this kindling in my arms?
This fire? They are not mine. I am not mine. In vain

– I am in your footsteps, in vain…

I know, my son, I am the father.
I lead you, the two of us walk together.

– I am not asleep. I am not awake.

I am asleep. My heart is awake
a ram bound by its black ribs.

A still stutter falls silent among the boughs
of time entangled in its day and night…

– Yes, I am here.

No!

◆

רַק הַיָּמִים וְהַיּוֹנִים,
רַק הַקְּמָטִים שֶׁבַּפָּנִים,
וְרַק הָרוּחַ, הַקְּרִיאוֹת,
הַלְּבָנוֹת הַמּוּזָרוֹת.

רַק הַחַמְסִין וְהַשְּׂרָפִים,
רַק הַדְּמָעוֹת וְהַצְּדָפִים,
וּפִי נוֹשֵׁק אֶת פִּיךְ בִּמְאֹד,
וְזֶה גָּלוּי וְזֶה הַסּוֹד.

♦

Just the days and the doves,
just the wrinkles by the eyes,
just the wind, the calling out,
cries unfamiliar and white.

Just the heat and tree amber,
just the broken shells and the bones,
just my mouth kissing your mouth,
this the revealed and this the unknown.

הלילה הזה

שֶׁבְּכָל הַיָּמִים חַיֵּינוּ כֶּהָרִים.
הַלַּיְלָה הַזֶּה
בְּהֵאָסֵף, גַּיְא.

הָיִינוּ כַּיַּעַר
הַלַּיְלָה הַזֶּה
עֵץ אֶחָד.

רוּחַ וְשֶׁמֶשׁ
סַנְוֵרִים.
בַּלַּיְלָה הַזֶּה, הַשֹּׁרֶשׁ.

שֶׁבְּכָל הַיָּמִים קָשִׁים
גּוּפֵינוּ שִׁרְיוֹן.
הַלַּיְלָה הַזֶּה
לְלֹא גְּבוּל

THIS NIGHT

As on all other days our lives were like the hills
This night
ingathering, a valley.

We were like a forest
This night
one tree.

Wind and sun
whirling, blinding.
This night, the root.

As on all other difficult days
our bodies are armored.
This night
unbordered

ילדים

שְׁנֵי יְלָדִים לִי: כָּחֹל וְיָרֹק,
שׁוֹמְרִים הֵם לִמְרַאֲשׁוֹתַי.

יְדֵיהֶם פַּרְפָּרִים, גּוּפָם סֻלָּם:
מַלְאָכִים יַעֲלוּ וְיֵרְדוּ

בְּאֵלֶם, בְּאֵלֶם רֹאשִׁי מֻטָּל
עַל אֶבֶן בֵּין עֵשֶׂב וְקוֹץ,

עֵינָיו צוֹדְדוֹת הַיָּרֹק, הַכָּחֹל
הַיָּרֹק, הַכָּחֹל צוֹדְדוֹת.

חֹמֶט מַבִּיט בֶּן תָּמֵהַּ מְאֹד,
שֶׁלְּדָג חוֹשְׁבָן דְּגִיגִים.

שְׁנֵי יְלָדִים סוֹכְכִים עָלַי,
כָּחֹל וְיָרֹק, יָרֹק וְכָחֹל:

צְחוֹק גָּדוֹל.

CHILDREN

Two children I have: blue-eyed and green,
guardians by my head.

Their hands are butterflies, their bodies ladders:
angels ascend and descend

silently, silently my head rests
on a stone between thorns and weeds,

his eyes hunt for the green, the blue
the green, the blue they seek.

A lizard looks at them in wonderment,
a pelican thinks they are goldfish.

Two children shelter me,
green and blue, blue and green:

What joy.

אָב עִם יָלוֹד

בָּשָׂר מוּזָר
רַךְ לָבַשׁ גּוּף
יָדוֹ רוֹשֶׁמֶת
נִשְׁכָּחוֹת בָּאֲוִיר

כְּתָב חַרְטֻמִּים
מִצְחוֹ הַקָּמוּט
כְּמִי שֶׁחוֹשֵׁב
עַל מַה הוּא חוֹשֵׁב

בְּרָאשֵׁי הַחִיּוּךְ
בֵּין שְׂפָתָיו לַבְנוֹנִית
חֲלֵב הַשֵּׁנָה
יָרֵחַ שׁוֹאֵל

עַל מָה אֲנִי כָּאן
מְעַט רָכוּן
כְּעַלְוֶה עַל צֶּלָּהּ
כְּלַחַשׁ עַל סוֹד

עֵינַיִם סוּמוֹת
נִפְקָחוֹת עַד־בְּלִי־דַי
בָּשָׂר מִבְּשָׂרִי
אַל תִּבְכֶּה בְּיָדִי.

24

FATHER AND INFANT

Strange flesh
embodied tenderness
his hand inscribing
old memories in the air

His wrinkled forehead
hieroglyphics
as though deep in thought
about what

In my mind I see the smile
of his lips with milky sleep
white pearled
a moon asks

Why am I here
hovering above
like leaves over their shadow
like a whisper over its secret

His closed eyes suddenly
open to infinity
Oh flesh of my flesh in my arms
don't cry.

שיר משפחה

בְּשֶׁקֶט אֲנִי חַי בֵּין
הָעֵצִים הַמְלַבְלְבִים וּבֵין הָעֵצִים הַמַּשִׁירִים,
בֵּין הַצִּפָּרְנִים וְהַצְּרִיחוֹת
אַתְּ עַל יָדִי וּמֵעָלַי
שְׂעָרֵךְ הַפָּרוּעַ בָּרוּחַ,
בִּכְאֵב, בְּתִקְוָה, בְּשֶׁקֶט
אֲנִי חַי מִתַּחַת לַמַּחֲשָׁבוֹת
אִתָּךְ, אֶת יְלָדַי, אֶת הַצִּפּוֹר וְאֶת הַחֹשֶׁךְ
מִתּוֹכִי, מִתּוֹךְ אִמִּי וְאָבִי מִתּוֹכִי
אֲנִי מַעֲלֶה מִלִּים,
עָנָן, קִינָה, נֶחָמָה, אַתְּ
בְּשֶׁקֶט חַיַּי, בִּצְעָקָה
אֲנִי חַי, לֹא עוֹד
בִּי, בָּאַחֵר.

A FAMILY SONG

I live quietly
between the blossoming and the shedding trees,
between the birds and the screams,
you by my side and above me
your wild wind-swept hair,
in sorrow, in hope, quietly
I live under the memories
with you, my children, the birds and the dark
from within me, from within my mother my father me
I bring forth words,
cloud, lament, you
in the quiet of my life, in a howl
I live, no longer
in me, in the other.

אֲחוֹתִי

1

הָלַכְתִּי לְחַפֵּשׂ לָךְ דְּמוּת,
עֶדְנָה בְּלִי גוּף,
תּוּגָה בְּלִי יָדַיִם וָמֵצַח,
הָלַכְתִּי לְחַפֵּשׂ אָבִיב
לָךְ, צִפּוֹר הַמְבַקֶּשֶׁת כְּלוּב,
הָלַכְתִּי דֶּרֶךְ לְחַפֵּשׂ
לִצְעָדַיִךְ,
מַזָּר לִשְׂעָרֵךְ, הָאָרֹךְ,
שְׁמוּרוֹת לְעֵינַיִךְ.

2

עִם עֲלִיַּת לְבָנָה שְׁלֵמָה תָּמִיד
מַשְׁחִירוֹת פְּנֵי אֲחוֹתִי,

צִפּוֹר עֲצוּבַת עֵינַיִם
בְּאִלָּן עֲזָבוּהוּ חַגָּיו.
תָּמִיד עִם חִדּוּשׁ לְבָנָה
מַשְׁחִירוֹת פְּנֵי אֲחוֹתִי,

שְׂפָתַיִם רֵיקוֹת בְּלִי קִדּוּשׁ
מְמַלְמְלוֹת מִלּוֹת צִפּוֹר.

הוּ הַשָּׁמַיִם הַגְּבוֹהִים הָאֵלֶּה,
מָה רַב בִּקַּשְׁנוּ מֵהֶם!
עוֹד מְעַט תְּטַשְׁטֵשׁ דְּמוּתָם כָּלִיל,
בְּלֹא דְּמָעוֹת.

MY SISTER

1

I went to find for you a form,
tenderness with no body,
sorrow with no hands no forehead,
I went to find for you
spring, a bird seeking a cage,
I walked a long way to find
your footsteps,
constellations for your long hair,
sanctuaries for your eyes.

2

Always when the full moon rises
my sister's face darkens,

sad-eyed bird in the branches
abandoned by its orbit.
Always when the moon is renewed
my sister's face darkens,

empty unblessed lips
muttering bird-words.

Oh these lofty skies,
how much we've asked of them!
Soon their image will be fully blurred,
bearing no tears.

דוד הזקן

עֵינַי רָאוּ יוֹתֵר מִדַּי.
עַמִּים רַבִּים מִדַּי הִגִּיעוּ עַד נַפְשִׁי.
בְּשִׁתִּי וָעֶרֶב גּוֹרָלוֹת אֲנִי שָׂרוּג.
הַגּוֹשְׁשׁוֹת, הַלֹּא־שְׁקֵטוֹת, יָדַי
אֲשֶׁר יָדְעוּ אִבְחַת הַחֶרֶב, רַעַד מֵיתָרִים –
מְלַמְלְמוֹת עַתָּה בְּחֹשֶׁךְ חֲרִישִׁי.
אֲנִי קוֹפֵא. עַד עֶמֶק נִשְׁמָתִי
אֲנִי קוֹפֵא. הַעוֹד אָרִים
עַצְמִי עַד אוֹר חַם וְנוֹשֵׁם שֶׁל גּוּף
הַשּׁוּנַמִּית שֶׁיְּמַהֲמַהּ מוֹתִי
עוֹד לַיְלָה זֶה סְפוּג רוּחַ הֶהָרוּג?
בְּהֶבֶל תְּנוּמָתָהּ תָּצוּף הַלְּבָנָה
וּבְרַקָּתִי הָרְכוּנָה
עַל שַׂעֲרָהּ הַחַי שׁוּב
יַהֲלֹם דָּמָן שֶׁל הַמִּלִּים
שֶׁבְּיָמִים קְדוּמִים הָיוּ בִּי לִתְהִלִּים.

30

OLD KING DAVID

My eyes have seen too much.
Too many nations have overwhelmed my spirit.
Through the warp and weft of destinies I am woven.
Fumbling, my unquiet hands
which once knew the sword's slaughter, the strings' quivering –
mumble now in the silent darkness.
I am freezing cold. To the depths of my soul
I am frozen. Will I raise myself once more
toward the light warm and breathing body
of the Shunamit so it may keep my death at bay
one more night drenched with the spirit of the dead?
The moon floats in the mist of its slumber
and in my head resting
on her living hair will beat
again the blood of words which
were once long ago sweet psalms in me.

II

AS LONG AS

♦

כְּשֶׁהֶחֵלּוּ הַפְּסָלִים לָנוּעַ
מִמָּקוֹם לְמָקוֹם, מִיַּבֶּשֶׁת לְיַבֶּשֶׁת
חַסְרֵי זְרוֹעוֹת וְחַסְרֵי פָּנִים
נִזְכַּרְנוּ בַּיָּמִים
בָּהֶם עָמַדְנוּ שְׁלוּבֵי מַבָּט
שָׁעוֹת אוֹ שָׁנִים
חֲלִילִים לָרוּחַ
לֹא אָמַרְנוּ דָּבָר וְהֵבַנּוּ כִּי דָּבָר לֹא אָבַד
כְּשַׁיִשׁ שֶׁל אֵשׁ הַשָּׁמַיִם הַזּוֹרְמִים
וְהַבָּרָק הָעוֹמֵד
וְיָדַעְנוּ, הַשָּׁעָה מְפַלֶּשֶׁת
וְאִישׁ מִבֵּינֵינוּ עוֹד לֹא הָיָה מֵת.

◆

When the statues started moving
from place to place, continent to continent,
armless and faceless,
it was then we remembered the days
we had stood with our gaze
interlocked for hours and years
flutes to the wind
saying nothing, knowing that nothing was lost
like the fiery marble of flowing skies
and the transfixed lightning
and we knew, the hours were stretched before us
and not one of us was dead yet.

שָׁם, אָמַרְתִּי

יָצָאתִי מִבֵּיתִי לְהַרְאוֹת לְבָנַי אֶת מְקוֹם מוֹצָאִי.
שָׁם, אָמַרְתִּי, שָׁכַבְתִּי עַל הָאָרֶץ
אֶבֶן לִמְרַאֲשׁוֹתַי, נָמוּךְ מִן הָעֵשֶׂב
כַּעֲפַר הָאָרֶץ
הַכֹּל שָׁם נִשְׁמַר.

עָבַרְנוּ בֶּהָרִים וּבַיְעָרוֹת שֶׁהָיוּ
מְעָרוֹת וְהַמַּיִם נִקּוּוּ בַּדֶּרֶךְ וְהַכְּבִישִׁים הָיוּ רָעִים.
הַמְּכוֹנִית דִּלְגָה עַל הַבּוֹרוֹת.

בָּאוֹר הַנּוֹטֶה הִגַּעְנוּ לְעִיר מוֹצָאִי.
מָה הָאֲוִיר הַמָּתוֹק הַזֶּה? שׁוֹאֲלִים בָּנַי.
מָה הַטִּיחַ הַנּוֹפֵל מֵהַקִּירוֹת?

אֵין דָּבָר, הִגִּידָה הַיְּשִׁישָׁה בַּחַלּוֹן.
כָּאן גַּם הֶעָתִיד עָבַר. וְסָגְרָה אֶת עֵינֶיהָ הַיְּבֵשׁוֹת
כְּעוֹף הָעוֹלֶה וְקוֹפֵל אֶת כְּנָפָיו וְצוֹלֵל.

כָּאן נוֹלַדְתִּי, אָמַרְתִּי לְבָנַי.
הוֹרַי וּזְקֵנַי נוֹלְדוּ כָּאן קָרוֹב.
נוֹלָדִים. כָּאן הָיָה בַּיִת
אָמַרְתִּי לְבָנַי וְהָרוּחַ עָבְרָה
בֵּינִי וּבֵין הַמִּלִּים.

בִּקַּשְׁתִּי לְהַרְאוֹת לְבָנַי מְקוֹם מוֹצָאִי, וּמָתַי
נֹאכַל, שׁוֹאֲלִים בָּנַי, וְאֵיפֹה
נָלוּן?

THERE, I SAID

I left my home to show my children where I came from.
There, I said, I lay on the ground
a stone for a pillow, my head lower than the grass
like the earth's dust –
everything is preserved there.

We passed hills and forests that were
caves, and water collected in pools along the way and the roads were bad.
The car lurched over the ditches.

In the waning light we reached the city of my birth.
What is this sweet air? my children ask.
What is that plaster falling from the walls?

It's nothing, said the old woman in the window.
Here, also the future is past. And she closed her dry eyes
like a bird that flies high, then folds its wings and dives.

I was born here, I told my children.
My parents and ancestors were born nearby.
Everyone is born. Here was a house
I told my children and the wind passed
between me and the words.

I wanted to show my children where I came from, and when
will we eat, they asked, and where
will we sleep?

איש יאמר

אִישׁ יֹאמַר לָהּ: אַתְּ
יֹאמַר לָהּ: אַתְּ
וְאֵין מַעֲנֶה.

הִי, נְהִי
אוֹבְדֶיהָ, קִינַת נְבוֹכִים

צֶלֶם זִכָּרוֹן: אָדָם חַי וְנוֹשֵׁם
חֲבִיבָה לַבְּרִיּוֹת
אִשָּׁה כּוֹרְעָה לָלֶדֶת.

מֵעוֹלָם לֹא יָדַעְנוּ אֶת צְפוּנוֹתֶיהָ.
עַד עוֹלָם לֹא נֵדַע אֶת קוֹלָהּ הַגָּלוּי.

SOMEONE WILL SAY

Someone will say to her: *You*
Will say to her: *You*
and there's no answer.

Oh, the wailing
of those who have lost her,
lament of the bewildered.

Image of a memory: a living, breathing person,
creation's beloved,
a woman crouching in labor.

We never knew her coded secrets.
We'll never know her unveiled voice.

הִיא הָיְתָה קְטַנָּה.
הִיא לָבְשָׁה שִׂמְלָה חֲדָשָׁה, הִיא עָנְדָה סִנָּר לָבָן.
הִיא נָשְׁמָה בִּכְבֵדוּת.
הִיא הִגִּישָׁה תֵּה בַּחֲדַר הָאֹכֶל.
רֶגַע נְטָלָה
כְּמוֹ עַיִן מִתּוֹךְ הַפָּנִים, כְּמוֹ
קוֹל מִתּוֹךְ הַגָּרוֹן.

הִיא לֹא צָעֲקָה. הִיא אָמְרָה
לֹא טוֹב לִי, לֹא טוֹב לִי, יָד

מְבַקֶּשֶׁת לַחֲבֹק
אֲוִיר. עֵינַיִם רוֹאוֹת
וְלֹא, אִישׁ
נוֹתַר לְבַדּוֹ בַּחֶדֶר הַבָּנוּי לִשְׁנַיִם

כְּחֹשֶׁךְ עַל פְּנֵי תְהוֹם, אִשְׁתּוֹ
בְּדַרְכָּהּ לָרוּחַ וְלַמַּיִם

נְשָׁמָה בְּזָכְרָהּ, מַה יַּעֲשֶׂה לָהּ בְּשָׁעָה שֶׁכָּל
הַשְּׁאָר דְּמָמָה

SHE WAS

She was small.
She wore a new dress, had on a white apron.
She was breathing heavily.
She served tea in the dining hall.
The moment excised her
like an eye from a face, like
a voice from the throat.

She didn't scream. She said
I don't feel good, don't feel good, her hand

grasping at
air. Eyes seeing
and not, a man
left alone now in a room built for two

like darkness over the deep, his wife
on her way toward wind and water

the soul upon remembering, what can be done for her now
everything else is silence

מן הצל בעיני

אַתְּ שֶׁצָּעַקְתְּ בַּלַּיְלָה, אֲבָל
הִנַּחְתְּ אֶת יָדֵךְ עַל הַפֶּצַע
מִבֹּהָלָה. הָלַכְתְּ בַּדֶּרֶךְ הַיּוֹרְדָה
רוּחַ פְּזוּרָה עַל פָּנַיִךְ
קְרִיאוֹת צִפֳּרִים. קוֹלֵךְ
הוּא קוֹלָהּ. מִי זֹאת עוֹלָה

עֵינַי אֶשָּׂא אֶל הֶהָרִים
הָרְחוֹקִים, הָאֲדִישִׁים, הַמֻּשְׁלָגִים, אֶל הַמַּיִם הָרַבִּים
הַנּוֹפְלִים. הָאֲנָחוֹת, הָאֲנָחוֹת. אֶל הַיְעָרוֹת
אֶל הַיְעָרוֹת הָרְחוֹקִים, אֶל הַמְּעָרוֹת
בַּיְעָרוֹת הַלֵּילִיִּים. מִי זֹאת עוֹלָה

מִן הַצֵּל בְּעֵינַי, לֹא עוֹד הִיא, לֹא עוֹד
הִיא. אַף אַחַת. לֹא
אֵדַע, לֹא אֵדַע לֹא אַחַת אֲבוּדָה
וּבַצֵּל בְּיָדָהּ
הַשְּׁלוּחָה אֶל פִּצְעִי וּבַצְּעָקָה הַקַּלָּה.

FROM THE SHADOW IN MY EYES

You who shouted out in the night, but
rested your hand on the wound
frightened. You walked the downturned path
winds scattering bird songs
across your face. Your voice
is her voice. Who is she who rises

I lift my eyes to the hills
the distant, the indifferent snow-covered hills, to the mighty waters
falling, the sighs and sighs. To the forests
the distant forests, to the caves
in the night forests. Who is she who rises

from the shadow in my eyes, no longer she, not
she. No one. No I'll not
know not she who is lost
and not the shadow in her hand
stretched toward my wound and her small cry.

החרב

הַקּוֹל הַצָּלוּל בָּעֶרֶב.
הַחֶרֶב בְּיָדוֹ
חוֹרֶתֶת לְאַט
בָּאֲפֵלָה הַמּוּאֶרֶת
תָּוֵי פָּנִים אֲשֶׁר אָהַבְתָּ.
מִתְהַפֶּכֶת בַּבָּשָׂר הַחַי.

THE SWORD

The crystal voice of evening.
With sword in its hand
it slowly carves
in the illuminated dark
the contours of a face that you loved.
The sword turns and twists in the living flesh.

תן לי לראות את פניך

תֵּן לִי לִרְאוֹת אֶת פָּנֶיךָ. אֲנִי רָכוּן בָּרוּחַ, אֲבָל
אֵינֶנִּי רוֹאֶה אֶת פָּנֶיךָ. צֵא מֵהַחֹשֶׁךְ וְהַדְּמָמָה.
קוֹל פִּצּוּחַ עֵצִים נִשְׁמָע וְהָאֲדָמָה מִתְכַּסָּה צִנָּה.
אָנָה אֲנִי. בָּא חֹרֶף. הַשֶּׁטַח הָרֵיק פָּתוּחַ לַקֹּר.
פְּתַח אֶת הַדֶּלֶת הַסְּגוּרָה

אַתָּה הָעוֹמֵד כָּפוּף בַּחַלּוֹן בִּזְרוֹעוֹת קוֹרְאוֹת לְעֶזְרָה.

LET ME SEE YOUR FACE

Let me see your face. I am bent to the wind, but
I cannot see your face. Come out of the darkness and silence.
The felling of trees can be heard and the ground is covered with frost.
Where am I. Winter is coming. The empty space is bare to the cold.
Open the closed door

you who stand bowed at the window your arms calling out for help.

דג

מִי שָׁם
שָׁמַע?

דָּג חַי נִזְרַק לַיַּבָּשָׁה.
בְּעַד פִּיו הַפָּעוּר עוֹבֵר הָרוּחַ.
הַכֹּל שָׁכוּחַ
מֵאֹפֶק עַד אֹפֶק
לוֹחֲשִׁים הַמַּיִם.

FISH

Who there
heard?

A live fish tossed on land.
The wind blows through its gaping mouth.
From one horizon to the next
all is forgotten
whisper the Waters.

הרחיקי, לא

הַרְחִיקִי
לֹא תַחְתְּמִי פִּי בְּפִיךְ
אֲדַבֵּר וְיִרְוַח לָךְ
נִשְׁלָח וְשָׁב הָרַעַד
צַעַד צַעַד בִּי תִּגְבְּרִי כַּיָּם
בְּשֵׁפֶל נוּחִי, שִׁכְבִי
לֹא תְכַבִּי
אַבִּיט בְּפָנַיִךְ, תִּרְאִי
פָּנַי כְּעוּרִי
אֵשׁ קוֹלֵךְ בְּקוֹל הָרוּחַ
פָּצוּעַ בִּי הַכֹּל פָּתוּחַ. הַרְחִיקִי, לֹא
תַּנִּיחִי יָדֵךְ עַל גּוּפִי, פִּיךְ עַל אָפְלוֹ.

DISTANCE YOURSELF, DON'T

Distance yourself
don't seal my mouth with your mouth
I'll speak and you'll be relieved,
the trembling dispatched and returned.
Step by step you'll increase in me like the sea,
at low tide lie down, rest,
don't turn off the lights
I'll study your face, you'll see
my ugliness
the fire of your voice in the voice of the wind
the wounded in me wide open. Distance yourself, don't
lay your hand on my body, your mouth on its darkness.

קבורה

עַכְשָׁו, רֵעִי, תִּחְיֶה
אֲשֶׁר רָאוּ עֵינֶיךָ
לְרֶגֶל הַיַּעַר הַמְעָנָן
אֲדָמָה פְּתוּחָה וְלַחָה, דַּם עָלִים
מָשְׁלָךְ, אִי-סֵדֶר זֶה שֶׁלַּטֶּבַע
בְּשָׁעָה שֶׁטָּמַנוּ גּוּפָהּ, יָדֶיהָ, פָּנֶיהָ, וְלֹא יִהְיוּ
אֶלָּא זֵכֶר יָמִים וְקוֹל
אֲשֶׁר שָׁמַעְתָּ גַּם תִּשְׁמַע
בַּיָּמִים הַבָּאִים בְּדָמְךָ
וּבְדַם הָעֵצִים הַסּוֹעֵר מֵעָלֶיךָ
וְנוֹטֵף עַל פָּנֶיךָ וְעַל יָדֶיךָ וּבְעָנָן וּבְכָל הַנִּפְתָּח
מִבִּפְנִים, בַּקַּיִץ וּבַסְּתָו עַד אֲשֶׁר
תִּשְׁכַּח גַּם תִּשְׁכַּח.

BURIAL

Now, my friend, you'll live
what your eyes have seen
at the foot of the cloud-covered forest
earth open and damp, blood of leaves
falling, nature's disorder
at the hour they buried her body, her hands, her face, now
they'll be only a memory of days gone by and the voice
you heard you'll hear
in the coming days in your blood
and the trees' blood swirling above you
and dripping on your face on your hands and in the clouds
in all that opens from within, in summer and autumn until
you forget are also forgotten.

יקיצה

אֵינִי מַתְחִיל
הַשִּׁיר מַתְחִיל
אוֹתִי, שׁוּב
דְּבַר־מָה מִתְרוֹמֵם מֵהֶחָלוֹל הַכָּבֵד, מְעוֹפֵף

וּכְבָר שָׁלֹשׁ שָׁנִים לְאַרְבָּעִים

שָׁנִים מֵעָלַי אוֹתָם שָׁמַיִם, בִּי
אוֹתוֹ מִדְבָּר, לְעֵינַי
עֵץ הַפִּלְפֵּל הַמְשֻׁנֶּה דּוֹמֵם מִפַּעַם וּמִפְעָם
וְהַיָּרֵחַ שֶׁעוֹלֶה בְּעוֹרְקַי
וְהַצִּפֳּרִים
בְּקֵן זָקֵן חֲבוּיִים שֶׁל
שְׂעָרֵךְ

לָרִאשׁוֹנָה
אָמַרְתִּי שׁוּב
לָךְ? לִי? לְמִי?
מִלִּים אֵלֶּה הַמַּתְחִילוֹת

AWAKENING

I don't begin
my poem begins
me, again
something lifting from the heavy sand, fluttering

And it's already three years to forty

years above me the same skies, in me
the same desert, before my eyes
the pepper tree from time to time changing silently
and the moon that rises in my veins
and the birds
in the hidden nests of
your hair

For the first time
I said again
For you? For me? For whom?
These words which begin

יקיצה (2)

בַּשָּׁנָה הַשְּׁחוּנָה הַזֹּאת אֲנִי
בַּחֹשֶׁךְ בְּלִי שָׂפָה
הֵיכָן אַתְּ

מִסְתַּתֶּרֶת
צִפּוֹר עֲשׂוּיָה אֵפֶר
בֵּין הָעֲשָׂבִים הַגְּבוֹהִים
שִׁירָה הָיְתָה
מִסְתַּתֶּרֶת בְּעֵינַיִךְ הָעֲגֻלּוֹת

שׁוּבִי, שׁוּבִי מֵהַמֶּלַח הָאָפֵל
בְּרִיסַיִךְ, גְּעִי
בִּי, פַּעַם אַחַת עוֹד

שְׂעָרֵךְ הָאָרֹךְ הַחוֹזֵר עַל פָּנַי מְכַסֶּה
הַאִם הוּא מְכַסֶּה הֵיטֵב אֶת גּוּפֵךְ הָרָזֶה
בַּקֹּר הַזֶּה

אַתְּ

אֵפֶר וְעֵינֵי צִפּוֹר
לְאַט
פּוֹתַחַת אֶת עֵינַי בְּקוֹל דְּמָעוֹת

AWAKENING (2)

In this parched sleep I am
in a wordless dark
where you are

hiding
bird of ash
in the high grass
poetry used to
hide in your round eyes

Come back, come back from the dark salt
on your lashes, touch
me, one more time

Your long hair before my eyes again covers
does it cover your thin body
in this cold

You

ash and bird eyes
slowly
opening my eyes with the sound of tears

לִשְׁלוֹחַ יָד אֶל תּוֹךְ הָעוֹלָם כְּעֶבֶד הָאוֹחֵז
בְּבֶרֶךְ אֲדוֹנוֹ. תֵּן לִי לָגַעַת בְּגַרְגֵּר וּבְצֵל שֶׁל עָלֶה
בְּכָל הַנּוֹשֵׁם כָּל הַמּוּאָר הָאָפֵל הַזֶּה וּקְצֵה כָּל אֶצְבַּע
הַלֵּל

רָאִיתִי הַרְבֵּה, רָאִיתִי מְעַט. עַכְשָׁו
לִשְׁלוֹחַ יָד אֶל הַקָּרוֹב, הַמְּבֹרָךְ. הָאוֹר
מַנְמִיךְ עֵינֵי בְּשֶׁקֶט רַב, רוּחוֹת בָּאִים בַּחֲשַׁאי
שָׁטִים עַל אֲדָמָה חֲרוּשָׁה רַגְלֵי אָדָם חוֹלְפוֹת חֲרִישִׁיּוֹת
בִּכְאֵב אוֹהֵב. אַל תְּסָרֵב. אַל־נָא תִּסְגֹּר אוֹתִי
בְּתוֹךְ לִבִּי. אֲנִי שׁוֹלֵחַ יָד –

◆

Reaching out into the world like a slave clutching
at his master's knee. Let me touch the grain, shade of the leaf,
all that breathes, this whole lit-up darkness and every fingertip
Praise

I've seen much, I've seen little. Now
reaching out toward what is near, what is blessed. Light
lowers my eyes most quietly, winds arrive in secret
sailing over the plowed land, man's feet pass by silently
with loving pain. Don't deny me. Please, don't close me up
in my heart. I'm reaching out –

לך, אם תוכל

לֵךְ, אִם תּוּכַל
בַּיְּעָרוֹת הַחוּמִים
שִׂים מִצְחֲךָ אֶל הַגְּזָעִים

לֹא תִזְכֹּר, אִם תּוּכַל
פְּעָמַי נִרְדָּף בַּיַּעַר
הָאֹזֶן לַנָּקֵר

עָלִים מְכַסִּים
עוֹד מְעַט הַלִּבְלוּב
הַנִּצָּנִים כְּבָר נִרְאִים בָּאָרֶץ

דַּע, אִם תּוּכַל
כִּי עַכְשָׁו אָבִיב. עַכְשָׁו אַתָּה עוֹד נוֹשֵׁם
בַּיְּעָרוֹת הַחוּמִים.

GO, IF YOU CAN

Go, if you can
into the brown forests
Rest your forehead against the tree-trunks

Don't remember, if you can
the heartbeats of the hunted in the forest
Listen to the woodpecker

The leaves cover everything
soon there will be blossoming
First buds are already seen in the homeland

Know, if you can
that now it's spring. Now you are still breathing
in the brown forests.

◆

שִׁירַת הַצִּפּוֹר הַקְּפוּאָה שֶׁל הַלַּיְלָה.
יָרֵחַ אֵינוֹ נִרְאֶה עוֹד
יָרֵחַ. דָּם לָבָן
דָּבֵק בָּאֲדָמָה הָעֲרֵמָה.
לֹא הָיוּ לֵילוֹת אֲחֵרִים.
אֵין לִזְכֹּר לֵילוֹת אֲחֵרִים שֶׁהָיוּ
מָעוֹן לָנוּ מִדּוֹר לְדוֹר בְּטֶרֶם יָלְדוּ הָרִים
הַרְרֵי הַקֹּר וַעֲצֵי הַדֹּק
וְהַפַּחַד וְהַכּוֹכָבִים הַנּוֹרָאִים
מֵעַל לֶחָזֶה הַגָּלוּי כַּאֲשֶׁר אֲנַחְנוּ בְּעֵינֵי צִפֳּרִים
וּבְגוּף שֶׁל שִׁירָה אָהַבְנוּ אָהַבְנוּ
שׁוֹב וָשׁוֹב
אֵין לִזְכֹּר.

♦

The song of the frozen bird of the night.
The moon no longer looks
like a moon. White blood
is glued to the naked earth.
There were no other nights.
There's no remembering other nights that were
for us a home, generation after generation, before hills were born
the hills of the cold and the heavenly trees
of fear and the terrible stars
above the exposed chest while we in the birds' eyes
and in the body of song loved and loved
again and again there's
no remembering.

♦

כָּל עוֹד אַתָּה אוֹמֵר
כִּי סוֹף, כִּי אֵין יוֹתֵר
לֹא כֵן לֹא לֹא
דַּי קְרָב. יֵשׁ

מִישֶׁהוּ אוֹמֵר
אֲנִי שׁוֹמֵעַ אֶת קוֹלוֹ
שֶׁל מִישֶׁהוּ, כִּי רַב
כִּי טוֹב, יֵשׁ מִישֶׁהוּ אוֹמֵר
לֵאמֹר יֵשׁ מִישֶׁהוּ
אֲשֶׁר נוֹשֵׁם עַכְשָׁו.

♦

As long as you say
it's over, because there's nothing left
not no not yes just
too much struggle, there's

Someone else saying
I can hear someone's
voice, it is many
it is good, there's someone who will say
there's someone
who is breathing now.

III

THE BATTLES OF THE NIGHT

LEFT BEHIND

קרבות הלילה הותירו

שָׁקֵט הַיּוֹם.
לוּ נִתַּן לִישֹׁן מְעַט.

יוֹם, יוֹם וְיוֹם, יוֹם וּשְׁנַיִם, יוֹם
וּשְׁלֹשָׁה יוֹם וְאַרְבָּעָה יוֹם וַחֲמִשָּׁה
יוֹם וְשִׁשָּׁה וְלַיְלָה אֶחָד –
הַהַכָּרָה לֹא חָזְרָה.

חֲפָצִים אֲחָדִים בְּלִי בְּעָלִים.
גּוּפִיָּה מְיֻזַּעַת, נְעָלִים שְׁחוּקוֹת.

בַּשָּׁרָב גַּם הַצֵּל הַבָּלוּי שֶׁל עֵץ אֶקָלִיפְּט רַחֲמָיו מְרֻבִּים.
שָׁעָה קַלָּה, רַק שָׁעָה קַלָּה, לְהַחֲלִיף כֹּחַ.

הָיָה מְחַיֵּךְ כְּשֶׁפָּנוּ אֵלָיו. לֹא דָּחַק וְלֹא הָיָה דָּחוּק.
אִשְׁתּוֹ בַּחֹדֶשׁ הָרְבִיעִי.

זְחִילַת תּוֹלָעִים אֵין סוֹף בַּמִּזְבָּלָה.
הָאֲדָמָה הָאֲדֻמָּה מִתְהַפֶּכֶת רֶגַע רֶגַע.
גֶּתֶה חָשַׁב, אַחַר פְּטִירָתוֹ תִּהְיֶה יָדוֹ אוּלַי פַּרְפַּר.

יֵשׁ חֲלוֹם שֶׁאַתָּה נִקְלָע בּוֹ, וְאֵין מוֹצָא.

THE BATTLES OF THE NIGHT LEFT BEHIND

The quiet of day.
If only sleep were possible.

A day, a day and another day, a day and two,
a day and three a day and four a day and five
a day and six and one night –
consciousness has not returned.

A few possessions with no owners.
A sweaty undershirt, worn-down boots.

In the heat-wave even the faded shade of a eucalyptus tree is great mercy.
A moment or two, no more, to restore energy.

He used to smile when turned to. He never pressed, was never pressured.
His wife is in her fourth month.

Endless crawling of the worms in the dunghill.
The red earth turns over moment by moment.
Goethe thought, after his death his hand would become perhaps a butterfly.

There are dreams you become entwined in, and there's no way out.

וּפְנֵי הָאֵם בַּכַּף

וְאִם הַפַּעַם זֶה בְּנָם שֶׁל הַשְּׁכֵנִים
אֲשֶׁר מִמֶּנּוּ לֹא נוֹתַר מְאוּם לֶעָפָר
וְאִם הַפַּעַם זֶה בְּנָם שֶׁל הַשְּׁכֵנִים
וְהָרוּחַ לֹא עָמַד וְהָעֵץ לֹא נֶעֱקַר וְהַכֶּלֶב נָבַח
וְאָמַרְנוּ נוֹרָא נוֹרָא הֲרֵי זֶה
נוֹרָא. תּוֹדָה לָאֵל, בְּנָם שֶׁל הַשְּׁכֵנִים
בָּרוּךְ הַשֵּׁם, בֶּן
הַשְּׁכֵנִים –
כְּלוּם לֹא שָׁנִים, כְּלוּם לֹא נִמְשַׁךְ שָׁנִים
כָּל רֶגַע שֶׁהָיִינוּ כְּרוּיִים
לַקּוֹל שֶׁיָּבוֹא מֵעֵבֶר לַקַּו וְיֹאמַר שָׁלוֹם לִי, אֲנִי שָׁלֵם, שְׁלוֹמִי טוֹב
עַד שֶׁנִּגְזַר הַכֹּל וְנֶחְתַּךְ וּבְלֹא רַחֲמִים
וְהוֹרָיו זְקֵנִים
וְזֶה הַסּוֹף. וְאֵיךְ לְהַבִּיט וְהֵם בְּנֵי אָדָם
מְאָבָּנִים. וּבַפָּנִים הַתְּוֹהוֹת בְּלִי נִיעַ פְּנֵי חַיָּה גּוֹסְסָה פְּנֵי הָאָב
וּפְנֵי הָאֵם שֶׁאֵינֶנָּה עוֹד אֵם וְאֵין לָהּ פָּנִים, בַּכַּף?

THE MOTHER'S FACE IN THE PALM OF HER HANDS

And if this time it's the neighbors' son
of whom nothing is left for dust
and if this time it's the neighbors' son
and the winds didn't stand still the trees weren't uprooted the dog
    kept barking
and we said *its terrible terrible* because it's
terrible. Thank god, the neighbors' son
thank god, the neighbors'
boy –
nothing lasts an eternity,
every second we were glued
to the voice speaking from the other end of the line
    which would say
I'm fine, I'm in one piece, I'm safe and sound
until everything was mercilessly ripped to shreds
and his parents are old
and this is the end. How are we to look now they are stone
people, and in their bewildered frozen faces, the face of a dying
    animal, the father's face
and the face of the mother who is no longer a mother, and no longer has
    a face, in the palm of her hands?

עיר זו

עקודה על סלעיה

עֲקוּדָה עַל סְלָעֶיהָ עוֹלָה
בְּאֵשׁ נִכְפֶּשֶׁת בְּאוֹר הַתָּמִיד
עִיר זוֹ הוֹמִיָּה
חוֹמָה לִפְנִים חוֹמָה
וּפֹה וָשָׁם מִגְדָּל
שׁוֹעָה דַּקָּה
רוּחַ זֵיתִים אֲפֹרָה
עִיר כָּנָף קְרוּעָה בֵּין הָרִים נִכְסֶפֶת
מֵאָדָם רֶשֶׁת נִצְחָהּ
לִפְרֹחַ
שְׁבוּיָה
בִּשְׁעָרִים חוֹרְגִים בִּפְנוֹת הַיּוֹם
לְהִפָּתַח לְהִפָּתַח

חֲתוּמָה מִכְוַת־אֵשׁ בְּיָדוֹ הַשְּׁחֹרָה שֶׁל הַמַּלְאָךְ

72

THIS CITY [JERUSALEM]

Bound on Her Boulders

Bound on her boulders a burnt offering
in flames trampled by light of the daily sacrifice
this teeming city, longing
in its walls within walls
scattered towers
thin outcries
grey wind of the olives
torn among the hills yearned-for city of wings
from her red thicket eternity
blossoming
imprisoned
in gates straying at day's end
to open and open

She is marked by a branding-iron in the Angel's black hand

אבן רוצה לזרם

אֶבֶן רוֹצָה לְזֶרֶם
עֵץ הַזַּיִת מְבַקֵּשׁ לְהִתְאַבֵּן

כְּנֵסִיּוֹת שׁוֹאֲלוֹת אֶת לִבָּן לָעוּף
עָנָן יוֹשֵׁב עַל הַר הַבַּיִת

שְׁמָשׁוֹת סָבְבוּ בַּחוּצוֹת, הָיוּ לְקוֹצִים
מִלְחָמוֹת שֶׁעָבְרוּ בָּהּ לַחֲלוֹמוֹת

צְלָלִים מְהַלְּכִים בִּמְאוֹר־פָּנִים
דְּמָמָתָהּ פַּעֲמוֹנִים פַּעֲמוֹנִים

אֲבָנֶיהָ זוֹרְמוֹת
עֵץ הַזַּיִת אֶבֶן

הַיָּשֵׁן וְלִבּוֹ עֵר יוֹדֵעַ בַּלַּיְלָה
עִיר כְּבֵדָה זוֹ עוֹלָה לָשׁוּט בַּלְּבָנָה

Stones Want to Flow

Stones want to flow
The olive tree wants to be stone

Churches long to fly
A cloud sits on the Temple Mount

Suns wandered on her outskirts, became thorns
Wars passed through and became dreams

Shadows walk around with bright faces
Her silence is bells and bells

Her stones flow
The olive tree is stone

He who sleeps and his heart is awake knows how at night
this heavy city ascends to walk with the moon

יום כמו לילה כמו

יוֹם כְּמוֹ לַיְלָה כְּמוֹ
שֶׁמֶשׁ אֵשׁ
כְּמוֹ בְּכִי בְּלִי קוֹל עִיר זוֹ אֵיפֹה
אֲנַחְנוּ בַּחֲלוֹם כְּמוֹ אוֹר
זְרוֹעַ מַקְפִּיא אֲבָנִים אֲבָנִים עַד
כְּמוֹ נֶצַח סֶלַע עִיר זוֹ
מְעָרוֹת אוֹ בָּתִּים כְּמוֹ
עֵיִם כְּמוֹ חָצָץ כְּמוֹ עָפָר עַד דַּק רוּחַ
כְּמוֹ הָיִינוּ כָּאן

יוֹם אוֹ לַיְלָה
כְּמוֹ בְּלִי קוֹל כְּמוֹ בַּחֲלוֹם מַמָּשׁ הָיִינוּ
כָּאן מְהַלְּכִים בְּעִיר זוֹ זֵכֶר
עָמוּם בְּכִי כְּמָבוֹא חָשׁוּךְ סִמְטָה
שְׁקוּעָה בְּסִמְטָה חַכִּי
חַכִּי אַל תֵּעָלְמִי רַק רֶגַע עוֹד רֶגַע כְּמוֹ
חַיִּים

76

Day Like Night Like

Day like night like
sunfire
like voiceless cries this city where
we live in a dream like sown lights
freezing the stones eternal stones
like rock-eternity this city
caves or homes like
ruins like gravel like unending wind-thin dust
as though we were here
day or night
as though voiceless as in a dream we were really
here wandering through this city remnants
of muted cries like a dark entryway an alley
sunken in the alley wait
wait don't vanish just one moment one more moment like
Life

שמים שקטים ופתוחים

שָׁמַיִם שְׁקֵטִים וּפְתוּחִים
מֵעַל עִיר שֶׁהָיְתָה אַחַת אֱלֹהִים
מֵעַל עִיר שֶׁהָיְתָה אֲחֻזָּה
מֵעַל עִיר שֶׁהָיְתָה
שָׁמַיִם פְּתוּחִים וּשְׁקֵטִים

Quiet and Open Skies

Quiet and open skies
above a City God's treasured possession
above a City that was God-possessed
above a City that was possessed
above a City that was open and quiet skies

ירח וכוכבים אשר כוננתה

בְּרוּרִים כְּמוֹ מִדְבָּר בָּאֲפֵלָה
הֵם מַשְׁקִיפִים עָלֵינוּ: צֶדֶק, מַאְדִּים וְהַצַּיָּד
– לֹא יָכְלוּ לַעֲצֹם אֶת עֵינָיו. עַל הַגַּב. קַו דָּם דַּק. פָּנָיו –
הוֹפְכִים פָּנֵינוּ צֵל וָצֵל אֲבָנִים שְׁבוּרוֹת.

MOON AND STARS THAT YOU CREATED

As clear as the desert in darkness
they look down on us: Jupiter, Mars and the Hunter
– But they couldn't close his eyes. There where he lies, on his back. Slender
   blood streak. And his face –
transforms our face into shadows, shades and broken stones.

קַיִץ

קַיִץ קוֹרֵא לַקּוֹצִים אֵשׁ
שָׁם בַּ־אֵין־לוֹמַר־זֹאת־שָׁמַיִם
מִתְגַּלְגֶּלֶת מֵת־
בּוֹסֶסֶת הַשֶּׁמֶשׁ

הַשָּׂדוֹת סָבִיב צְרוּבִים. פֹּה שָׁם
כִּתְמֵי תִּירָס יָרֹק כְּמוֹ
פְּצָעִים שֶׁלֹּא הִגְלִידוּ. זֹאת הָאֱמֶת
אֵין לְכַחֵד תַּחַת הַלָּשׁוֹן
הַבּוֹעֶרֶת הַמְּשֻׁרְבֶּבֶת תַּחַת
אֵיךְ־קוֹרְאִים־לָזֶה הַשָּׁמַיִם

הַמֵּתִים, אֵין לְכַחֵד, הַמֵּתִים
הָרַבִּים מִתְרַבִּים מִיּוֹם לְיוֹם
נִבָּטִים בְּעֵינַיִם, אֵין לוֹמַר זֹאת, מָתוֹת
וְאֵין לְכַחֵד. הָאַלְמָנוֹת
צְעִירוֹת. אָזְנֵי אִמָּהוֹת
כְּבֵדוֹת. פָּנֵינוּ

הַצִּדָּה. זֹאת הָאֱמֶת, הַמִּלְחָמָה
אֵין לְכַחֵד, טוֹרֶפֶת
עוֹד קַיִץ עוֹד קַיִץ
בָּאֲדָמָה מְשֻׁגַּעַת־מָוֶת, חוֹלֶמֶת דָּם.

SUMMER

Summer calls forth its fire thorns
and there in the can't-be-called-a-sky
the sun is spinning turning wal-
lowing

The fields all around are singed. Here and there
are patches of corn green like
open sores. This is the truth
there's no concealing it under the burning
stuck-out tongue under the
what's-it-called sky

The dead, there's no denying it, the many dead
are multiplying day by day, gazing
with eyes that are, it-shouldn't-be said, dead
and there's no denying. The widows
are young. The mothers
deaf. We turn our faces

away. This is the truth, the War
there's no denying, devours
another summer and then another
in this death-demented, blood-dreaming land.

המדבר האחרון

בָּעַר. כְּמוֹ קְרִיאוֹת קַלּוֹת
הָאֵשׁ בְּקוֹצָיו. קְצָת
קִרְעֵי קוֹלוֹת.
אַחַר אָכַל.

אֵין לְהַבְדִּיל בֵּין חוֹל לְחוֹל

אֵיפֹה   מִי

מַה

פְּנֵי הַמִּדְבָּר הַמְּחוּקוֹת.

תִּפְרַחַת דְּמָמָה.

THE LAST DESERT

Burned. The fire in its thorns
like faint callings. A few
ragged voices. Then
was devoured.

There's no distinguishing sand from sand

Where   who

What

The desert's erased face.

Silence breeding.

פיאטה רונדניני

עוֹד רֹאשְׁךָ לְכְתֵפִי, עוֹד יָדִי
אָנָה יָדֶיךָ?
עוֹד שְׁנֵינוּ קֶשֶׁת אַחַת
עוֹד הַצְּעָקָה בָּאֶבֶן. עוֹד
אַתָּה
הַחוֹמֶק, הַגּוּף הַחוֹמֶק, לֹא
לֹא
בְּנִי

RONDANINI PIETÀ

Still your head on my shoulder, still my hand
where is your hand?
Still the two of us one arc
still the scream in stone. Still
you
slipping away, the body slipping away, no
no
my son

1

בַּיִת
לֹא בַּיִת.
חָלָל.

שַׁרְווּל הַקְּטֵעַ יוֹדֵעַ
אֶת הַחֹם
שֶׁהָיָה בּוֹ.

דְּמוּת אֵינָהּ רַק דְּמוּת. מָחוּק מוֹתִיר עֲקֵבוֹת.

אֵשׁ פּוֹרַחַת בָּעֵץ. קוֹל
סוֹבֵב בָּרוּחַ. הוֹלֵךְ סוֹבֵב
דּוּמָה. גְּמְגּוּם. יְבָבָה.

הוּא שֶׁהַכֹּל הָיָה לְפָנָיו

אַחֲרָיו
רֶגַע לֹא אָכַל.

2

לְהָבִין
מַה לְהָבִין
אֲנִי שׁוֹמֵעַ
אֲנִי נוֹשֵׁם
אֲנִי הוֹלֵךְ עַל שְׁתַּיִם

3

מַה נָּבוֹן
שֶׂכְוִי
מַבְחִין בֵּין יוֹם לְלַיְלָה

1983

1
Home
is not a home.
A hollow.

The amputee's sleeve knows
the warmth
it once had.

An image is not just an image. The erased leaves tracks.

Flames blossom in the tree. A voice
swirls in the wind. Whirling
in silence. A stutter. A whimper.

He who had everything before him

after him
every moment burns and burns.

2
To understand
understand what
I hear
I breathe
I walk on two

3
How clever
is the rooster
who distinguishes between day and night

4

לְדַבֵּר
לְדַבֵּר –
אֲנִי חוֹפֵר וְחוֹפֵר
וְעָפָר עִם עָפָר מִתְחַבֵּר

5

מִלִּים זוֹנוֹת
אַחֲרֵי הַמָּוֶת
אוֹמְרוֹת הָלַךְ
אָבַד
הִסְתַּלֵּק
חֹרֶף, קַיִץ, רוּחַ בָּעֵצִים, אוֹר, אֲוִיר

6

בְּנִי שֶׁאָבַד
בֶּן זְקוּנַי
שָׁב
מָצָא מַחְבּוֹא
סָמוּי בְּעֵינַי –
לֹא תִּירָא רַע
יָדִי עַל פָּנַי.

90

4
To talk
and talk –
I dig and dig
until dust unites with dust

5
Words are whores
after the death
they say *He went*
Is lost
Left
Winter, summer, wind in the trees, light, air

6
My son who was lost
my youngest son
came back
found a secret
hiding place
in my eyes –
Fear no harm now
my hands cover my face.

פרידה מידיד

לדן פגיס

לֹא בִּרְצוֹן אֲנִי נִפְרָד מִמְּךָ.
אַל תִּתְמַהְמַהּ.
הֲלֹא אֵינְךָ אוֹהֵב לִנְסֹעַ בַּחֹשֶׁךְ.

צֵרוּף מַפְתִּיעַ אֵינֶנּוּ מַפְתִּיעַ עוֹד.
פִּתְרוֹן שָׁנוּן שׁוֹרֵט בָּאֲוִיר.

מַה טַּעַם בִּדְמוּי מְחַבֵּר שָׁמַיִם וָאָרֶץ?
בַּחֲרוּז מְזַוֵּג נִפְרָדִים?

הֵיטַבְתָּ עִמִּי. הֵיטַבְתִּי עִמְּךָ?

רַעַשׁ קַל וְחוֹלֵף

שְׁנֵינוּ הָלַכְנוּ יַחְדָּו כָּל אֶחָד לְדַרְכּוֹ.
מוֹתֵנוּ וְחַיֵּינוּ בְּיַד לָשׁוֹן.
אָמַרְנוּ בְּלִבֵּנוּ: אִם לֹא נְדַבֵּר אֶל לֵב
נִפֹּל חָלָל.

קוֹל כְּמוֹ

עֲזָבוֹ דָמוֹ.

מִתְאַפְלֶלֶת גִּבְעַת הַמּוֹרֶה.
הַר־גַּעַשׁ כָּבוּי מִשֶּׁכְבָר הַיָּמִים.
עוֹד נִרְאֶה בֵּית־הַקְּבָרוֹת הַקָּטָן בְּצַלְעוֹ.
הַר עִקֵּשׁ וְאִלֵּם.

הַאִם הוּא מְבַקֵּשׁ לְהַמְרִיא
גּוּשׁ אָפֹר זֶה, רָחוֹק מִלִּהְיוֹת מְפֹאָר
פּוּגִ׳יָמָה זָעִיר, מְאָבָּק, בְּלִי פִּסְגַּת־שֶׁלֶג?

מָה עוֹד אוּכַל לוֹמַר.
שׁוּב אֵינֶנִּי רוֹאֶה מְאוּם.

92

FAREWELL FROM A FRIEND

For Dan Pagis

Not willingly do I bid you farewell.
But don't tarry.
After all, you don't like traveling in the dark.

A surprising collocation is no longer surprising.
A clever solution scratches at the air.

What good is an image connecting earth and sky?
In a rhyme coupling the separate?

You graced my days. Did I grace yours?

A small noise, then gone.

We walked together each on his own path.
Our deaths and our lives in the power of words.
We said in our hearts: if we don't talk to the heart
we'll fall among the fallen.

A voice like
the blood-less.

Moreh Hill darkens.
A volcano extinguished long ago.
We'll still see the small graveyard in its shadows.
A mute and stubborn hill.

Does it want to soar
this gray lump, far from grand
a tiny Fujiyama, dust-covered, no snow-cap?

What else can I say.
Again I see nothing.

IV

A GRAVEN AND A MOLTEN IMAGE

הנפילה

אֵצֶל שָׁאגָאל מִשְּׁמֵי־שָׁמַיִם
הוּא נוֹפֵל. כְּנָפָיו כְּלֶהָבוֹת כֵּהוֹת
סוֹמְרוֹת מֵעַל גַּבּוֹ לְלֹא הוֹעִיל.
הוּא כְּמוֹ עֻבָּר שָׁמוּט מֵרֶחֶם.
בְּאֵיזוֹ מְהִירוּת
הַכֹּל חוֹלֵף, הוֹפֵךְ אֲוִיר, בִּיעָף
הַנַּסִּים הַלָּלוּ, כָּל הָעֲיָרָה
שֶׁהִתְאַסְּפָה לְקִרְאַת הַמַּחֲזֶה, הַפַּחַד
הוֹתִיר בַּתָּוֶךְ שֶׁטַח רֵיק,
זְרוֹעוֹת שְׁלוּחוֹת, נָשִׁים כּוֹרְעוֹת לָלֶדֶת, אֲחֵרִים
מֵתִים מִצְּחוֹק – כְּבָר עֲצוּמִים כְּמוֹ עָנָן
וּמְכַסִּים חַיָּו שֶׁעוֹד לְהֶרֶף־עַיִן
שָׁם מֵעַל, מַזָּל מוּזָר,
תּוֹעִים בְּמָבוֹךְ נְפִילָתוֹ.

לֹא כָּכָה אֵצֶל בְּרֵכֶל. כָּאן
רַק רֶגֶל זְעִירָה עוֹד מִזְדַּקֶּרֶת מַעְלָה
בְּעוֹד שֶׁהַשְּׁנִיָּה כְּבָר שְׁטוּפָה גַּלִּים קְטַנִּים.
דַּיָּג עָסוּק בְּחַכָּתוֹ.
בְּמִפְרָשִׂים גְּדוֹלִים נוֹסַעַת אֳנִיָּה.
רוֹעֶה, גַּבּוֹ לַיָּם, מַבִּיט בְּעֵץ כְּבְפֶלֶא מִשָּׁמַיִם.
אִכָּר מַמְשִׁיךְ בַּחֲרִישׁוֹ, כִּי אֵין לְהִשְׁתַּמֵּט
מֵעַצְבוֹנָהּ שֶׁל אֲדָמָה וּמִטְּרַחַת הַיּוֹם.
אִיקָרוֹס? מִי?
הַשֶּׁמֶשׁ כְּבָר נוֹטָה. הַחֲשֵׁכָה קְרוֹבָה.

THE FALL

In Chagall's painting, he falls
from heaven's heights. His wings like dark flames
stiffen from his back, to no effect.
He is like a fetus dropped from the womb.
How quickly
it all passes by, becomes air, in a rush.
Those dwarves, the whole village
that has gathered to watch the spectacle, fear
creating an empty space in the middle,
arms outstretched, women crouching to give birth, others
dying of laughter – they are already huge like a cloud
covering his life that still for an instant
up there, strange luck,
wanders through the labyrinth of his fall.

Not so in Brueghel. Here
only a tiny leg still protrudes upward
while the other is already being rinsed in small waves.
A fisherman is busy with his rod.
A ship with billowing sails passes by.
A shepherd, his back to the sea, stares at a tree as though it were heaven's
    wonder.
A farmer continues his plowing, because there's no avoiding
the land's toil and the day's chores.
Icarus? Who?
The sun is already setting. Darkness draws near.

למה

(גולגולת בדולח, אינדיאנית קדומה, המוזיאון הבריטי)

גֻּלְגֹּלֶת הַבְּדֹלַח צְלוּלָה מְאֹד.
מְלֶאכֶת מַחֲשֶׁבֶת לְעֵלָּא וּלְעֵלָּא.
תַּרְבּוּת מַיָּה, כִּמְדֻמֶּה.

הָאוֹר נוֹגֵעַ בָּהּ וְנִבְלָע.

עֶצֶם בִּדְמוּת דִּמְעָה
צָרָה צוּרָה לַדְּמָמָה.

אֵינָהּ מְשִׁיבָה. אֵינָהּ שׁוֹאֶלֶת.

לָמָה אַתָּה נִגְרָר לִרְאוֹתָהּ
כְּסַהֲרוּרִי
הֲלוֹם חֲלוֹמָהּ?

מֵאַרְבּוֹת עֵינֶיהָ נִבָּט שָׁחוֹר.
אֵיזוֹ אֲפֵלָה שֶׁאֲפִלּוּ אֲפֵלָה
אֵינֶנּוּ שָׁמָּה.

WHY

The crystal skull is crystal clear.
A stunning work of art.
Mayan, I believe.

Light touches it and is swallowed up.

Bone in the shape of a tear
gives shape to silence.

It answers no question. It asks none.

Why are you drawn to look at it
like a sleep-walker
struck by its dream?

From its eye sockets peers out a black flame.
This is darkness that even darkness
is not its name.

המצביא

(מוזיאון האקרופוליס, אתונה)

הַמַּצְבִּיא לוֹטֵשׁ עֵינַיִם.
יֵשׁ בָּהֶן בָּרָק מוּזָר.

רֹאשׁ הַנַּעַר מִמּוּלוֹ מְסָרֵב.
שְׂפָתָיו קְמוּצוֹת, לְבָנוֹת.
עֵינָיו לְבָנוֹת.
דָּמוֹ נִמְלַט מִמֶּנּוּ.
גּוּפוֹ נִמְלַט מִמֶּנּוּ.

הַמַּצְבִּיא הַגָּדוֹל צוֹפֶה לְמֶרְחוֹק:
לַמִּדְבָּר, לַנֶּצַח
עָסוּק בְּתִכְנוּן נִצְחוֹנוֹ הַסּוֹפִי.
הַבְּרוֹנְזָה שֶׁלּוֹ הֶעֱלְתָה יְרֹקֶת.
שׁוֹמֵר הָאוּלָם מְנַגֵּב אֶת הָאָבָק מִלִּבּוֹ.

THE COMMANDER

(Museum of the Acropolis, Athens)

The Commander stares and stares.
His eyes are strangely aglow.

The head of the boy across from him declines.
His lips are clenched, white.
His eyes are white.
His blood has fled him.
His body has fled him.

The Great Commander looks off into the distance:
to the desert, to eternity,
busy with plans for his final victory.
His bronze is rusty.
The hall's guard wipes the dust from his heart.

הַנְּעָרִים

(אתונה)

תָּמִיד הֵם מְחַיְּכִים הַנְּעָרִים הַלָּלוּ
וְהַגְּבָרִים שֶׁאֵין לָהֶם גִּיל.
אֲפִלּוּ אֵינָם אֶלָּא טוֹרְסוֹ
אַתָּה מְדַמֶּה לִרְאוֹת אֶת הַחִיּוּךְ עַל פְּנֵיהֶם.
הֵם מְחַיְּכִים פְּנִימָה אֶל תּוֹךְ עַצְמָם.
נְקֻדַּת כֹּבֶד מַשֶּׁהוּ מִתַּחַת לַלֵּב.
הֵם הוֹלְכִים בְּנוּחָם וְנָחִים בְּלֶכְתָּם
שׁוֹמְרֵי־מִפְתָּן אֵלֶּה שֶׁל הַחֲלוֹמוֹת.

בְּיוֹם רִאשׁוֹן בַּבֹּקֶר יָצָא הַבֵּן אֶת הָאָרֶץ.
פָּנָיו לַדְּרָכִים הַמַּפְלִיגוֹת,
לַמַּיִם הַמִּתְפַּלְּגִים תַּחְתָּיו.
הוּא יִפְנֶה לְכָאן וּלְכָאן.
אֵין לָדַעַת מָתַי יָשׁוּב.
בַּת שְׂחוֹק חֲבוּיָה מִבַּעַד לְפָנָיו.
מְהַלְּכוֹת אַגָּדוֹת לְמִינֵיהֶן.

עֵינֵיהֶם הָרֵיקוֹת רוֹאוֹת גַּם בַּחֹשֶׁךְ.
מִפְּנֵי עִוְרוֹנָן אֵין מָנוֹס.
הֵן זוֹכְרוֹת אֶת אִיגֵאוּס, הַמִּפְרָשׂ הַשָּׁחוֹר.
יְדֵיהֶם קְמוּצוֹת כָּלְשֶׁהוּ, צְמוּדוֹת לְגוּפָם.
"חַיִּים הֵם מָוֶת וּמָוֶת גַּם הוּא חַיִּים"

THE YOUTHS
(*Athens*)

They are always smiling, these youths
and the men who are ageless.
Even though they are only torsos
you imagine you can see the smile on their faces.
They are smiling inwardly.
Their center of gravity is somewhere beneath the heart.
They walk while resting, rest while walking
these threshold dream-guardians.

On Sunday morning the son left the country,
heading towards distant paths,
towards waters parting beneath him.
He'll go here and there.
There's no knowing when he'll return.
A small, half-hidden smile on his face.
Tales of every type are starting to spread.

Their empty eyes can see also in the dark.
There's nothing to do about the blindness.
They remember Aegeus, the black sail.
Their hands are clenched, held close to their bodies.
"Life is death and death is also life"

הַחִיּוּךְ

תָּמִיד הֵם מְחַיְּכִים הַנְּעָרִים הַלָּלוּ
וְהַגְּבָרִים שֶׁאֵין לָהֶם גִּיל.
אֲפִלּוּ אֵינָם אֶלָּא טוֹרְסוֹ
אֵין הַחִיּוּךְ סָר מֵעֲלֵיהֶם.
הֵם הוֹלְכִים בְּנוּחָם וְנָחִים בְּלֶכְתָּם
שׁוֹמְרֵי־מִפְתָּן אֵלֶּה שֶׁל הַחֲלוֹמוֹת.

הַכִּכָּר בַּחוּץ – מִשְׁכַּב חַמָּה.
בָּתֵּי הַקָּפֶה בַּחֲצִי הַגֹּרֶן הוֹמִים מֵאָדָם.
אוֹהֲבִים צוֹחֲקִים מְמַזְּגִים אֶת פְּנֵיהֶם.

גַּם פָּרָשׁ בֵּינֵיהֶם. הַסּוּס אָבַד.
רָאוּי לִזְכֹּר אַף אֶת הָאִישׁ הַשּׁוֹכֵחַ לְאָן מוֹלִיכָה הַדֶּרֶךְ.
מָוֶת הוּא אֲשֶׁר רוֹאִים הָעֵרִים, אֲבָל בַּשֵּׁנָה

"חַבֵּק אוֹתִי קְצָת וְאַל תַּחֲלֹם שָׁם,
בּוֹא וְנַשֵּׁק אוֹתִי, חַיְכָן אֶחָד!"

THE SMILE

They are always smiling, these youths
and the men who are ageless.
Even though they are only torsos
the smile never leaves their lips.
They walk while resting, rest while walking
these threshold dream-guardians.

The square outside – the sun's resting place.
Cafes in a half-circle are crowded.
Lovers are laughing, their faces entwined.

There's a horseman among them. The horse is lost.
It's worth remembering also he who forgot where the road leads.
Death is what the wakeful see, but in sleep –

"Embrace me a little and don't dream there,
come and kiss me, you smiling one!"

האסטלה

(אתונה)

הַנִּפְטָר נִפְרָד מִן הַנּוֹתָר בִּתְקִיעַת יָד
בְּכָל הַמַּצֵּבוֹת (אוֹ כִּמְעַט בְּכֻלָּן)
מוֹשִׁיט הַמֵּת יָד לֶחִי.
תָּמִיד הַשְּׁנַיִם.
אִישׁ אֵינוֹ מְדַבֵּר.

בְּמַצֶּבֶת קֶבֶר אַחַת מִן הַמֵּאָה הָרְבִיעִית
יֵשׁ גַּם שְׁלִישִׁי: כֶּלֶב חַי.
הָאִישׁ הַפּוֹנֶה וְעוֹבֵר לִהְיוֹת צֵל
יָדוֹ הַפְּנוּיָה מַצְבִּיעָה עָלָיו.
בַּהֲמֻלָּה הַקָּמָה פִּתְאֹם בָּאוּלָם הַמָּלֵא הֲמוֹן תַּיָּרִים
נָע וָנָד מִמָּקוֹם לְמָקוֹם
מִתְעַטֶּפֶת, חֲרִישִׁית כְּשַׁיִשׁ,
הַיְבָבָה הַדַּקָּה.

THE GRAVESTONE
(Athens)

On all the tombstones, or almost all,
the deceased bids farewell with an outstretched hand –
the dead reaches out to the living.
Always there are both.
Neither speaks.

On the tombstone of one grave from the fourth century
there's a third figure: a dog.
The man who is leaving, becoming a shadow,
points at it with his free hand.
In the commotion suddenly astir in the hall full of tourists
moving from place to place
one can hear, quiet as marble,
its thin whimper.

פָּנִים

(ארון מצרי, המוזיאון הבריטי)

אָרוֹן בְּתוֹךְ אָרוֹן זְכוּכִית. פָּתוּחַ. חָנוּט.
אֲנִי עוֹבֵר וּמַבִּיט, עוֹבֵר וּמַבִּיט.
אֲחֵרִים עוֹבְרִים עַל פָּנַי, עַל יָדִי
הֲמוֹן רוֹחֵשׁ דְּמָמָה. נַעֲרָה שְׂעָרָהּ אֵשׁ. אִישׁ
עַל קַב. יָשִׁישׁ פָּנָיו פְּנֵי מַיִם קְמוּטִים. כִּתָּה
שֶׁל בֵּית־סֵפֶר, כִּמְעַט תִּינוֹקוֹת. פָּנַי אֶל
פְּנֵי הֶחָנוּט דּוּמָם נִבָּטִים בַּזְּכוּכִית פָּנִים
עַל פָּנִים

בְּהֵעָלֵם
הָאָרֶץ הַחֲלוּמָה עַל לַחְמָהּ וְתִירוֹשָׁהּ וּנְהָרָהּ וְאוֹרָהּ
כְּצֵל לָבָן, כְּחֶמֶת חֲלוּלָה בַּמִּדְבָּר
שְׁאֵרִית גְּרוּמָה, מְטַל מָה,
מֶלֶךְ הַחֲלוֹמוֹת, צָדוּף, מַשְׂחִיר פָּנִים, מוּאָר
מִזְוִית מִסְתֶּרֶת מִין שֶׁמֶשׁ תַּחְתִּית
דֶּרֶךְ אֵיזוֹ שִׁמְשָׁה

אֲנִי מַבִּיט וּמַבִּיט

FACE

(*Egyptian sarcophagus, British Museum*)

An open sarcophagus inside a glass casement. A mummy.
I walk by it and stare, walk by again and stare.
Others pass by me, near me
a crowd of rustling whispers. A girl with fire hair. A man
on crutches. An old man with the face of wrinkled waters. A group
of schoolchildren, almost babies. I face
the face of the mummy silently looking out from the glass face
to face

With the disappearance
of the dreamt-of land, with its breads and wines and rivers and light
like white shadows, like the desert's hollow rage,
these skeletal remains are what remain, somewhat imposed,
this King of Dreams, encrusted, face blackening, illuminated
from a hidden angle, an underworld sun from a dark elsewhere
shining on it through the pane

I stare and stare

תמונה ודו־שיח
(מכס ארנסט, "כל העיר כולה")

הַמָּאוֹר הַקָּטָן הוּא הַמָּאוֹר הַגָּדוֹל.
הָאֲוִיר רְאִי שֶׁל מַיִם מְאָרָרִים.
בְּאוֹר הָרַע, בַּשְּׁתִיקָה
מוּטֶלֶת עִיר, נָפְלָה יְרֵכָהּ, כְּשֶׁרֶץ מְפֻתָּל.
רֹאשָׁהּ, פָּחוּס, בְּעַיִן מְאֻבֶּנֶת
נִבָּט בְּעֵין הָאֶבֶן שֶׁל הַמַּה־שֶּׁמָּם־שָׁם שָׁמַיִם.

– "אֵיזֶה צְבָעִים," אָמַרְתְּ, "אֵיזֶה צְבָעִים! כַּמָּה חַיִּים!"
– "כְּמוֹ," אָמַרְתִּי חֵרֵשׁ וּמִתְּשׁוּקָה
רָעַד קוֹלִי. "כְּמוֹ חַיִּים.
צָרִיךְ לָזוּז. יַקִּירָתִי, צָרִיךְ לְאַט
לָזוּז. הוֹלְכִים וּמְכַבִּים, סוֹגְרִים,
סוֹגְרִים אוֹתָנוּ עוֹד מְעַט."

A PAINTING AND A CONVERSATION
(after Max Ernst's "The Entire City")

The lesser light is the greater light.
The air is a mirror of cursed waters.
In the evil light, in the silence
the city sprawls, fallen to its haunches, like a twisted creeping thing.
Its head, squashed, with a petrified eye
gazes at the stone's eye of the what's-its-name-there sky.

– "What colors," you said, "what colors! How much life!"
– "Like," I said softly, my voice
trembling with passion. "Lifelike.
We must move, my dear, we must
move on. They are turning off the lights, closing up,
they'll lock us in soon."

סוס ורוכבו

(סימונה מרטיני, "ג'ודוויצ'ו פוליאנו")

רָכוּב עַל גַּב סוּס.
בִּשְׁנוֹת הַשְּׁמוֹנִים שֶׁל הַמֵּאָה הָעֶשְׂרִים
מָה עוֹשֶׂה אוֹתוֹ אִישׁ רָכוּב עַל גַּב סוּס?
הוּא אִטִּי
הוּא אִטִּי מְאֹד.
אֵין טַעַם לַחֲזֹר.
עִתּוֹתָיו בְּיָדָיו כְּמוֹשְׁכוֹת שְׁמוּטוֹת.
אַחֲרָיו חוֹמוֹת. לְפָנָיו חוֹמוֹת.
גְּדֵרוֹת מְחֻדָּדוֹת וַחֲנִיּוֹת עֲזוּבוֹת פֹּה וָשָׁם.
הַשָּׁמַיִם אֲפֵלִים לְבִלְעַ.
אוֹר הָאָרֶץ חִוֵּר כַּמָּוֶת.
וַאֲנִי אֵינֶנִי
אֶלָּא מְדַבֵּר.
מֵאַיִן רוֹכֵב הָאִישׁ עַל גַּב סוּס?
לְאָן רוֹכֵב הָאִישׁ עַל גַּב סוּס?
אֵין טַעַם לְהַמְצִיא תַּחְבִּיר חָדָשׁ.
סוּס וְרוֹכְבוֹ, בֵּין כֹּה וָכֹה.
הוּא לֹא הִתְקַדֵּם גַּם לֹא פְּסִיעָה אַחַת.
גַּם לֹא מִכָּאן עַד כָּאן.
אֵין טַעַם לַחֲזֹר בָּאוֹר הַזֶּה.
הוּא מַבִּיט נִכְחוֹ.

HORSE AND HIS RIDER
(after Simone Martini's "Guidoriccio da Fogliano")

Seated on the back of a horse.
In the 1980s of the twentieth century
what is a man doing on the back of a horse?
He's slow.
He's very slow.
There's no point in turning back.
His days are in his hands like fallen reins.
Behind him, walls. Before him, walls.
Sharp-edged fences and abandoned spears all around.
The sky is a swallowing darkness.
The earth's light is as pale as death.
And I am not
but speaking.
Where is the man on the horse riding from?
Where is he riding to?
There's no point inventing a new syntax.
It's a horse and his rider, any way you put it.
He hasn't advanced even a single step.
Not even from here to here.
In this light there's no point in turning back.
He stares straight ahead.

המכתב

(ורמר, "אשה קוראת מכתב")

מַפַּת הָעוֹלָם בָּרֶקַע, בַּצֵּל
עוֹמֶדֶת אִשָּׁה צְעִירָה שְׁקוּעָה
– הוּא רָחוֹק וְלֹא
הִיא קוֹרֵאת –
כֻּלָּהּ בְּאוֹר
מִכְתָּב

אַהֲבָה

THE LETTER

(after Vermeer's "Woman in Blue Reading a Letter")

A map of the world in the background, in the shadows
a young woman stands, immersed in thought
– he is far and not
she is reading –
all in light
a letter

of love

רשומי מלאכים של פאול קליי וצבע מים אחד

1

מלאך שכחן

גַּם אֲנִי רוֹצָה לִמְצֹא חֵן
וּלְעוֹפֵף לְפִי הָאָפְנָה.
אֲבָל שָׁכַחְתִּי...
כְּנָפַי מְגַמְגְּמוֹת
וְאֵינֶנִּי נָע.

2

התקפה

לֹא שֶׁבַח לֹא הַלֵּל
לֹא חֵן לֹא חָכְמָה.
אֲנִי חַי בַּחֲצוֹת הַלֵּיל
בְּלֵב לִבָּהּ שֶׁל חַמָּה.

3

מבחן עמס

עַל רֹאשִׁי רַק רֶמֶז שֶׁל אֶבֶן
וּכְבָר אֲנִי עַל בִּרְכַּי.
אֲנִי מְנַסֶּה רוֹם־עֵינַיִם

אֲנִי מַלְאָךְ לֹא־כְדַאי.

PAUL KLEE'S ANGELS:
EIGHT DRAWINGS AND ONE WATERCOLOR

1

Forgetful Angel

I too want to be adored
and fly in the day's fashion.
But I've forgotten how...
My wings stutter
and I do not move.

2

Attack

Not praise not glory
Not wisdom not grace.
I live in night's midnight
in the sun's heart of hearts.

3

Weight-Bearing Test

On my head just the hint of a stone
and already I'm on my knees.
I try haughtiness

I am an angel, useless.

4

מלאך, מכער עדין

הִנְנִי מַה שֶׁהִנְנִי.

כְּלִי מְבַקֵּשׁ הֶלָל.

לֵב לֹא מְכֻוָּן.

כִּמְעַט לֹא נוֹצַרְתִּי. אֵינֶנִּי.

אֲנִי מַשְׁחִיר

וְהַשֶּׁטַח נָקִי וְלָבָן.

5

מלאך לא גמור

קָרַעְתִּי עֵינִי. לֹא רָאִיתִי.

גַּם רָאשֵׁי הַמּוֹרָם מְרֻכָּן.

כְּנָפַי מְרַטְטוֹת: אֵשׁ צָרֶבֶת.

סְבוּכוֹת וְחַדּוֹת, צְמוּחוֹת פְּנִימָה –

אֲנִי מִשְׁתָּרֵךְ, מְקֻרְטָע. אֲנִי

אֵינֶנִּי מוּכָן.

6

ספק מלאך

(אנגלוס דוביוזוס)

אֲנִי טוֹעֵן? אֲנִי פּוֹרֵק.

אֲנִי דּוֹגֵר עַל הַסָּפֵק.

זִכְרוֹן שְׁלִיחוּת... עָנָן זוֹהֵר...

אֲנִי יוֹשֵׁב וּמְהַרְהֵר.

עֵינַי קְרוּעוֹת כְּשֶׁל יַנְשׁוּף.

בְּכָל אַחַת אִישׁוֹן בּוֹעֵר.

4
Angel, Still Ugly

I am what I am.
A vessel desiring praise.
Unaligned heart.
I was almost not created. I am not.
I am blackening
while the space is white and clean.

5
Unfinished Angel

I tore out my eyes. I can't see.
Even my raised head is bowed.
My wings quiver: fire burning.
Entangled and honed, burgeoning inward –
I fidget, twist and turn. I am
not ready.

6
Dubious Angel

Do I plead? I break free.
I hatch doubt.
Memory of a calling… Luminous cloud…
I sit and ponder.
My eyes are torn like an owl's.
In each one a pupil burns.

7

זה בוכה

עֲנָנִים הָיוּ לִי כְּנָפַיִם
כְּלִיל הַחֹרֶשׁ פָּרַח בְּעֵינַי.
עַכְשָׁו אֲנִי מָטָל
כְּמוֹ דְּמָעוֹת לְרַגְלַי.

8

מלאך, עוד לא

קְצָת שֶׁל אַוִּיר	קְצָת שֶׁל עָפָר
קְצָת שָׁבִיר	קְצָת מִתְעַקֵּשׁ
יָד? כָּנָף?	קְצָת מִתְבַּלְבֵּל
חוֹשֵׁב כִּי עָף	הוֹלֵךְ וְשָׁח
קְצָת מִשָּׁם	קְצָת מִכָּאן
דַּבְּרָן מַחְשָׁן	לֹא מְתֹאָם
שָׁב וְלֹא שָׁב	נוֹשֵׁם וְלֹא

לֹא הִסְתַּיַּמְתִּי גַּם עַכְשָׁו

7

It Weeps

Clouds have become my wings.
In my eyes blossomed the red-bud tree.
Now I am crestfallen
like tears at my feet.

8

Angel, Not Yet

A bit of dust	A bit of air
A bit stubborn	A bit fragile
A little confused	Hand? Wing?
Wandering about	Thinking he flies
A bit of here	A bit of there
Misaligned	Loquacious form-maker
Breathing and not	Returning and not

I am not yet finished even now

מלאך חדש

פָּנַי בְּעָרְפִּי. לְנֶגֶד עֵינַי
עֲיֵי חֲרָבוֹת, עֲיֵי חֲרָבוֹת.
תִּקְווֹת זְעוּמוֹת נִתְעוֹפְפוּ, חֲרוּכוֹת
צָנְחוּ אֶל הָאֹפֶל.
נִפְלַטְתִּי.
עָלִיתִי.
נוֹלַדְתִּי שֵׁנִית
שָׁקוּף כַּעֲשָׁן.

הַזְּמַן הָאִלֵּם
נוֹשֵׁב מִגַּן אִילָנוֹת הַיַּלְדוּת,
דּוֹחֵק בְּלִבִּי הָעִקֵּשׁ,
פּוֹשֵׁק אֶת כְּנָפַי.
אֲנִי נִדְחָף אָחוֹר לַבָּאוֹת.
מָתַי יָבוֹא הַבָּא לְכַבּוֹת אֵשׁ עֵינַי?

ANGELUS NOVUS

My face is on my back. I see
heaps and heaps of ruins.
Tiny hopes were tossed aloft, scorched
they plummeted into the dark.
I was spewn out.
I rose up.
I was reborn
translucent as smoke.

Mute time
blows from childhood's pine groves,
presses on my stubborn heart,
spreads my wings.
I am pushed back toward what is coming next.
When will he come, the one to extinguish the fire in my eyes?

דומם

חָתוּל שָׁחֹר
בְּדֶשֶׁא יָרֹק.
דּוֹמֶה, מִשֶּׁל מַאטִיס.
אֲבָל אֵינֶנּוּ.
הַדֶּשֶׁא רָטֹב מִגֶּשֶׁם.
הַפַּרְוָה רְטֻבָּה מֵהַדֶּשֶׁא.
הַשְּׂעָרוֹת דְּבִיקוֹת.
הַגּוּף חֵמֶת חֲלִילִים
פּוֹלֵט אֶת אֲוִיר הָאָבִיב.
אַחַר כָּךְ דּוֹמֵם.

STILL LIFE

Black cat
in green grass.
Like a Matisse.
But not.
The grass is wet from rain.
The fur is wet from the grass.
The hair is sticky.
The body of bagpipes
ejects the spring air.
Then it is still.

צבע מים שחרים

(האנס הרטונג, "קומפוזיציה")

נוֹף מְקֻטָּע, כְּמוֹ תָּפוּר קְרָעִים קְרָעִים.
בְּקוֹל לֹא קוֹל יוֹרְדִים הַמַּיִם הַשְּׁבוּרִים.
פְּנֵי אֲחוֹתִי הִבְלִיחוּ וְכָבוּ בֵּין הֶהָרִים.

הַבְּקָרִים, יוֹם אַחַר יוֹם, כְּמוֹ בּוֹרוֹת.
יְמֵי הַיַּלְדוּת עֵינֵיהֶם אָבֶן. אַל תָּרִים.
הָאֶבֶן מְקִירָה דְּמָעוֹת שְׁחֹרוֹת.

THE COLOR OF BLACK WATERS
(after Hans Hartung's "Composition")

The landscape is torn, as though stitched from tatters.
In a voice-not-a-voice fall the broken waters.
My sister's face among the hills flickered and disappeared.

The mornings, day after day, are like deep pits.
The eyes of childhood are stone. Don't lift it.
The stone drips black tears.

הזכרון

בַּחֲדַר הַחֹשֶׁךְ הַלֵּב
מְפַתֵּחַ
עוֹלָם מָלֵא בִּצְבָעִים.
שׁוּב אוֹתָהּ צְפִיָּה חַסְרַת־מָנוֹחַ.

בֵּין פַּסֵּי הָרַכֶּבֶת עוֹלֶה הַיָּרֹק הַבָּהִיר
הָרַךְ, בְּלִי דַעַת, מֵנִיעַ
כְּנָפַיִם זְעִירוֹת כְּאִלּוּ לָעוּף, זוֹחֵל
לְכָל סֶדֶק, פִּתְאֹם אָפֹר.

אַלְפִּית שֶׁל שְׁנִיָּה אָדָם בָּאֲוִיר
(חַלּוֹנוֹת הַבַּיִת הַמֵּט – לַהֲבוֹת הַשְּׁקִיעָה)
כְּמוֹ צִפּוֹר שִׁכּוֹר, שָׁחֹר. אֲבָל לְמַטָּה
בָּרְחוֹב עֶרֶב רַב, הַדָּם נִגָּר בְּכָל גּוֹנָיו.

אַחַר כָּךְ נַעֲרָה עֲטוּפָה בִּשְׂעָרָהּ כְּבָאֵשׁ
עַל רֶקַע רָקִיעַ בְּצֶבַע עֲצָמוֹת.
הִיא מִשְׁתַּהָה, כְּמוֹ כְּלוּאָה בִּזְכוּכִית.
בּוֹאִי, קַלָּה, כְּעָנָן, קוּמִי, צְאִי!

אַחַר כָּךְ כָּל אֵלֶּה שֶׁאֵין לְהַבְדִּיל בְּקַלּוּת בֵּינָם
לְבֵין רוּחַ. כִּתְמֵי צֶבַע
כֵּלִים, נֶעְלָמִים בָּאֵד, צַוָּאר נָטוּי,
יַד פְּרִידָה בָּאֲוִיר.

שְׁמֵי עָשָׁן סְגֻלִּים, אַחַר צְהֻבִּים,
מִתְפּוֹרְרִים. זוּג אוֹהֲבִים
מְעוֹפֵף, פַּרְפָּרִים שֶׁל אֵפֶר.

אַחַר כָּךְ הַסֶּרֶט נָקִי.
הַאִם קָרָה מַה שֶּׁקָּרָה?
הַאִם מַמְשִׁיךְ לִקְרוֹת?

THE MEMORY

In the darkroom the heart
develops
a world full of color.
Again that same restless anticipation.

Between the railroad tracks a light green grows
the tender one, unknowingly, moves
tiny wings as though to fly, crawling
into every crevice, suddenly grey.

For a millisecond there's a man in the air
(windows of the crumbling house – the flames of sunset)
like a drunk bird, black. But below
the street is crowded, blood flowing in its every hue.

Then a girl wrapped in her hair as in fire
against the backdrop of a bone-colored sky.
She tarries, as though glass bound.
Come, little bride, light as a cloud, rise and flee!

Then, all the others who are not easily distinguished
from the wind. Splashes of color
becoming extinct, vanishing in the mist, a neck extended,
a hand in the air waving farewell.

A smoke sky of purple, after yellow,
crumbling. A pair of lovers
flying, ash butterflies.

Then the film is blank.
Did something happen?
Is something still happening?

מגדל בבל (1)
(פיטר ברויגל)

הַמִּלִּים כְּמוֹ צִפֳּרִים
זְעִירוֹת כִּמְעַט
אֵין לְהַבְחִין שָׁם
לְמַעְלָה שׁוּם דָּבָר
מַשֶּׁהוּ מֵרִים מַשֶּׁהוּ נוֹפֵל
קִיר אַחַר קִיר פְּעִימוֹת
הַלֵּב טָרוּף
מִתְהַדֵּק עָנָן חוֹנֵק
שֶׁמֶשׁ מַתֶּכֶת פּוֹלֵחַ
רֹאשׁחוֹר
הַפְּתָחִים זָבִים אֲפֵלָה
גּוּפִים רְחוּפִים צְלָלִים
כְּנָפִים נִטְרָפִים נוֹצוֹת
הַמִּלִּים מִתְהַפְּכוֹת
בָּרוּחַ הַיּוֹרֶדֶת? הָעוֹלָה?

130

THE TOWER OF BABEL (1)
(*after Pieter Brueghel*)

The bird-like words
are tiny almost
imperceptible there
above where nothing
something is lifting something falling
wall after wall the heart
is beating madness
tightening a strangling cloud
a metal sun cuts into
a blacksummit
the openings ooze gloom
bodies hover winged
shadows feather-blended
the words tumbling in
the descending wind? Ascending?

מגדל בבל (2)

הַקּוֹלוֹת הַכְּלוּאִים בַּמִּגְדָּל הָאוֹבֵד בְּמָבוֹאוֹתָיו טוּרִים טוּרִים
עִוְרִים פְּרוֹזְדוֹר מִסְתַּבֵּךְ בִּפְרוֹזְדוֹר קוֹמָה עַל קוֹמָה
קוֹרֶסֶת אֵין מוֹצָא אֵין
לְהָבִין מִלָּה
הֵד
הֲבָרָה
שָׁבוּר
אַתָּה תוֹעֶה בְּעֵינַיִם מִתְרוֹצְצוֹת
מִסּוֹף עַד סוֹף
הַבִּנְיָן בְּרֹאשׁוֹ עָנָן
הָאָבָק גַּרְגְּרִים פּוֹרְחִים בָּאֲוִיר זְעִירִים
קוֹלֵנוּ הִתְעַקֵּל בַּמִּסְדְּרוֹנוֹת,
נֶעְלַם בְּפִנָּה לַחָה.

שָׁמַעְנוּ, הָעֲגוּרִים חָלְפוּ מֵעַל.
הָעֲגוּרִים, הַחֲסִידוֹת, הַזַּרְזִירִים, הַקִּיוְיוֹת.
מִנַּיִן כָּל הַמִּלִּים הַלָּלוּ?
בְּרָקָן בָּאֲפֵלָה כִּבְרַק נְחֹשֶׁת קָלָל.

מִגְדָּל זֶה עַז מַדָּעֵתֵנוּ.

עַכְשָׁו עוֹלָה מִמַּחֲשַׁכָּיו מַנְגִּינָה.
אֵיזוֹ מַנְגִּינָה עוֹלָה מִמַּחֲשַׁכָּיו.
לֹא שָׁמַעְנוּ מֵעוֹדֵנוּ מַנְגִּינָה כְּמוֹתָהּ.

THE TOWER OF BABEL (2)

The voices imprisoned in the lost tower in its entryways row after row are
blind corridors entangled in corridors floor after floor
falling with no exit no
understanding a word
echo
syllable
broken
you stray with wild eyes
from end to tower's end
cloud at its summit
the dust is tiny seeds sprouting in the air
our voice angles in the hallways,
disappears in a damp corner.

We heard, the cranes passed above us.
The cranes, the storks, the starlings, the kiwis.
Where are all these words from?
Their glow in the gloom is like burnished bronze.

This tower is bolder than our thoughts.

Now a melody rises from its darkness.
What melody rises from its darkness.
We've never heard a melody like this.

מגדל בבל (3)

"אֲנַחְנוּ חוֹפְרִים אֶת פִּיר בָּבֶל" (פרנץ קאפקא)

קוֹל חֲבוּט, קוֹל דִּרְדּוּר.

עָפָר.

חֹמֶר.

עָפָר.

אֶבֶן עַל אֶבֶן.

אֲבוֹתֵינוּ הִתְחִילוּ.

אֲנַחְנוּ הִתְחַלְנוּ.

שַׂמְנוּ אֶבֶן עַל אֶבֶן,
חוֹמָה עַל חוֹמָה.
"קִנַּנּוּ נָשִׁים בֵּין כּוֹכָבִים."

הַחֹשֶׁךְ גּוֹבֵר.

קָרַעְנוּ פְּתָחִים לְמַרְאֶה עֵינַיִם.
בָּרוּךְ בּוֹרֵא מַרְאֵה עֵינַיִם
וְעֵינַיִם רוֹאוֹת מַרְאֶה.

מְסַפְּרִים, עָנָן נִצָּב מֵעָלֵינוּ וְאֵינֶנּוּ עוֹבֵר.

לְחִישׁוֹת הַנָּשִׁים הִנְשִׁימוּ עוֹרֵנוּ,
זַהֲרוּרִים זְעִירִים בַּחֲשֵׁכָה.
"מִי אַתְּ, מִי?"

THE TOWER OF BABEL (3)

"We are digging the pit of Babel" (Franz Kafka)

The sounds of beating, of rocks sliding.
Dirt.
Mortar.
Dirt.
Stone on stone.

Our forefathers began this.

We began this.

We put stone on stone,
wall on wall.
"We'll place our nest among the stars."

The darkness grows stronger.

We broke open portals to see.
Blessed is He who created sight
and eyes to enrapture light.

They say a cloud is stationed above us and will not move.

The women's whispers breathe life into our skin,
small sparks in the dark.
"Who are you, who?"

הסעודה האחרונה

הַצְּבָעִים דָּהוּ.
תָּוֵי הַפָּנִים מְטַשְׁטְשִׁים.
טֶמְפֶּרָה עַל טִיחַ!
דְּבָרִים אֲחֵרִים הֶעֱסִיקוּ אֶת הַצַּיָּר. אֲבָל
עוֹד יוֹשְׁבִים כֻּלָּם לְאוֹתוֹ שֻׁלְחָן,
עוֹד נִבְצָע הַלֶּחֶם,
עוֹד נִצֶּבֶת הַכּוֹס, עוֹד נוֹף גְּבָעוֹת כְּחַלְחַל בַּגַּב.
וְגַם כִּי לֹא יִהְיֶה
אֶלָּא כֹּתֶל סָדוּק עִם כַּמָּה כְּתָמִים,
וְגַם כִּי לֹא יִהְיֶה
אֶלָּא כֹּתֶל סָדוּק עִם כַּמָּה כְּתָמִים,
וְגַם כִּי יְטֻאְטָא הַכֹּתֶל –
שִׁמְעוֹן הָיָה, יַעֲקֹב הָיָה, וְכָל הַשְּׁאָר, לְתָמִיד.
הָרוּחַ הַהוֹלֵךְ סוֹבֵב סוֹבֵב עַל פְּנֵי הַשֶּׁטַח הָרֵיק
נוֹשֵׂא צִבְעֵיהֶם כְּמוֹ אֲבַק הַפְּרִיחָה,
כְּמוֹ אָבָק. גַּם כִּי בָּגַד הַבּוֹגֵד,
הַנִּבְגָּד לֹא הוּקַע, לֹא אָבַד.

THE LAST SUPPER

The colors are faded.
The faces are blurred.
Tempera on plaster!
Others things preoccupied the painter. But
still they are all sitting at the same table,
still the bread is cut,
still the goblet stands, the blue-hued hills behind.
And even if it's
nothing but a cracked wall with a few color stains,
and even if the wall were swept clean – still
Simon was there, James was there, and all the rest, forever.
The wind swirling around the empty space
carries their colors like pollen, like dust.
And even if the betrayer betrayed,
the betrayed is not cast out, not lost.

ההורדה מהצלב
(רמבראנדט)

שַׂק קֶמַח עָבֵשׁ, נֹאד
לָבָן, נָפוּחַ, הַמּוֹשִׁיעַ
מוּרָד מִן הָעֵץ הַמֻּכְתָּם הָרֹאשׁ־
לֹא־רֹאשׁ נָפוּל, שָׁמוּט כְּמוֹ
כַּדּוּר־פּוֹרֵחַ זָעִיר
חֲסַר אֲוִיר. אֶחָד אוֹחֵז בִּזְרוֹעַ
הַבֻּבָּה הַכְּעוּרָה הַזֹּאת,
נוֹעֵץ בָּהּ עֵינַיִם בְּתִמָּהוֹן,
חֶמְלָה וָפַחַד. אֲחֵרִים נוֹשְׂאִים
וְנוֹתְנִים וְלוֹקְחִים בְּפָנִים
תוֹעִים בֵּין מַעְלָה וּמַטָּה.
שֶׁמֶן עָטוּר מִצְנֶפֶת
עוֹמֵד וּמִתְבּוֹנֵן
מְרֻצֶּה מִכִּרְסוֹ הַחַיָּה שֶׁל עַצְמוֹ.
עַל רֶקַע הָרָקִיעַ הָאָפֵל
מִתְכּוֹפֵף אֶחָד, מַנִּיחַ
לְאַט לַסָּדִין לִצְנֹחַ.
הַכֹּל אָפֵל סָבִיב. גַּם הָעֵצִים.
רַק הַגּוּפָה זוֹהֶרֶת.

לֹא. לֹא כָּךְ. עוֹד פַּעַם. מֵהַתְחָלָה.
בָּשָׂר לָבָן וָרֹד, כְּמֻדְמֶה,
חַי, נוֹשֵׁם, מֵנִיעַ זְרוֹעוֹת,
אֲפִלּוּ אוֹהֵב. מִחוּץ לַמִּסְגֶּרֶת,
יֵשׁ לְשַׁעֵר יְנִיחוּהוּ בְּבוֹר.
יְנִיחוּהוּ? יָנוּחַ? מְנוּחַת עוֹלָמִים.

לֹא, לֹא כָּךְ.

138

DESCENT FROM THE CROSS
(after Rembrandt)

Moldy sack of flour, white
wineskin, swollen, the Savior
is removed from the stained wood, his head-
not-head fallen, drooping like
a small hot-air balloon
airless. One man clutches his arm
this ugly rag-doll,
staring at it in wonder,
in pity and fear. Others hold him
passing him one to the next their gazes
straying up and down.
A fat man adorned in a turban
stands to the side and observes,
satisfied with his own living belly.
Against the backdrop of the gloomy skies
another stoops over, letting
the sheet slowly drop.
Everything around is dark. The trees too.
Only the body shines.

No, not exactly. Try again. From the beginning.
Soft white flesh. As though
living, breathing, moving its arms,
even loving. Outside the frame,
one guesses they'll put him to rest in the ground.
Put him to rest? Will he rest? Eternal rest.

No. Not exactly.

הַדְּמוּת דְּמוּת, אֲבָל
רַק לְכָאוֹרָה. הַמַּחֲזֶה יָדוּעַ,
לִכְאוֹרָה. הַדְּמָיוֹת,
הָעֵץ הַדָּמוּם, הָרָקִיעַ
צְבָעִים. הַצְּבָעִים צְבָעִים –
אֲבָל מִנַּיִן וּלְאָן? אֲפֵלָה. הַתְּמוּנָה
תְּלוּיָה בְּמִינְכֶן. רָאִיתִי.
רָאִיתִי? הֲלֹא
הִיא מֵאֲחוֹרֶיהָ, הִיא מִלְּפָנֶיהָ,
הִיא מִתַּחַת הִיא מֵעַל לְבַדָּהּ
כַּצִּפּוֹר הַפּוֹרַחַת
בְּהֶבֶל פֶּה אַחֲרוֹן, מְרַחֶפֶת רֶגַע
מֵעַל פָּנִים שֶׁהָיוּ
מֻכָּרוֹת, וְלֹא עוֹד, מְדַמָּה
לַנְּשָׁמָה –

The figure is a figure, but
only seemingly. The scene is well-known,
presumably. The images,
the still-bleeding wood, the dark-hued
heavens. The colors in colors –
but from where and whence? Darkness. The painting
hangs in Munich. I saw it.
I saw it? Isn't it
behind it, before it,
it's beneath it's above on its own
like a bird flying
in a last empty breath, hovering for a moment
above a face that was
known, and no more, now imagined
a soul –

זכר אשה במחלקה המצרית

אֵיךְ אֶמְצָא אוֹתָהּ בָּעֲיֵפוּת הַזֹּאת
בֵּין חֲלוֹם וְהָקִיץ
בֵּין הָאֲרוֹנוֹת הַמִּצְרִיִּים
נֶעֶלְמָה הָאִשָּׁה הַזָּרָה בַּקָּהָל הַזָּר
אֵיךְ אֶמְצָא אוֹתָהּ
בְּעֵינַיִם מִתְקַשְּׁרוֹת בִּדְמָעוֹת שָׁם עָמְדָה
בּוֹכָה בַּמִּסְתָּרִים בִּרְאוֹתָהּ אִישׁ מִצְרִי מֵת
מְצֻיָּר עַל מִכְסֵה אֲרוֹנוֹ
בְּעֵינַיִם שְׁחֹרוֹת כִּשְׁקֵדִים
עָמְדָה רוֹאָה בִּדְמָעוֹת
אֶת הַיֹּפִי הַזֶּה

"בַּעֲשִׂירִי בְּיוּלִי אֶלֶף תְּשַׁע מֵאוֹת וְשִׁבְעִים בְּשָׁעָה אַחַת־עֶשְׂרֵה בַּבֹּקֶר"

MEMORY OF A WOMAN IN THE EGYPTIAN WING

How will I find her despite this fatigue
between wakefulness and dream she
vanished among the Egyptian sarcophagi
foreign woman in a foreign crowd
how will I find her
with her eyes welling up with tears there she stood
secretly crying on seeing the dead Egyptian man
drawn on his casket cover
her eyes as black as almonds
she stood there gazing through tears
at all that beauty

"On the tenth of July nineteen seventy at eleven o'clock in the morning"

V

POSTCARDS FROM

הרחק

1

הָיִיתִי הָרְחֵק.

חָזַרְתִּי.

הַנְּשָׁמָה עַתִּיקָה מְאֹד. יֵשׁ אוֹמְרִים
קַיֶּמֶת לָעַד, אֲפִלּוּ בְּלִי גּוּף.
פַּעַם כָּאן פַּעַם שָׁם וְגַם בְּשׁוּמָקוֹם.
פַּעַם חָשָׁה עַצְמָהּ בְּטוֹב וּפַעַם
הִיא זָרָה לְךָ, אֲבוּדָה, גַּם לְעַצְמָהּ.
קָשֶׁה לָדַעַת אֵיפֹה הִיא עַכְשָׁו.
אֵין לִרְאוֹת אוֹתָהּ, לִשְׁמֹעַ אוֹתָהּ, אִי אֶפְשָׁר
לָגַעַת בָּהּ, לִטְעֹם אוֹתָהּ, לְהָרִיחָהּ.
אֲבָל מַה יַּעֲשֶׂה הַגּוּף בִּלְעָדֶיהָ.

2

בְּשֶׁכְּבָר הַיָּמִים אָמַרְתִּי בִּצְחוֹק
אֲנִי צֶאֱצָא שֶׁל עֵץ, אֲבוֹת־אֲבוֹתַי
הָיוּ עֵצִים, אֲנִי מַרְגִּישׁ הֵיטֵב
מַה זֶּה לִהְיוֹת תָּקוּעַ בָּאֲדָמָה, בְּלִי יְכֹלֶת לָזוּז, בְּעוֹד
הָרֹאשׁ לְמַעְלָה, נוֹשֵׁב עִם הָרוּחַ
וּמַה זֶּה לַעֲמֹד קֵרֵחַ מִכֹּל
בַּכְּפוֹר הַקָּרֵב.

146

FAR AWAY

1
I was far away.
I came back.

The soul is very old. There are those
who say she exists forever, even without a body.
Sometimes she's here or there and sometimes nowhere.
Sometimes she feels she is well and sometimes
she's a stranger to you, lost, even to herself.
It's hard to know where she is now.
She can't be seen or heard, it's impossible
to touch her, or taste or smell her.
But what would the body do without her.

2
Once I said in jest
I am the descendent of trees, my forefathers
were trees. How well I know
what it's like to be stuck in the ground, unable to move while
one's head is up high, being blown with the winds,
and what it's like to stand bare and bald
before the coming frost.

גלויה מפרשבורג־ברטיסלוה

בְּרַטִיסְלַוָה הִיא פְּרֶשְׁבּוּרג הִיא פּוֹז'וֹנִי.
בִּשְׁבִילִי הִיא פְּרֶשְׁבּוּרג.
מוֹרִי, מַר ווֹרְם מֵהָעֲמָמִי
הוֹצִיא מִמְּגֵרָתוֹ אֶת תַּצְלוּם הַכִּתָּה וְהִצְבִּיעַ:
זֶה הָיָה נָאצִי וְגַם זֶה וְזֶה. הַהוּא
הָיָה אַכְזָרִי בִּמְיֻחָד. הַלָּה נָפַל בְּרוּסְיָה
וְאוֹתוֹ גֵּרְשׁוּ. מִי מֵהַתַּלְמִידִים הַיְּהוּדִים
שָׂרַד וָחַי – אֵינִי יוֹדֵעַ.
פְּרֶשְׁבּוּרג הָיְתָה עִיר תְּלַת־לְשׁוֹנִית. הַלָּשׁוֹן הָרְבִיעִית
הִיא הַשְּׁתִיקָה.
הַאִם הָיוּ פַּעַם גְּבוּלוֹת לָרַע?
פְּרֶשְׁבּוּרג שׁוֹכֶנֶת לְיַד הַדָּנוּבָה, בִּקְצֵה שְׁלוּחוֹת הַקַּרְפָּטִים.
בְּקִרְבַת הַקָּתֶדְרָלָה עָמַד בֵּית־הַכְּנֶסֶת שֶׁל הַנֵּיאוֹלוֹגִים
בְּסִגְנוֹן מָאוּרִי כָּלְשֶׁהוּ. לְמַטָּה שָׂרוּעָה כִּכַּר הַדָּגִים
לְמַעְלָה הִתְחִיל רְחוֹב הַיְּהוּדִים. הַדָּנוּבָה זוֹרֶמֶת כְּמוֹ תָּמִיד.
אֲנִי זָקֵן. אֵינִי יָכוֹל לְהִתְקַדֵּם אֶלָּא לְאַט.
בִּפְרֶשְׁבּוּרג נוֹלַדְתִּי. הָיוּ לִי אֵם, אָב וְאָחוֹת.
הָיְתָה לִי, כִּמְדֻמֶּה, יַלְדוּת קְטַנָּה מְאֻשֶּׁרֶת בִּפְרֶשְׁבּוּרג.
פַּעַם קָפְאָה הַדָּנוּבָה כָּל־כֻּלָּהּ.
הַקֶּלְטִים בָּנוּ כָּאן מִבְצָר, וְגַם נְסִיכֵי
מוֹרַבְיָה רַבָּתִי. הָרוֹמָאִים קָרְאוּ לַמָּקוֹם
פּוֹזוֹנְיוּם. זֹאת עִיר בָּאָה־בַּיָּמִים.
כֹּה בָּאָה־בַּיָּמִים עַד שֶׁאֵינִי יוֹדְעָהּ עוֹד.
לְהִתְרָאוֹת אֲהוּבָה, קָשֶׁה לְשַׁעֵר.

148

A POSTCARD FROM PRESSBURG-BRATISLAVA

Bratislava is Pressburg is Pozsony.
For me it is Pressburg.
My teacher, Mr. Wurm from the elementary school,
pulled a class photo from his drawer and started pointing:
"This one was a Nazi, and this one and that one too. This one
was especially brutal. This one fell in Russia
and that one was deported. Which of the Jewish pupils
survived – I do not know."
Pressburg was a tri-lingual city. Its fourth language
is silence.
Were there once borders to evil?
Pressburg lies adjacent to the Danube, at the edges of the Carpathian slopes.
Near the Cathedral the Neologist Synagogue once stood
built in some kind of Moorish style. Below is Fish Square,
above is where the Street of the Jews began. The Danube flows as always.
I am old. I can walk only slowly now.
I was born in Pressburg. I had a mother, a father, a sister.
I had, I believe, a small and happy childhood in Pressburg.
Once, the Danube froze solid.
The Celts built here a fortress, as did the princes
of greater Moravia. The Romans called this place
Possonium. This is an old old city.
So old I barely know her anymore.
Farewell, beloved, it's unimaginable.

גלויה מששטין: מדורות סתו

שָׁשְׁטִין, סְפֵק עֲיָרָה סְפֵק כְּפָר, קְרוֹבָה לִגְבוּל מוֹרַבְיָה.
מָקוֹם עֲלִיָּה לָרֶגֶל שֶׁל נוֹצְרִים, עִם כְּנֵסִיָּה גְּדוֹלָה וּמְפֹאֶרֶת
עֲצֵי עַרְמוֹן בַּחֲזִיתָהּ, מִנְזָר שֶׁל סִילֶזְיָאנִים
קְיוֹסְקִים גְּדוֹשִׁים פִּסְלֵי קְדוֹשִׁים וּמַמְתַּקִּים בִּימֵי חַג וְיָרִיד.
בַּזִּכָּרוֹן אֵין זְמַן עָבָר.
כְּבָר הַשּׁוּק כְּבָר מְכֻסֶּה בֶּטוֹן, הַמְּתוֹפֵף תּוֹפֵף עַל תֹּף הַפַּח
מַכְרִיז בְּקוֹל חֲדָשׁוֹת שְׁנַת 34 אוֹ 36, מִכָּל מָקוֹם בְּטֶרֶם
שָׁשְׁטִין נֶהְפְּכָה. לִפְנֵי
42.
אָז נֶאֶלְמָה דַּם שָׁשְׁטִין, לֹא הוֹצִיאָה הֶגֶה כַּאֲשֶׁר
הַמְתִּינָה הָרַכֶּבֶת – מִשְּׂמֹאל לַכְּבִישׁ, לְיַד בֵּיתוֹ שֶׁל
ד"ר נוֹבוֹמֶסְקִי אִם בָּאתָ מִכִּכַּר הַשּׁוּק שָׁם עוֹמֵד
הַבַּיִת שֶׁל הַסַּבִּים, הוֹרַי וַאֲחוֹתִי שׁוֹהִים אֶצְלָם
(הַאִם הוֹלְכִים הֵם עַל מִזְוְדוֹתֵיהֶם בָּרֶגֶל אֶל הַתַּחֲנָה, הַאִם עוֹדָם
מַפְנִים אֶת רֹאשָׁם לְאָחוֹר לִרְאוֹת אֶת עֵין הָאוֹכְרָה שֶׁלַּבַּיִת? –
(הַיּוֹם אֵין לְהַכִּיר) – וְנָסְעָה צָפוֹנָה.
יִשּׁוּב קָטָן סְתָמִי, לְמְרוֹת פְּאֵר הַכְּנֵסִיָּה, מַשִּׁימִים בְּסַךְ הַכֹּל. לִנְשֹׁם בּוֹ
אִי אֶפְשָׁר. הַכֹּל עָשָׁן. לֹא כְּלוּם לְהִתְבּוֹנֵן. אַף לֹא אֶחָד
לִקְשֹׁר שִׂיחָה. לֹא כְּלוּם לִכְתֹּב עָלָיו.

A POSTCARD FROM SHASTIN: AUTUMN FIRES

Shastin, half-village half-town, sits near the Moravian border.
A place of Christian pilgrimage, with its huge ornate church,
chestnut trees at the entrance, Silesian monastery,
stalls full of saint figurines and sweets on feast days.
There's no past in its memory.
The market square is already covered with concrete, the drummer
drumming on the tin drum
announces the news of '34 or '36, in any case from some time before
Shastin was completely changed. Before
June '42.
Then Shastin fell silent, uttered not a word when
the train waited there – left of the road, beside the house of
Dr. Novomesky if you came from the market square where the house
of my grandparents stands, my parents and sister are staying with them
(do they walk with their suitcases to the station, do they still
look back to see the house's ochre eye? –
                    today unrecognizable) – then traveled north.
An insignificant village, despite the grandeur of the church, dreary in the end.
There's no breathing there, everything is smoke. Nothing to see. Not
        a single person
to talk to. Nothing to write about.

בְּבוּדַפֶּשְׁט אֲנִי קוֹרֵא עַל בּוּדַפֶּשְׁט. חִקּוּי שֶׁל חִקּוּי
אוֹמֵר קְלָאוּדְיוֹ מַגְרִיס, חִקּוּיָהּ שֶׁל וִינָה
הַמְחַקָּה פָּרִיס. אָדָם שָׂמֵחַ (לֹא תָּמִיד) לִקְרֹא דְּבָרִים
אוֹתָם חָשׁ בְּעַצְמוֹ. עִיר נִגּוּנִים שֶׁל צוֹעֲנִים
בְּבֵית-קָפֶה. עִיר נֵיאוֹ-גּוֹטִיקָה וְנֵיאוֹ-רֶנֶסַנְס יַחְדָּו.
מָתַי אוֹמְרִים בָּהּ מַה שֶׁמַּרְגִּישִׁים, מָתַי
מַה שֶׁרָאוּי לוֹמַר? מַה בָּהּ צוּרָה לַנֶּפֶשׁ וְעַד מָה
סְמוּיוֹת הֵן הַדְּמָעוֹת שֶׁבַּדְּבָרִים?
הַדּוּנָה (הַדָּנוּבָּה) הַגְּדוֹלָה חוֹצָה הָעִיר לִשְׁתַּיִם
בְּגַן הַמְצוּדָה זְגוּגוֹת שֶׁל צְעִירִים (כַּמָּה יָפוֹת
הַבַּחוּרוֹת כָּאן) מַחֲלִיפִים פָּנִים.
הָרְחוֹבוֹת שֶׁל בּוּדָה – זִכָּרוֹן רָדוּם.
פֹּה שָׁם בֵּית יַיִן, יֶרֶק, שֶׁקֶט.
הַבִּנְיָנִים שֶׁל פֶּשְׁט מַעֲמִידִים פָּנִים, כִּי אֵין בָּם
יַד הַזְּמַן הַמְקַלֵּף אֶת חֲזִיתוֹתֵיהֶם.
הַמַּיִם בַּנָּהָר תָּמִיד אוֹתָם עַצְמָם תָּמִיד שׁוֹנִים.
עִיר כָּפֵל הַפָּנִים. בִּפְנִים אֶחָד מֵחֲדָרֶיהָ
בּוֹרֵר לוֹ אִימְרֶה קֶרְטֶשׁ מִלּוֹתָיו
לִמְצֹא אֶת מַה שֶׁמִּתְחַיֶּה בֵּינָן וּבַעֲדָן, לוֹמַר
אֱמֶת לַאֲמִתָּהּ.

A POSTCARD FROM BUDAPEST

In Budapest I read about Budapest. An imitation of an imitation,
says Claudio Magris, an imitation of Vienna
imitating Paris. A man is happy (not always) to read things
he felt himself. City of gypsy songs
in the cafes. A city neo-gothic and neo-renaissance both.
When does one speak here what one is feeling, and when
what is supposed to be spoken? What is soul-shaped here, and how
hidden are the tears of things?
The large Duna (the Danube) cuts the city in two,
in the Citadel garden young couples pass by (how
beautiful are the young women here).
The streets of Buda – a dormant memory.
A few wine houses, greenery, quiet.
The buildings of Pest pretend, as though time
hasn't stripped away their facades.
The water in the river is always itself always different.
A two-faced city. Inside one of its rooms
Imre Kertesz is choosing his words with great care
to find what can be revived between and for them, to speak
the absolute truth.

גלויה מלונדון

אֶת הַגְלוּיָה הַזֹּאת אֲנִי כּוֹתֵב מִלּוֹנְדּוֹן.
לוֹנְדּוֹן גְּדוֹלָה מִדַּי בִּשְׁבִילִי.
אֲנִי מִסְתַּפֵּק בַּנַשְׁיוֹנַל גָּאלֶרִי.
הַנַשְׁיוֹנַל גָּאלֶרִי גְּדוֹלָה מִדַּי בִּשְׁבִילִי. אֲנִי מִסְתַּפֵּק
בַּדְּיוֹקָן הָעַצְמִי שֶׁל רֶמְבְּרַנְדְט בִּהְיוֹתוֹ
בֶּן שִׁשִּׁים וְשָׁלוֹשׁ. הַתַּאֲרִיךְ הוּא 1669
שְׁנַת חַיָּיו הָאַחֲרוֹנָה. הַיּוֹם אֲנִי
גָּדוֹל מִמֶּנּוּ בְּאַחַת-עֶשְׂרֵה שָׁנִים. אַךְ "הַתְּמוּנָה
לֹא יָכְלָה לִהְיוֹת צְנוּעָה יוֹתֵר, הַחֲקוּר הָעַצְמִי
לֹא נִמְרָץ יוֹתֵר," כָּתוּב בַּקָּטָלוֹג.
(אֲנִי אוֹהֵב מוּבָאוֹת, אֶפְשָׁר לְהִסְתַּמֵּךְ עֲלֵיהֶן
בָּאִים לִידֵי שִׂיחָה, גַּם לַאֲחֵרִים יֵשׁ מַה לוֹמַר
נוֹצֶרֶת מֵעֵין פּוֹלִיפוֹנְיָה): "בַּפּוֹרְטְרֶטִים מִשְׁנוֹתָיו
הָאַחֲרוֹנוֹת הוּא מַצִּיג אֶת עַצְמוֹ כְּצַיָּר וּכְאָדָם הַמִּתְדַּיֵּן
עִם הָעוֹלָם כְּמִתְגָּרֶה בּוֹ אוֹ נִכְנָע לוֹ וּמְוַתֵּר. בַּדְּיוֹקָן
הַזֶּה, דּוֹמֶה, אֵין הָעוֹלָם אֶלָּא אֵי-שָׁם בָּרֶקַע." לוֹנְדּוֹן
הָעִיר הַפּוֹלִיפוֹנִית שֶׁאֲנִי מַכִּיר, כֻּלָּהּ בָּרֶקַע.
טְרַפַלְגַּר סְקְוֵיר כִּמְעַט בְּלִי קוֹל, סֶנְט גֵ'יְמְס פַּרְק
עִם צִפֳּרֵי הַמַּיִם וְהַקִּיוֹסְק הַגָּדוֹל, וְסְטְמִינְסְטֶר
הַפַּרְלָמֶנְט וְצֶ'רִינְג קְרוֹס, סֶנְט פּוֹל, הַטָּאוּאָר
אַחַר כָּךְ הַתַּמְזָה בְּכִוּוּן לַיָּם – בָּרֶקַע. הַמִּזְחִים הַזְּעִירִים
הַבִּנְיָנִים, הָאֳנִיּוֹת וְהַסִּירוֹת, גְּרִינִיץ', הַזְּמַן הַמְּדֻיָּק.
הָעֵינַיִם הַלָּלוּ
הָעֵינַיִם הַקְּשׁוּבוֹת, הָעֲיֵפוֹת, הַיּוֹדְעוֹת הַלָּלוּ
רוֹאוֹת כָּל זֶה וְלֹא רוֹאוֹת. רַק קֶנְווּד הָאוּס רוֹמֵז עוֹד מֵרָחוֹק
וְהַדְּיוֹקָן, תֵּשַׁע שָׁנִים צָעִיר יוֹתֵר, טַבְלַת צְבָעִים בַּיָּד, וּבְמַבָּט דּוֹמֶה.
(הַאִם הוּא מַאֲזִין לַמְנַגֶּנֶת שֶׁל וֶרְמֶר?)
"הַצֶּבַע הֻנַּח בְּחַסְכָנוּת גְּאוֹנִית."
הַיָּדַיִם שְׁלוּבוֹת, אוֹחֲזוֹת זוֹ בָּזוֹ בְּרִפְיוֹן.
שׁוּב אֵינָן רוֹצוֹת לִתְפֹּס דָּבָר אוֹ לְהַחֲזִיק בּוֹ.
לוֹנְדּוֹן רְחוֹקָה, אֵינָה אֶלָּא גְלוּיָה, הֱיִי שָׁלוֹם.

A POSTCARD FROM LONDON

I'm writing this postcard from London.
London is too large for me.
I content myself with The National Gallery.
The National Gallery is too large for me. Rembrandt's
self-portrait when he was sixty three
is enough for me. The year is 1669,
the last year of his life. Today I am
eleven years older than he was. But "the painting
could not be more modest, the self-investigation
more fervent," states the catalogue.
(I like quotations, one can depend on them
in conversation, that others also have something to say,
a type of polyphony created): "In the portraits from his last
years he presents himself as a painter and person debating
the world as it taunts him, or finally surrenders to him and gives in.
In this portrait, it seems the world exists only as the backdrop." London
the polyphonic city that I know, all backdrop.
Tralfagar Square is almost voiceless, Saint James Park
with its water birds and large kiosk, Westminster,
the Parliament and Charing Cross, Saint Paul's, the Tower
then the Thames on its way to the sea – backdrop. The tiny piers,
the buildings, the boats and ships, Greenwich, the exact time.
Those eyes
the listening weary eyes, those knowing eyes
that see it all and don't see. Only Kenwood House hints already from a distance
and the portrait, nine years younger, color palate in his hand, and with
    a similar look. (Is he listening to Vermeer's musician?)
"The paint was applied with genius economy."
His arms are crossed, holding each other lightly.
They don't want to reach for anything else anymore.
Distant London, it is nothing but a postcard, farewell to you.

גלויה מתל־אביב

תֵּל־אָבִיב עִיר צִבְעוֹנִית מְאֹד לְבָנָה.
מִשְׁתַּנָּה כָּל רֶגַע וְנִשְׁאֶרֶת מַה שֶׁהִיא.
תֵּל־אָבִיב עִיר נְקִיָּה מְלֻכְלֶכֶת.
זֶה תָּלוּי בָּעֵינַיִם.
תֵּל־אָבִיב כִּמְעַט נְיוּ־יוֹרְק.
מְיֻחָם מְלַקֵּק הַיָּם אֶת יַרְכֵי תֵּל־אָבִיב וְלֵב
תֵּל־אָבִיב לָבָן.
בְּנֵי אָדָם כָּאן אֵינָם שַׁיָּכִים לְאִישׁ.
גַּם לֹא לְעַצְמָם.
תֵּל־אָבִיב עִיר קוּפְסָאוֹת וּתְרִיסִים.
בְּתֵל־אָבִיב תֵּיאַטְרוֹנִים, אוֹפֵּרָה, הַתִּזְמֹרֶת הַפִילְהַרְמוֹנִית
מוּזִיאוֹנִים וְיָפוֹ.
אוֹמְרִים כִּי הַסַּרְסוּרִים רוֹצִים לִמְכֹּר אֶת יָפוֹ
וְיָפוֹ יְפַת יָמִים (כָּתַב עַגְנוֹן) הָיְתָה
זְמַן רַב לִפְנֵי תֵּל־אָבִיב. זְמַן רַב, רַב, רַב.
אֲפִלּוּ אַנְדְּרוֹמֶדָה הַכִּירָה אֶת נִמְלָהּ
וּתְּוּקָה אֶל סֶלַע עַד שֶׁפֶּרְסֵאוּס בָּא
וְשִׁחְרֵר אוֹתָהּ. שׁוּם פֶּרְסֵאוּס
לֹא יָבוֹא וְיִגְאַל אֶת תֵּל־אָבִיב.
רֶצֶנְזֶנְטִים רַבִּים מִדַּי מְאַיְּמִים
עַל רְחוֹבוֹתֶיהָ, שׁוֹכְבִים עִם נָשִׁים בַּחֲדָרֶיהָ
שְׁטוּפֵי זֵעָה. מְשׁוֹרֵר אֶחָד כָּתַב כִּי
אַהֲבַת בַּחוּרוֹתֶיהָ בֵּין רַגְלֵיהֶן.
דָּבָר כָּזֶה קַיָּם בְּתֵל־אָבִיב.
מִי שׁוֹמֵעַ אֶת מִי בָּרַעַשׁ הַזֶּה?
חֲמֵשׁ דַּקּוֹת גֶּשֶׁם וְתֵל־אָבִיב מוּצֶפֶת.
אֲנָשִׁים זְקֵנִים כִּשְׁרוֹצִים לַחֲצוֹת רְחוֹב
מַפְשִׁילִים אֶת שׁוּלֵי מִכְנָסֵיהֶם. אֲנָשִׁים זְקֵנִים
אֵינָם שׁוֹמְעִים אֶת שִׁירַת בְּנוֹת הַיָּם בְּתֵל־אָבִיב.
מַפְסִידָנִים יוֹשְׁבִים בְּלִי נִיעַ בְּבָתִּים מְפֹאָרִים מִתְקַלְּפִים

A POSTCARD FROM TEL AVIV

Tel Aviv, a colorful city, is very white.
She changes all the time and stays always what she is.
Tel Aviv is a clean, dirty city.
It depends on how you look at her.
Tel Aviv is almost New York.
The sea, in heat, licks at her thighs and her heart
is white.
People here belong to no one.
Not even to themselves.
Tel Aviv is a city of boxes and shutters.
There are theatres in Tel Aviv, opera, the philharmonic,
museums and Jaffa.
They say that the pimps want to sell Jaffa
though Jaffa, Belle of the Sea (wrote Agnon) existed
a long time before Tel Aviv. A long, long time.
Even Andromeda knew Jaffa's port,
bound there on her rock until Perseus came
and freed her. No Perseus
will come and redeem Tel Aviv now.
Too many critics threaten
her streets, sleep with women in her sweat-drenched
rooms. A poet wrote that
the love of her women is between their legs.
That's how it is in Tel Aviv.
Who can hear anyone in all this noise?
Five minutes of rain and Tel Aviv floods.
Old people who want to cross the street
have to wear the bottoms of their trousers rolled. Old people
cannot hear the mermaids in Tel Aviv.
Losers sit motionless in fancy, peeling houses

נוֹעֲצִים עֵינַיִם בַּתִּקְרָה עַד שֶׁמַּפְצִיעַ הַשַּׁחַר.
הַאִם יֵשׁ מַלְאָכִים בְּתֵל־אָבִיב?
דְּבָרִים נוֹרָאִים קָרוּ בְּתֵל־אָבִיב.
דְּבָרִים נוֹרָאִים קוֹרִים בְּתֵל־אָבִיב.
מִי פֵּלֶל שֶׁכָּךְ יִהְיֶה?
הַאִם תֵּל־אָבִיב תֵּל־אָבִיב?
מִי הִמְצִיא אֶת תֵּל־אָבִיב?

158

staring at the ceiling until dawn.

Are there angels in Tel Aviv?

Horrible things happened in Tel Aviv.

Horrible things happen in Tel Aviv.

Who ever imagined it would be this way?

Is Tel Aviv really Tel Aviv?

Who invented Tel Aviv anyway?

גלויה מאזור חברון

חֶבְרוֹן עִיר עַתִּיקָה מְאֹד.
אַבְרָהָם אָבִינוּ עִם שָׂרָה אִשְׁתּוֹ קְבוּרִים בָּהּ
אוֹמְרִים. דָּבָר קָדוֹשׁ בְּאֶרֶץ הַחַיָּה עַל הַמָּוֶת.
בַּבֹּקֶר אוֹכְלִים בְּחֶבְרוֹן פִּתָּה וְזֵיתִים וְלַבָּנֶה בְּשֶׁמֶן זַיִת.
בִּימֵי חַג שׁוֹחֲטִים טָלֶה.
אַנְשֵׁי חֶבְרוֹן אוֹהֲבִים אֶת הַשְּׁחִיטָה.
הַאִם לָמְדוּ אוֹתָהּ מִשִּׁמְעוֹן וְלֵוִי בְּנֵי יַעֲקֹב?
זְמַן רַב
עָבַר מֵאָז.
גַּם אֵרְעוּ כָּל אֵלֶּה בִּשְׁכֶם, שׁוֹנִים הָיוּ פְּנֵי הַדְּבָרִים בְּדוּרָה, בִּסְבִיבַת חֶבְרוֹן.
בְּדוּרָה חֲסֵרִים הַיּוֹם שְׁלֹשָׁה אָבוֹת לְיַלְדֵיהֶם.
אֲזוֹר חֶבְרוֹן יָדוּעַ לִשְׁמְצָה: אֲזוֹר קְשֵׁה עֹרֶף.
בְּ־1929 רָצְחוּ בְּחֶבְרוֹן שִׁשִּׁים וּשְׁמוֹנָה תַּלְמִידֵי יְשִׁיבָה, אִישׁ אִשָּׁה וָטַף.
הוּ קֶבֶר אַבְרָהָם אָבִינוּ (אוֹמְרִים), אָבִינוּ וַאֲבִיהֶם.
הוּ הַחַיָּלִים הַצְּעִירִים הַפּוֹחֲדִים. הוּ הָעֲשָׂרָה בְּמַרְס 1998.
כִּמְעַט יָרֵחַ מָלֵא, אַךְ הָיָה עוֹד אוֹר יוֹם. פּוֹעֲלִים מֵאֲזוֹר חֶבְרוֹן
נָסְעוּ הַבַּיְתָה. בִּכְבִישׁ חֶבְרוֹן, בְּתַרְקוּמְיָא, יֵשׁ מַחְסוֹם.
לְיַד הַמַּחְסוֹם עָמְדוּ חַיָּלִים. נַהַג הַמְּכוֹנִית אִבֵּד שְׁלִיטָה. מְכוֹנִיתוֹ
דָהֲרָה אֶל הַמַּחְסוֹם. מְפַקֵּד הַמַּחְסוֹם
נִפְגַּע וְנֶהְדַּף לַכִּוּוּן הַנֶּגְדִּי.
יֵשׁ גַּם גִּרְסָה אַחֶרֶת.
חֲבֵרָיו סָבְרוּ כִּי רוֹצִים לְדָרְסוֹ.
קָשֶׁה לָדַעַת לְמִי לְהַאֲמִין וּלְמָה.
פָּתְחוּ בָּאֵשׁ כְּהֶרֶף־עַיִן.
לְפִי הַהוֹרָאוֹת. לְפִי הַפְּקֻדּוֹת.
בְּאֵיזוֹ מְהִירוּת זֶה מִתְרַחֵשׁ. בְּאֵיזוֹ מְהִירוּת
פּוֹשְׁטִים צוּרָה, הוֹפְכִים לְאַחֵר:
בְּלִי נִיעַ, פְּנֵי גֶּבֶס, עֵינֵי זְכוּכִית.
אוֹ אַחַר כָּךְ זְרוֹעוֹת רְפוּיוֹת, שׁוּב מִלִּים בַּפֶּה, לֹא צְעָקוֹת.
אֶתְמוֹל עוֹד פִּתָּה וְזֵיתִים וְלִפְנוֹת בֹּקֶר אוּלַי מִשְׁגָּל.

A POSTCARD FROM THE HEBRON REGION

Hebron is a very ancient city.

Abraham our father with Sarah his wife are buried there

so they say. A sacred thing in a land that lives on its dead.

In the morning in Hebron they eat pita and olives and *labane* drenched in
   olive oil.

On feast days they slaughter a lamb.

The people of Hebron like the slaughtering.

Did they learn it from Shimon and Levi the sons of Jacob?

Much time

has passed since then.

Also in Nablus they ate pita and olives this morning, though things were
   different in Dura, near Hebron.

In Dura today three fathers are missing.

The Hebron region is notorious: stiff-necked and stubborn.

In 1929 sixty-eight Jews were murdered in Hebron, man woman and child.

Oh, the grave of our forefather Abraham (they say), our father and their
   father.

Oh, the soldiers, young and frightened. Oh the tenth of March 1998.

Almost a full moon night, but there was still the light of day.

Laborers from near Hebron traveled home. On the Hebron road, at
   Tarkumiyah, there was a roadblock.

Near the roadblock the soldiers stood. The driver lost control. His

car sped toward the roadblock. The commander of the roadblock

was hit and thrown to the opposite side.

There are other versions told.

His friends surmised that they wanted to run him down.

It's hard to know who to believe, and what.

In a split-second, the soldiers opened fire.

Following the protocol. Following their orders.

How fast it all happens. How fast

אֶתְמוֹל עוֹד לוֹגְרִיתְמִים, הִסְטוֹרְיָה, נְעָרוֹת עַל שְׂפַת הַיָּם. וּפֶתַע
הַכְּבִישׁ מְזֹהָם כְּתָמִים אֲדֻמִּים. הַיָּרֵחַ כִּמְעַט מָלֵא, לָבָן כְּעַצְם.
הִתְרוֹצְצוּת אָנֶה וָאָנָה, קְרִיאוֹת, הָלְאָה עִם זֶה, אַחַר כָּךְ הָאֲבָנִים.
הַאִם מִתְרַבּוֹת הָאֲבָנִים? לְאַט לְאַט, אֵין לַעֲצֹר, פָּרוֹת וְרַבּוֹת הָאֲבָנִים.

162

one form is stripped off, another put on:

Unmoving, mask faces, glass eyes.

Or later, slackened arms, again words in their mouths, no shouting.

Yesterday more pita and olives in the early morning, maybe love-making.

Yesterday more logarithms, history, girls on the beach. Then suddenly

the road is stained red. The moon is almost full, bone white.

Rushing around here and there, calling out, let's get on with it, then stones.

Are the stones multiplying? Slowly, unstoppable, the stones are being fruitful

and multiplying.

גלויה מווינה

זְרוֹעַ שְׁלוּחָה אֶפְשָׁר גַּם לְהוֹרִיד
מֵעַל־יָד – לְהַרְפּוֹת.
פֶּה מָלֵא צְרָחוֹת מְסֻגָּל גַּם לְדַבֵּר.
צְוָחוֹת שִׂמְחָה עֲשׂוּיוֹת לְהִתְגַּלְגֵּל בִּשְׂחוֹק.
לֹא בְּהֶכְרֵחַ יֵשׁ לְנַקּוֹת מִדְרָכוֹת בְּמִבְרֶשֶׁת־שִׁנַּיִם
וְאַף־עַל־פִּי־כֵן וִינָה עִיר יָפָה וּנְקִיָּה לְמִשְׁעִי
בַּעֲלַת עָבָר עָשִׁיר. הַרְבֵּה מוּזִיקָאִים
הִתְגּוֹרְרוּ בָּהּ, שַׂחְקָנִים, סוֹפְרִים לָרֹב.
עִיר שֶׁיֵּשׁ לָהּ בַּמֶּה לְהִתְפָּאֵר.
בַּהֶלְדֶּנְפְּלַץ מְקַשְׁקְשִׁים הַדְּרוֹרִים
הַהֶמְיָה הָעֲמוּמָה מְקוֹרָהּ בַּתְּנוּעָה הָעֵרָה.
מְרַצֵּחַ אֵינוֹ צָרִיךְ לְהִתְבַּיֵּשׁ כִּי
הָיָה מְרַצֵּחַ. גַּם הַדָּנוּבָּה
לָאו דַּוְקָא כְּחֻלָּה.
הַטּוֹב בְּמוּבָן מְסֻיָּם מַשְׁמִים, רָשַׁם קַפְקָא
וּלְלֹא נֶחוּמִים. הֱיִי שָׁלוֹם.

A POSTCARD FROM VIENNA

An outstretched arm can be dropped,
a raised hand – lowered.
A mouth full of screams can also speak.
Screeches of joy may roll into laughter.
One doesn't necessarily have to scrub the pavements with a tooth-brush.
And still, Vienna is a beautiful city, immaculate,
with a rich and illustrious history. Many musicians
lived here, actors, writers in abundance.
A city that has much to be proud of.
At the Heldenplatz the sparrows are chattering
An indistinct hum emanates from the steady traffic.
A murderer doesn't have to be ashamed at having been
a murderer. The Danube too
isn't necessarily blue.
In a certain sense Good is charmless, wrote Kafka,
and comfortless too. Farewell to you.

גלויה מירושלים

יְרוּשָׁלַיִם יָצְאָה מִירוּשָׁלַיִם וְהִסְתַּלְּקָה לָהּ.
זֶה שָׁם לְמַעְלָה בָּאֲוִיר, הֲלֹא לֹא יִתָּכֵן שֶׁזֹּאת יְרוּשָׁלַיִם?

A POSTCARD FROM JERUSALEM

Jerusalem took leave of Jerusalem and vanished.
There, up in the air, there's no way that could be Jerusalem?

גלויה מסיאנה

אֲהוּבָתִי, סִיְאָנָה, בְּטִפְטוּף אַדְמוֹנִי
כְּכַר הַצֶּדֶף, יָצָאת זֶה עַתָּה
מֵהַפְלָצוֹ פּוּבְּלִיקוֹ נִפְרֶדֶת לְשָׁלוֹם
מִגְ'וּידוֹרִיצְ'יוֹ דָּא פּוֹלִיאָנִי
לִפְנֵי הַקְּרָב עִם קַסְטְרוּצְ'יוֹ קַסְטְרָקָנִי, שֶׁבּוֹ נִצַּח.
דָּבָר לֹא נִכָּר בּוֹ, אָמַרְתְּ, מִנִּצְחוֹנוֹ-לֶעָתִיד.
הוּא בּוֹדֵק בְּצוּרִים בְּשֶׁקֶט רַב
אָמַרְתְּ, לְאַט-לְאַט. הַשָּׁמַיִם כִּמְעַט שְׁחֹרִים
וְהָאוֹר חִוֵּר. אוֹר טוֹב לְצִלּוּם, אָמַרְתִּי
מַחֲזִיק בַּמַּצְלֵמָה חֶסְרַת הַבּוּשָׁה אֶל מוּל
הַקִּירוֹת הַחוֹשְׂפִים אֶת סוֹדָם שִׁכְבָה
אַחַר שִׁכְבָה. אָמַרְתִּי. אַרְבַּע שָׁנִים מִקֹּדֶם
מַרְטִינִי נָשָׂא לְאִשָּׁה אֶת בִּתּוֹ שֶׁל מָמוֹ מֶמִּי.
מַזָּל טוֹב, אָמַרְתְּ, אֲבָל לָמָּה
כָּל הַשְּׁתִיקָה הַזֹּאת? הַגֶּשֶׁם הַקַּל סִנֵּן אֶת הָעִיר.
בַּגָּלֶרְיוֹת הִתְחַבְּאוּ רַבֵּי"אָמָנִים שֶׁל פַּעַם.
הַכֹּל כָּאן מֵאִיר כְּמוֹ מִבִּפְנִים, אָמַרְתִּי, חָזָק בְּהַרְבֵּה
מִן הַחִוָּרוֹן שֶׁל מַעְלָה. חֲבֵרִים מֵתִים
אָמַרְתְּ, כָּל-כָּךְ רַבִּים, וּמָה
אֲנַחְנוּ עוֹשִׂים כָּאן? הַבַּטְתִּי סָבִיב. רֵיק
רֵיק וְהוֹלֵךְ. אֲבָל, אָמַרְתִּי, הַאִם בֶּאֱמֶת
אֲנַחְנוּ כָּאן, הַאִם בֶּאֱמֶת, אָמַרְתִּי
הָיִינוּ כָּאן?

A POSTCARD FROM SIENNA

My beloved, Sienna, Shell Square
in a red-hued drizzle – you've just left
the Palazzo Pubblico bidding farewell to
Guidoriccio da Fogliano
before his battle with Castruccio Castracan, the battle he won.
Nothing of the triumph to come, you said, shows on him.
He's checking fortifications, very quietly
you said, one by one. The skies are almost black
and the light is pale. A good light for photographing, I said
holding my shameless camera up to
the walls revealing their secrets layer
after layer. Four years earlier, I said,
Simone Martini took the daughter of Memo Memmi as his wife.
Congratulations, you said, but why
all this silence? The light rain cooled the city.
The Masters from long ago hid in the galleries.
Everything here is lit as though from within, I said, much stronger
than the paleness above. So many friends
are dead, you said, and what
are we doing here? I looked around. Empty
and emptier. But are we really
here, I said? Were we ever, I said,
really here?

טיוטה של גלויה בלתי אפשרית

לִכְתֹּב לְךָ מֵהַמָּקוֹם הַזֶּה – כִּמְעַט מִגְּחָךְ.
מֵהַמָּקוֹם הַזֶּה לֹא כּוֹתְבִים. שׁוּם דָּבָר הַחוּצָה.
אֲנִי מִגְּחָךְ. אֲנִי כּוֹתֵב.
הַמָּקוֹם הַזֶּה רֵיק וְשָׁטוּחַ, אִם כִּי
לֹא יָשָׁר. גַּם שְׁבִילִים יֵשׁ בּוֹ, מִמָּקוֹם
לְמָקוֹם. בִּקְצֵהוּ צוֹנְפִים סוּסִים. מֵעֵבֶר
חַיּוֹת עוֹד פָּרוֹת, אוֹמְרִים, בִּזְכוּת חֲלָבָן. אֲבָל
כְּלָבִים לָרֹב מִתְרוֹצְצִים וְרוֹבְצִים בּוֹ, וְהֵם
נוֹבְחִים מִשִּׂמְחָה. גַּם בְּנֵי אָדָם
מְהַלְּכִים כָּאן, אוֹ מַה שֶּׁנִּרְאֶה כָּךְ. מִתּוֹךְ הַשִּׂיחִים
מֵגִיחוֹת פְּנֵי מַסֵּכוֹת. הַגּוּף לֵאֶה.
הַכְּאֵבִים אֲטוּמִים. אֵין מְדַבְּרִים עַל מַה
שֶּׁאֵין צֹרֶךְ לְדַבֵּר. מַה שֶּׁהָיָה הָיָה וְאֵין צֹרֶךְ
לִזְכֹּר. הַמָּקוֹם דּוֹאֵג לְאַנְשֵׁי הַמָּקוֹם
בְּמִדָּה שֶׁהוּא דּוֹאֵג. לַצִּפֳּרִים אֵין לִדְאֹג:
הֵן בָּאוֹת וְהוֹלְכוֹת לִרְצוֹנָן. יֵשׁ בֵּינֵיהֶן
שֶׁשָּׁרוֹת. אִלְמָלֵא הָיִיתָ כָּאן הָיִיתָ שׁוֹמֵעַת
יֹפִי שֶׁל שִׁירָה

DRAFT OF AN IMPOSSIBLE POSTCARD

Writing you from this place – it's almost absurd.
One doesn't write from this place. At least nothing outgoing.
I'm absurd. I'm writing.
This place is empty and flat, though not
straight. It also has pathways, connecting one area
to another. At the edges of this place, horses whinny. And beyond
there are still cows, kept alive for their milk, they say. Many
dogs run around and lie about, barking
joyfully. People too
walk around here, or so it seems. Masked faces
jump out from the bushes. The body is weary.
Pain is sealed off. No one talks about what
doesn't need mentioning. What was was and there's no need
remembering. The place looks after the local people
as much as it does. The birds have no cares:
they come and go at will. There are those among them
that sing. If you were here you would hear
their beautiful song

השתניות

אֵיךְ הַשֶּׁמֶשׁ מִזְדַּוֶּגֶת עִם עָנָן!
אֵיךְ הָרוּחַ מְשַׁנֶּה צוּרוֹת עֵצִים!
רֵיחַ גֶּשֶׁם בָּאֲוִיר!
הוֹ, כָּל הַשִּׂמְחָה הַזֹּאת!

גַּם אַחֲרַי.

TRANSFORMATIONS

How the sun couples with a cloud!
How the wind shifts the shapes of the trees!
There's the fragrance of rain in the air!
Oh, all this joy!

Even after me.

VI

HOW DO WE END THAT WHICH

HAS NO END

קָרְבָּן וָשׁוּב

הֱיוֹת קָרְבָּן וָשׁוּב וְשׁוּב קָרְבָּן –
אֵיזֶה תַּפְקִיד! גַּם כָּאן גַּם שָׁם.
קָרְבָּן מוֹלִיד מַקְרִיב, מַקְרִיב מוֹלִיד סַכִּין
סַכִּין מוֹלִיד פַּחַד, פַּחַד
מוֹלִיד שִׂנְאָה, שִׂנְאָה – רְשָׁעוּת
רְשָׁעוּת כְּמוֹ אַרְבֶּה אוֹכֶלֶת מְלוֹא הַפֶּה

חֶלְקָה אַחַר חֶלְקָה שֶׁל אֶרֶץ
מְדַמֶּמֶת כְּמוֹ רַגְלָיו שֶׁל יֵשׁוּ עַל הַצְּלָב
מִדַּדָּה עַל קַבַּיִם, מִשְׁתָּרֶכֶת
עַל כִּסְאוֹת גַּלְגַּלִּים, סוּמָא –

חֲמִשָּׁה יְלָדִים בְּדַרְכָּם לְבֵית הַסֵּפֶר בְּחַאן יוּנֶס דָּרְכוּ עַל מַשֶּׁהוּ.
בֶּן רֶגַע הָיוּ בָּשָׂר קָרוּעַ, סְמַרְטוּטֵי בָּשָׂר. יֶלֶד שִׁשִּׁי נוֹרָה שָׁם בְּאוֹתוֹ הַיּוֹם,
עֶשְׂרִים וּשְׁלוֹשָׁה בְּנוֹבֶמְבֶּר אַלְפַּיִם וְאַחַת. הַצָּבָא... בּוֹדֵק... חוֹקֵר...
מֵאוֹתוֹ מָקוֹם... נוֹרוּ פְּצָצוֹת מַרְגֵּמָה... מַבִּיעַ... צַעַר... עֹמֶק...

הַנַּחְלִיאֵלִי שׁוּב עוֹלֶה יוֹרֵד, עוֹלֶה יוֹרֵד בְּנַדְנֵדַת אֲוִיר
הַפָּשׁוֹשׁ מְפַשְׁפֵּשׁ בַּשִּׂיחִים וְגַם אָדָם־הֶחָזֶה נִגְלָה.

מִי עוֹד שׁוֹמֵעַ מַשֶּׁהוּ בָּרַעַשׁ הַנּוֹרָא

שִׂנְאָה וּפַחַד וְשִׂנְאָה וּפַחַד
בִּגְוֵי שִׂנְאָה וּפַחַד

אֵיךְ לְסַיֵּם דְּבָרִים שֶׁאֵין לָהֶם סִיּוּם?

VICTIM, AGAIN

Being a victim, again and again a victim –
what a job! Here and there both.
A victim begets a victimizer, a victimizer begets a knife
a knife begets fear, fear
begets hatred, hatred – wickedness
wickedness like locusts eats greedily

parcel after parcel of a land
bleeding like the feet of Jesus on the cross
worthless, plodding along
in wheelchairs, blind –

In Khan Younis five children on their way to school stepped on something.
In one second they became torn flesh, ragged flesh. A sixth child was shot
there the same day, on the twenty-third of November 2001. The army… is
checking… investigating… from that same spot… artillery fire was shot…
expresses...deep… sorrow…

The wagtail is again rising and falling, rising and falling on air currents
the warbler is warbling in the bushes and the robin too has been spotted.

Who else hears something in this terrible noise

Fear and hatred and hatred and fear
contempt of hatred and fear

How do we end that which has no end?

קולות (2)
(במחסום)

הַשָּׁבוּי
יָדָיו כְּפוּתוֹת.
רַגְלָיו כְּפוּתוֹת.
הַיְּרִיָּה מְעִיפָה אֶת כָּל הַצִּפֳּרִים.

קָשֶׁה לָשֵׂאת.
הַשֶּׁמֶשׁ אֶבֶן לוֹהֶטֶת.
הַצֵּל קָצָר מִדַּי.

לָמָּה הִיא נִדְחֶקֶת?
לָלֶדֶת? אֶפְשָׁר?
יֵשׁ כָּאן מִישֶׁהוּ?
אִי אֶפְשָׁר?

אַתָּה זוֹכֵר אֵיךְ מַמְלִיטָה כִּבְשָׂה?
– אֲבָל זֶה בָּאָבִיב
– מְלַקֶּקֶת לְאַט אֶת הַשִּׁלְיָה
וּבֶן־רֶגַע עוֹמֵד הַטָּלֶה עַל רַגְלָיו

אֵיזוֹ שִׂנְאָה בָּעֵינַיִם
אֵיזֶה צְעָקוֹת.
יֵאוּשׁ. אָדָם אֵינוֹ יָכוֹל לִשְׁמֹעַ
אֶת עַצְמוֹ.

הַשָּׁמַיִם נְחֹשֶׁת.
הָאֲדָמָה שְׂרוּפָה.
לֹא שָׁרַנוּ הַרְבֵּה כִּילָדִים
שֶׂחַקְנוּ בְּלַהֲרֹג.

אֵין צֹרֶךְ בְּמִלִּים גְּבוֹהוֹת.
מַה זֶּה דָּם מְבִינִים.
שֶׁל יֶלֶד גָּדוֹל – מָה אֲנַחְנוּ?
דַּם יֶלֶד קָטָן

178

VOICES (2)
(at a West Bank roadblock)

The prisoner
His hands are bound.
His legs are bound.
The single shot scatters all the birds.

It's hard to bear.
The sun is a scorching stone.
The shade is too narrow.

Why is she being pushed, pushing?
In labor? Is that possible?
Is there anyone here?
How can this be?

Do you remember how the ewe gives birth?
– But that's in spring
– Slowly she licks away the placenta
and instantly the lamb stands on its feet

What hatred in the eyes
what shouts.
Despair. A man can't hear
himself.

The sky is bronze.
The land is burnt.
We didn't sing much as children
we played killing games.

There's no need for fancy words.
We know what blood is.
Of a grown boy – but what are we?
The blood of a little boy

עוֹד מְפַחֵד?

מַה נִּקְרַע מִגּוּפְךָ רִאשׁוֹן
רֹאשׁ אוֹ לֵב?
גַּם יָד יָמִין אוֹ רֶגֶל שְׂמֹאל?
סַמֵּן בְּצֶלֶב.
עָפְתָּ? עִם צִפֳּרִים אוֹ בְּלִי?
עֲנֵה כֵּן/לֹא.
מְחַק אֶת הַמְיֻתָּר.
בָּאתָ מִ־
סַמֵּן בְּצֶלֶב.
הָלַכְתָּ לְ־
עֲנֵה כֵּן/לֹא.
מִשְׁקָל, גֹּבַהּ, צֶבַע עֵינַיִם?
מְחַק אֶת הַמְיֻתָּר.
אֵילוּ מַחֲלוֹת הָיוּ לְךָ?
אֵילוּ תְּרוּפוֹת אַתָּה לוֹקֵחַ?
עֲנֵה כֵּן/לֹא.
סַמֵּן בְּצֶלֶב.
סַמֵּן בְּצֶלֶב.
סַמֵּן בְּצֶלֶב.
סַמֵּן בְּצֶלֶב.
דָּתִי? חִלּוֹנִי? חָרֵד?
סַמֵּן בְּצֶלֶב.
לֹא רָאִיתָ עוֹד אֶת בִּנְךָ?
הָיָה עַל־יָדְךָ?
מַרְגִּישׁ נוֹחַ?
רוֹצֶה לִשְׁאֹל?
מַשֶּׁהוּ לֹא בָּרוּר?

STILL AFRAID?

What was ripped from your body first
head or heart?
Right hand or left foot?
Mark the box.
Did you fly? With the birds or without?
Answer yes or no.
Cross out the extraneous.
You came from-
Mark with an x.
You went to-
Answer yes or no.
Weight, height, eye color?
Cross out the extraneous.
What illnesses did you have?
What drugs do you take?
Answer yes or no.
Mark with an x.
Mark with an x.
Mark with an x.
Mark with an x.
Religious? Secular? Orthodox?
Mark with an x.
You never saw your son again?
Was he beside you?
Are you comfortable?
Is there anything you want to ask?
Is anything unclear?

הצפרים של אודרי

צִפֳּרִים נִפְלָאוֹת שֶׁל אֵימָה
פָּרְחוּ מִתּוֹךְ יָדֶיהָ
צוֹלְלוֹת עַל טַרְפָּן.
פְּדוּ אוֹתִי פְּדוּ אוֹתִי, קוֹרֵא הַלֵּב הַקָּטָן.
קְחוּ אוֹתִי קְחוּ אוֹתִי, קוֹרֵא הַלֵּב הַגָּדוֹל
צִפֳּרֵי חֲלוֹם.
הַמַּקּוֹר בַּלֶּהָבוֹת.
דֹּם אָדָם! אוֹמֶרֶת צִפּוֹר גַּן הָעֵדֶן
הַשֶּׁמֶשׁ צָהֲבָה?
הַשֶּׁמֶשׁ שְׁחֹרָה?
וְאוֹסֶפֶת אֶת כְּנָפֶיהָ.

AUDREY'S BIRDS

(after a painting by Audrey Bergner)

These wondrous birds of terror
took flight from her hands
and dive toward their prey.
Rescue me rescue me, cries the small heart.
Take me take me, cries the large heart
of dream birds.
The beak of disasters.
Red, stand ready! commands the Bird of Paradise
Is the sun yellow?
The sun is black!
she says, gathering her wings inward.

איש עם בית
(ציר לא ידוע)

הָאִישׁ עִם הַפֶּה הֶעָקֹם
הָאִישׁ עִם הָעַיִן הָאַחַת
עַיִן יַנְשׁוּף עָיֵף
הָאִישׁ עִם הָרַגְלַיִם הַקְּצָרוֹת מִדַּי
הָאִישׁ הַיּוֹשֵׁב גֵּאֶה כְּבוּל עֵץ
הָאִישׁ הָעֵצִי הַזֶּה, בַּעַל הַקְּלִפָּה הַצְּהֻבָּה
הַאִם הוּא אִישׁ הַאִם הוּא צֵל?
הָאִישׁ הַמִּתְחַבֵּא בְּתוֹךְ עַצְמוֹ
הָאִישׁ הַמַּחֲזִיק תְּמוּנָה בְּיָדָיו
בַּתְּמוּנָה יֵשׁ בַּיִת, בַּיִת וְסוּס
הָאִישׁ עִם בֵּיתוֹ הַנָּטוּשׁ
הַפָּלִיט הַזֶּה
לֹא יָזוּז עוֹד, לֹא יוּכַל עוֹד
לָקוּם וְלָלֶכֶת
וּלְאָן יֵלֵךְ
כְּשֶׁהַבַּיִת רַק בַּיִת מְצֻיָּר?

MAN WITH A HOUSE
(*Unknown artist*)

The man with the crooked smile
the man with one eye
a tired owl eye
the man with legs that are too short
the man who sits there proud as a tree-stump
this oaken man, with the yellow bark
is he a man or a shadow?
The man who is hiding himself within
the man who is holding a picture in his hands
in the picture is a house, a house and a horse
the man with his abandoned house
this refugee
will move no more, he can no longer
stand up and walk away
and where would he go
when his house is just a picture?

זה שנים

זֶה שָׁנִים
שֶׁמִּפְלָצוֹת הֵחֵלּוּ מְהַלְּכוֹת בֵּינֵינוּ
תְּחִלָּה לֹא יָדַעְנוּ, קָשַׁרְנוּ לָהֶן כְּתָרִים
קִשַּׁטְנוּ אוֹתָן בְּדִבְרֵי הַלֵּל, הֶאֱכַלְנוּ אוֹתָן פְּרִי מְגָדִים
סִמַּנּוּ בָּתִּים, אֲנָשִׁים נֶעֶלְמוּ, הַמִּפְלָצוֹת חִזְּכוּ בַּנִּימוּס, מָצְאוּ
כִּתְמֵי דָם, לֹא יָדְעוּ דָם שֶׁל מִי, כְּלֵי מַשְׁחִית גֻּנְחוּ, בְּנֵי אָדָם
נִתְפַּחֲמוּ צְעִירִים, הַמִּפְלָצוֹת נִגְּבוּ פִּיהֶן בְּגַב יָדָן, הַלֶּחֶם הִשְׁחִיר
וְהִתְאַבֵּן, הַגֶּשֶׁם נָאֱטַם, הַשָּׁמַיִם נִכְרְכוּ תַּכְרִיכִים, תִּינֹקֶת נוֹרָתָה
לָקוּצִים לֹא אִכְפַּת, גַּם לֹא לַבִּלְיָנִים, הַמִּפְלָצוֹת נִטְמְעוּ, שָׁבְרוּ עֲצָמוֹת
צוֹפְפוּ אֲכְלוּסִין וּגְדֵרוֹם, הַיָּאוּשׁ טָוָה חוּטִים, אַחַר כָּךְ חֲבָלִים, אַחַר כָּךְ
חַבְלֵי-חֲבָלִים, הָאֲוִיר מָלֵא מֵהֶם, יֵשׁ שֶׁתָּלוּ עַצְמָם, יֵשׁ שֶׁקָּפְצוּ מִקּוֹמָה
שֶׁבַע אוֹ שְׁלֹשִׁים, אֲחָדִים לָקְחוּ רַעַל, יֵשׁ שֶׁאָנְסוּ נָשִׁים בְּטֶרֶם דִּקְרוֹן
שָׁתַקְנוּ, מְפַחֲדִים אוֹ סְתָם שׁוֹתְקִים, אֶחָד מֵעִיר וּשְׁנַיִם מִמִּשְׁפָּחָה עָזְרוּ
לַחֲבוּלִים, אִמָּהוֹת קוֹנֵנוּ, פֹּה וְשָׁם יְלָלָה, רֹאשׁ וְלַעֲנָה רֹאשׁ וְלַעֲנָה
רְשָׁרְשׁוּ רְשָׁרְשׁוּ, אֲבָל הַמּוּזִיקָה, אֵיךְ לְוַתֵּר עַל הַמּוּזִיקָה, אֲהָהּ, עַל
הַפּוֹתַחַת פֶּתַח בְּאֵין-מוֹצָא, אֵיךְ גַּם עָלֶיהָ? אֵיכָה, אָמַר אִישׁ
אֶרֶץ הוֹפֶכֶת חַטָּאת, אֶרֶץ אֻמְלָלָה אוֹי, אֲחֵרִים צָחֲקוּ צְחוֹק חָלוּל
אַחַר כָּךְ עַצְמָם הָיוּ חֲלוּלִים.
הַמִּפְלָצוֹת הִתְרַבּוּ בְּכָל הַשְּׁכָבוֹת, בְּכָל הַמַּעֲמָדוֹת, הַדְּרָגוֹת
בּוֹרוֹת נִפְעֲרוּ פִּתְאֹם, הַשּׁוּלַיִם קָרְסוּ, הֶהָרִים נִזְדַּעְזְעוּ, שׁוּם
עֶזְרָה, שׁוּם עֶזְרָה, עֵינַיִם נִשְׂאוּ, נִשְׂרְפוּ הַיְּעָרוֹת, הַשִּׂיחִים
שְׂדוֹת הַבָּר חַיּוֹת הַבָּר, הָאֵשׁ אָכְלָה אֶת הָאֹפֶק, הַמַּיִם הִתְיַבְּשׁוּ,
הֵחֵלּוּ לְגָרֵשׁ אֶת מִי שֶׁמְּצָאוּ לְגָרֵשׁ, אֵיךְ לָשִׂים לָזֶה סוֹף
וְאֵין סוֹף

IT'S BEEN YEARS

It's been years
since the monsters started walking among us.
At first we didn't know, we crowned them with laurels,
adorned them with praise, fed them the finest fruits.
Houses were marked, people disappeared, the monsters smiled polite-
ly, bloodstains were found, no one knew whose, the tools of destruction
groaned, humans were burned-to-coal still young, the monsters wiped their
mouths on the back of their hands, bread blackened became stone, the rain
stopped, the sky wrapped itself in shrouds, a baby girl was shot, the thorns
didn't care, neither did the revelers, the monsters blended in, broke bones,
crowded populations together fencing them in, despair wove threads, then
ropes, then roped agony, the air thick with it, there were those who hung
themselves, those who jumped from the seventh or thirtieth floor, a few took
poison, there were those who raped women before stabbing them, we were
silent, afraid or just silent, one or two helped the battered, mothers wailed,
cries scattering, rack and ruin wormwood and root rustling, rustling, but the
music, how can we relinquish the music, oh, that which opens its mouth at
the dead-end, how can we give up on it too? How, oh how, said the lamenting
man does a land become sinful, oh miserable land, others laughed a hollow
laugh then they themselves became hollow.
The monsters multiplied, in every class, every rank and place, pits suddenly
gaped open, eyes looked to the hills, forests burned down, the shrubs, the wild-
fields and wild animals, fires devoured the horizon, the waters dried up, they
started deporting whomever they could deport, how oh how to end this when
there is no end

187

הערות שוליים למסה על איוב

1

שְׁמַע, זֶה אָדָם, זֶה.
– כֵּן, אוּלַי.
וְאוּלַי לֹא?
– מִי יוֹדֵעַ.

2

הִצְטַמֵּק, הִצְטַמֵּק, הִתְכַּדֵּר!
מִי יַכִּיר אוֹתְךָ עוֹד?
הֲרֵי אַתָּה אֵינְךָ אַתָּה.

3

אַל תִּבְרַח.
מִמֵּילָא אַתָּה לְבַד.

4

נְשֹׁךְ אֶת יָדְךָ. הַצְּעָקָה
בְּלִי קוֹל.

5

אָהַבְתָּ?
שָׁכַח. שָׁכַח.

6

הַמַּכִּירְךָ הַיּוֹם
לֹא יַכִּירְךָ מָחָר.

FOOTNOTES TO THE BOOK OF JOB

1

Listen, this is a human being, this.
– Yes, maybe.
Maybe not?
– Who knows.

2

Become smaller and smaller, roll yourself
into a ball! Who will know you now?
After all, you are no longer you.

3

Don't flee.
Anyway, you're alone.

4

Bite your hand. The soundless
scream.

5

Did you love someone?
Forget all about it.

6

He who knows you today
will not know you tomorrow.

7

צֶדֶק אוֹ עָוֶל –
מִי טוֹעֵן?

8

הָאָדָם שָׁמִישׁ
אַךְ לֹא כְּאָדָם.

9

שְׂרָרָה אֵינֶנָּה בְּרֵרָנִית.
אַל תִּהְיֶה מְפָנָק.

10

הַנּוֹתֵן־אֵמוּן יוֹנֶה.
לֵב הַפֶּצַע כָּלֶה לְדָם.

11

חָכְמַת הַשָּׂטָן – אֵינְךָ יוֹדֵעַ?
הוּא מְשַׁכְנֵעַ אוֹתְךָ שֶׁאֵינֶנּוּ קַיָּם.

12

בתודה לאינגר כריסטנסן

אַתָּה זוֹכֵר אֶת הַשְּׂחוֹק?
אֶת הָאַהֲבָה?
הֵם הָיוּ, כֵּן, הֵם הָיוּ.

אֶת שְׁקִיעוֹת הַחַמָּה בַּסְּתָו?
הָעֵינַיִם שֶׁאֵינָן חַדֵלוֹת?
הֵן הָיוּ, כֵּן, הָיוּ.

190

7
Justice or Injustice –
depends who's arguing the case.

8
The human being is of use.
Just not as a human being.

9
Authority isn't choosy.
Don't pamper yourself.

10
He who trusts will be tortured.
Heart of the wound ends in blood.

11
The Devil's shrewdness – don't you know?
He convinces you he doesn't exist

12
With thanks to Inger Christensen

Do you remember the laughter,
the love?
They existed, yes, they did.

The autumn sunsets?
The endless eyes?
They existed, yes, yes.

אֶת הַכְּבָשִׂים בַּמִּרְעֶה? אֶת הַטְּלָאִים בָּעֵשֶׂב?
אֲוִיר הַחֲדָרִים? הַשַּׁעֲשׁוּעִים בַּחֲשֵׁכָה?
הָיוּ, הָיוּ

אֶת הַבִּלְבּוּל הַמְמֻשְׁקָף? אַל תִּהְיֶה חֵרֵשׁ.
אֶת הֶחָלִיל בִּגְרוֹנוֹ, הָעֲלַעְלִים בְּעֵץ הַפֶּקָן?
הָיוּ, הָיוּ, כֵּן, הָיוּ

כֵּן כֵּן כֵּן כֵּן כֵּן כֵּן

13
מִי שֶׁעוֹמֵד בָּזֶה עוֹמֵד בָּזֶה.
מִי שֶׁאֵינֶנּוּ עוֹמֵד – אֵינֶנּוּ.
הַמִּתְעַלֵּל בְּלִי קָרְבָּן
דָּבָר רֵיק הוּא, סְתָם פִּטְפּוּט.

בָּרוּךְ הַשֵּׁם.

The sheep in the pasture? The lambs in the grass?
The air of orange blossoms? The games in the dark?
Yes, they existed, existed.

The bespectacled songbird? Don't play dumb and deaf.
The flute in his throat, the small leaves in the pecan tree.
They existed, yes, yes, they existed

Yes yes yes yes yes yes

13
He who can endure, endures.
He who cannot – does not.
The victimless persecutor
is an empty thing, pointless.

Blessed be his name.

מכה ועוד מכה

הַכָּחֹל לְמַעְלָה לְבֶן־פָּנִים.
בָּאָחוּ כַּלָּנִיּוֹת, טַבְּלַת־צְבָעִים גַּם יְרֻקָּה גַּם אֲדֻמָּה.
כָּךְ מִצְטַיֵּר יוֹמְךָ כְּמוֹ בְּנִים־לֹא־נִים
וְקוֹל דְּמֵי אָחִיךָ עוֹלִים אֵלֶיךָ חֶרֶשׁ מִן הָאֲדָמָה.

הַצְּפַרְדְּעִים הַצְּפַרְדְּעִים בְּכָל מָקוֹם, בַּכֹּל
קוּקְקוּק־פְּלַפְּלַפּ עַד אֵין לָשֵׂאת.
אֵיךְ לָאֹטֶם אָזְנַיִם מִפְּנֵי מַבּוּל הַקּוֹל
הַמַּחֲרִישׁ בְּקִשְׁקוּשָׁיו אָשָׁם וָחֵטְא?

כֻּנִּים כְּבָשׁוּךְ, אֶרֶץ הַצְּבִי.
וּמָצְצוּ דָּמַיִךְ. אִישׁ וָאִישׁ כָּשֵׁל.
הַנַּעֲשֶׂה אֵין לְהָשִׁיב. תִּיבַּבְי.
נָתַתְּ בִּידֵי הַטַּפִּילִים אֶת הַמִּמְשָׁל.

עֶרֶב עִבְרִית בְּלוֹעֲזִית. הַכֹּל מֻתָּר.
מִי כָּאן יִקְבַּע מַה טּוֹב מַה רַע.
רַק אֵצֶל שַׁמְרָנִים יִקֹּב הַדִּין עוֹד אֶת הָהָר.
אֲנַחְנוּ חָפְשִׁיִּים, הֵידָד, הוּרָה!

אֶתְמוֹל דָּבָר שֶׁלֹּא בָּא לָעוֹלָם. הַיּוֹם זֶה דָּבָר.
הָרוּג וְעוֹד הָרוּג יוֹם אַחַר יוֹם, יָמִים, יָמִים.
מַה שֶּׁנֶּחְשַׁב שָׁלֵם הָיָה לְשֶׁבֶר
וְאָנוּ מִתְרַגְּלִים וַהֲמוּמִים וּמִתְרַגְּלִים וַהֲמוּמִים.

194

ONE PLAGUE AND ANOTHER

The Blue above is bleached deep through.
Anemones speckle the meadow green and red.
Thus your days are painted in half-wakefulness half-sleep.
And the blood of your brother cries out from the land silently.

The Frogs the frogs are everywhere, in everything
the *ribbit ribbit ribbit* pushing us past endurance.
How can we seal up our ears from the flood of sound
deafening with its chattering *guilt guilt and sin?*

Lice have conquered you, Land of the Deer.
And they've sucked your blood. Everyone has failed.
What's been done cannot be undone. Now weep and wail.
For you've ceded rule and command to the leeches.

Sweet-Swarming is Hebrew on a foreign tongue. All is allowed.
What's good and what's bad – who's to rule?
Only among conservatives does the law still curse the hill.
We are free to do as we wish, heydad and hurray!

In Past Days, a thing unknown. Today, a pestilence.
Another slain then another, day after day after day.
What was once whole has become shards
we adapt and are stunned and adapt and are stunned again.

הַלֵּב שָׁחוּן. הַדָּם הַמְלַכְלֵךְ זוֹרֵחַ.
אַתְּ, אֲנִי, אַתָּה.
מַה שֶּׁעָשִׂינוּ גַם אֵל מָלֵא רַחֲמִים אֵינוֹ סוֹלֵחַ.
וּבְהוֹלֵים מִתְרוֹצְצִים בְּעִיר שֶׁל בְּעָתָה.

אֲוִיר הָיָה לְכַדּוּרִים שֶׁל קֶרַח.
אֵפֶר קָפָא פְּתוֹתִים פְּתוֹתִים.
הַנְּשִׁימוֹת הַחֲנוּקוֹת שֶׁל הַמֵּתִים
אַט יְכַסּוּ הַכֹּל בְּאֵפֶר קֶרַח.

הַרְבֵּה קָרָה, הַרְבֵּה קוֹרֶה שֶׁאֵין
לוֹ תְּקוּמָה, אֲפִלּוּ נֶהְפַּךְ עוֹרֵנוּ.
כְּמוֹ אַחֲרֵי אַרְבֶּה כָּל שֶׁחָבוּי הָיָה גָּלוּי לְעֵין
הַשֶּׁמֶשׁ. עֲרָמָה עִירֵנוּ.

הָהּ, הַלְוַאי שֶׁחֹשֶׁךְ יְכַסֶּה עֵינֵינוּ!
לְאָן נִבְרַח מִקּוֹל לִבֵּנוּ הַטּוֹעֵן
הֲלֹא יָדֵינוּ שֶׁשָּׁפְכוּ דָּמֵנוּ!
לְאָן נִבְרַח עוֹד מִפָּנֵינוּ?

זֹאת לֹא רָצִינוּ, לֹא, זֹאת לֹא רָצִינוּ.
בִּלְעֲדֵיהֶם מָה אָנוּ וּלְשֵׁם מַה?
לֹא כָּךְ חָשַׁבְנוּ. לֹא רָצִינוּ, לֹא, זֹאת לֹא רָצִינוּ
שֶׁכָּךְ תִּבְלַע הָאֲדָמָה.

The Heart is Parched. The dirty blood shines.
You, me, he.
What we have done even God, Full of Compassion, will not forgive.
And the panicked run wild through the City of Terrors.

The Air has Become ice bullets.
Ash has frozen in every pale crumb.
Slowly all will be covered in ice dust,
those strangled breaths of the dead.

Loathsome, what has happened, is happening, so much
is unredeemable, even if we shed our skins.
Like after the locusts, the hidden all bared
to the sun's eye. Our city, in naked sin.

Oh Let the Darkness cover our eyes!
Where can we flee from the sound of our hearts
proclaiming: was it not our hands that spilt our blood!
To where can we still run from ourselves?

This Is Not what we wanted, no, no, not this.
Without them, who are we and what is ours?
We didn't want this, no, not this, we didn't think it would be like this:
that the Land would devour and devour.

שאלה

כַּמָּה שָׁנִים אֶפְשָׁר
לִשְׁמֹר עַל שִׁוּוּי־מִשְׁקָל
עַל פִּי הַתְּהוֹם?

A QUESTION

How many years can one
maintain one's balance on
the edge of the abyss?

VII

HISTORY

אָבִי הוּמַת.

אִמִּי הוּמְתָה.

אֲחוֹתִי הוּמְתָה.

סָבִי הוּמַת.

סָבָתִי הוּמְתָה.

שְׁאֵרֵי בְּשָׂרִי הוּמְתוּ.

חֲבֵרִים הוּמְתוּ.

נוֹבֵחַ כֶּלֶב. יֶלֶד בּוֹכֶה. רוּחַ נִלְכְּדָה בָּעֲלָוָה.

דּוֹדִי נִצַּל.

דּוֹדָתִי נִצְּלָה.

עָדָה נֶהֶרְגָה.

לוּדְוִיג מֵת.

לֵאָה מֵתָה.

דּוֹדִי מֵת.

יַעֲנְקֶלֶה מֵת.

מוֹרָן נֶעְדַּר

שְׁמוֹנֶה-עֶשְׂרֵה שָׁנִים.

שְׁמוֹנֶה-עֶשְׂרֵה שָׁנִים

נֶעְדַּר מוֹרָן.

לֹא לַחֲשֹׁב! לֹא לַחֲשֹׁב!

דָּן מֵת.

אֵילוּ צְעָקוֹת שָׁם בַּחוּץ. מְכוֹנִית מִשְׁטָרָה מְיַלֶּלֶת.

דּוֹדָתִי מֵתָה.

וֶרְנֶר מֵת.

אַיָּה מֵתָה.

שְׁמָמִית עַל רֶשֶׁת הַחַלּוֹן.

אַוָּה מֵתָה.

נָתָן מֵת.

אֶרְנֶסְט מֵת.

עוֹזֵר מֵת.

◆

My father was murdered.
My mother was murdered.
My sister was murdered.
My grandfather was murdered.
My grandmother was murdered.
My kinsmen were murdered.
My friends were murdered.
A dog barks. A child cries. A wind is trapped in the leaves.
My uncle was saved.
My aunt was saved.
Ada was killed.
Ludwig died.
Lea died.
My uncle died.
Yankeleh died.
Moran is missing
eighteen years.
Eighteen years
Moran has been missing.
Inconceivable!
Dan died.
Those are shouts outside. A police car wailing.
My aunt is dead.
Werner is dead.
Aya is dead.
There's a lizard on the window screen.
Eva is dead.
Natan is dead.
Ernest is dead.
Ozer is dead.

שָׁכַחְתִּי מִישֶׁהוּ?
בִּלְבַּלְתִּי אֶת הַסֵּדֶר?
אֲנִי הוֹלֵךְ לְמַרְאָה
מַבִּיט:
אֲנִי עוֹצֵם עֵינַיִם.
אֲנִי פּוֹקֵחַ עֵינַיִם.
מַה לֹּא נָכוֹן?

Have I forgotten anyone?
Have I confused the order?
I go to the mirror
and look:
I close my eyes.
I open my eyes.
What's wrong with this image?

יוֹם־יוֹם הֶחֱלִיף אֶת חֲלִיפָתוֹ

חֻלְצָתוֹ, לְבָנָיו, גַּרְבָּיו, נַעֲלָיו, אֶת הַכֹּל.

לָנוּ שָׁמַר אֱמוּנִים.

יוֹם־יוֹם אַחֲרֵי שֶׁאָכַל צָהֳרַיִם, הָיָה מְנַמְנֵם

עַל גַּבֵּי הַסַּפָּה עֶשֶׂר דַּקּוֹת בְּדִיּוּק

וְאוּלַי שְׁתֵּים־עֶשְׂרֵה. הוּא לֹא הִסְתִּיר אֶת הַחֹר

שֶׁהָרְמָץ מֵאַחַד הַסִּיגָרִים שֶׁלּוֹ (שִׁשָּׁה מִדֵּי יוֹם בְּיוֹמוֹ)

שׁוּב שָׂרַף בָּאֲרִיג הָאַנְגְּלִי. בְּנוֹסָף עַל אֵלֶּה גַּם עָשָׁן

אַרְבָּעִים "מִצְרִיּוֹת" (מוֹנוֹפּוֹל הַטַּבָּק הָאוֹסְטְרִי)

שֶׁשָּׁלַף מִקֻּפְסָה דַּקִּיקָה בְּצֶבַע כָּתֹם.

פַּעַם לָקָה בְּהַרְעָלַת נִיקוֹטִין.

בִּסְפָרִיָּתוֹ מֵאֲחוֹרֵי זְכוּכִיּוֹת עָמַד לְצַד הַיַּיְנָה יוּלִיסֶס שֶׁל ג'וֹיְס.

הַאִם הִזְמִין אֶת הַסֵּפֶר מֵרֹאשׁ, אוֹ קִבְּלוֹ מַתָּנָה?

דַּרְכּוֹ הַיּוֹמִית לֹא הוֹבִילָה אוֹתוֹ אֶלָּא עַד מִשְׂרָדוֹ וְחָזֹר.

בְּיוֹם א' יָכֹלְתָּ לִסְמֹךְ עָלָיו כְּשֶׁצָּעַד, מַקְלוֹ בְּיָדוֹ

בְּמִכְנְסֵי נִיקֶרְבּוֹקֶר קִילוֹמֶטֶר אוֹ שְׁנַיִם עַד לַפֻּנְדָּק בַּיַּעַר

לְיַד בְּאֵר־הַבַּרְזֶל, מַה שֶּׁכִּנָּה אַחַר־כָּךְ "טִיּוּל".

יָדוֹ הִבְטִיחָה שַׁלְוָה, עֵינָיו – עָתִיד טוֹב יוֹתֵר.

לְאָמוֹן כְּמוֹ שֶׁלּוֹ לֹא זָכִיתִי מֵעוֹדִי.

הַאִם חָשַׁשׁ בְּלִבּוֹ? כְּבוֹנֶה חָפְשִׁי נֶאֱמָן

לֹא גִּלָּה אֶת סוֹדוֹ. הוּא רָקַם תָּכְנִיּוֹת

וְכִמְעַט הִגְשִׁימָן. הוּא, שֶׁנָּסַע בָּרַכֶּבֶת רַק בְּכִסְיוֹת

וְאָכַל סֶנְדְוִיץ' בְּסַכִּין וּמַזְלֵג –

יִהְיֶה לְלוֹלָן, יְנַקֶּה זֶבֶל־עוֹפוֹת בְּשָׁבֵי צִיּוֹן!

הַמִּלְחָמָה שֶׁפָּרְצָה סִכְּלָה אֶת הַכֹּל.

הוּא עָמַד קְצָת בַּצַּד וְהִזְלִיג דִּמְעוֹתָיו פְּנִימָה

כַּאֲשֶׁר נִפְרַדְנוּ בְּתַחֲנַת הָרַכֶּבֶת וְשׁוּב לֹא נוֹתַר מִמֶּנּוּ אֶלָּא

נִפְנוּף שֶׁל יָד.

פַּעַם אַחַת עוֹד רְאִיתִיו בַּחֲלוֹם: בָּבָה לְבָנָה

כֻּלּוֹ עָטוּף גֶּבֶס, הֻזְדַּקֵּר בְּמַלְקָסָן בִּמְכוֹנִית דְּחוּסָה

MY FATHER

Every day he changed his suit
his shirt, his underwear, his socks, his shoes, everything.
To us he was ever loyal.
Every day after he ate lunch he would nap
on the sofa for exactly ten minutes,
maybe twelve. He didn't hide the hole
that an ember from one of his cigars (six a day)
burnt again in his suit's English fabric. In addition to those, he also smoked
forty "Egyptians" (Austrian tobacco monopoly)
he would pull out from a slender orange packet.
Once he got nicotine poisoning.
In his library behind the glass panes Heine stood beside Joyce's *Ulysses*.
Did he order the book ahead of time, or receive it as a gift?
His daily path led him only to his office and back.
On Sundays I could depend on him striding, walking-stick in hand,
in his knickerbockers the kilometer or two to the village tavern
near the iron-well, what was later called "a hike."
His hand promised peace, his eyes – a better future.
No one has ever believed in me as he did.
Was he afraid? As a faithful Freemason
he never told his secrets. He made plans
and almost fulfilled them. He, who always wore gloves when travelling by
train and ate a sandwich with knife and fork –
he would be a chicken farmer, clean the chicken-manure in Shavei Zion!
The war that erupted thwarted everything.
He stood a bit apart and shed tears only inward when
we said good-bye at the train station, and then there was nothing left of him
but the wave of a hand.
Once I saw him again in a dream: a white doll
completely wrapped in plaster, protruding sideways from a crowded car

שֶׁבָּאָה מִכִּוּוּן הַדָּנוּבָּה.
הַיּוֹם מִסְתַּכֵּל הוּא בִּי מֵהַקִּיר וְשׁוֹאֵל בְּעֵינָיו
אִם אֵדַע, בֶּאֱמֶת אֵדַע, שֶׁאֵין לְהַפְרִיד
בֵּין חַיִּים וּבֵין מָוֶת, וְכִי לְשׁוֹן לְעִתִּים אֵינֶנָּה
אֶלָּא אֲבֵלוּת עַל עֶדְנָה שֶׁאָבְדָה.

coming from the direction of the Danube.

Today he gazes at me from the wall and asks me with his eyes

if I know, do I really know, that one cannot separate

life from death, and that language is sometimes nothing more than

the mourning of lost tenderness.

אִמִּי

מֵאֹפֶל אִמִּי
הַמּוּאָר כֻּלּוֹ בְּאוֹר לְבָבָהּ
יָצָאתִי אֶל אוֹר הָעוֹלָם.

לֹא יָנַקְתִּי חָלָב שָׁחֹר מִשְּׁדֵי אִמִּי.
לֹא יָשַׁבְתִּי זְמַן רַב עַל כֵּס הַכָּבוֹד שֶׁל בִּרְכֶּיהָ.

אִמִּי הַיָּפָה נַעֲשָׂתָה צְעִירָה כְּשֶׁנָּשְׂאוּ הַשְּׁעָרִים
עַל גַּבָּם הָרָחָב אֶת הַקַּיִץ, אֲוִיר הָעֶרֶב צִרְצֵר
הַצְּפַרְדְּעִים נָתְנוּ אֶת קוֹלָן בְּשִׁיר.

כְּלוּם לֹא הָיְתָה הָעִיר כְּמָחוֹךְ לָהּ
וּבֵיתֵנוּ – תְּחוּם מֶמְשַׁלְתָּהּ – כְּלוּב זָהָב?

אָז לֹא יָדַעְתִּי. הַיּוֹם אֲנִי יוֹדֵעַ:
חוּט אַהֲבָה קָשַׁר אֶת לִבִּי אֶל לִבָּהּ.

עַכְשָׁו אֵינֶנִּי רוֹאֶה אֶלָּא צְדוּדִיתָהּ
בְּהִירָה, חֲרֵת בֵּין הַסְּפָרִים שֶׁעַל הַמַּדָּף
שְׂפָתֶיהָ צֵל שֶׁל חִיּוּךְ שֶׁאֵינוֹ מְחַיֵּךְ, כִּמְעַט אֲבוּדָה
הִיא שְׁקֵטָה מְאֹד, נוֹכַחַת רַק כִּבְיָכוֹל, מַבִּיטָה

הַעוֹדֶנָּה פּוֹרֶשֶׂת יָדֶיהָ כְּמוֹ לְחַבְּקֵנִי לִפְרֵדָה־לֹא־פְּרֵדָה?

210

MY MOTHER

From my mother's darkness
illuminated in full by the light of her heart
I came into the light of the world.

I didn't nurse on black milk from my mother's breasts.
I didn't sit for long in the honored seat of her lap.

My pretty mother became young when the bulls carried
the summer on their wide backs, the evening air chirping,
the frogs lifting their voices in song.

The city was but a boned bodice to her
and our house – her kingdom – a golden cage?

Then I didn't know. Today I know:
a thread of love tied my heart to hers.

Now I cannot see but her fair profile
pale among the books on the shelf,
on her lips the shadow of an unsmiling smile, almost lost
she's very quiet, present only as if, watching –

Is she still opening her arms as though to embrace me in farewell-not-fare-
     well?

ליל ירח

אֵין שִׁכְחָה.
הַכּוֹכָבִים שְׁחֹרִים.
אִם לְבָנָה אֲבוּדָה תּוֹעָה
בִּסְבַךְ הַחֹשֶׁךְ.

MOONLIT NIGHT

There's no forgetting.
The stars are black.
A lost mother, white, wanders
through the night thicket.

תצלום

עֵינַיִם בְּגוֹן הַשָּׁמַיִם בַּחֹרֶף.
אֵפֶר. עָנָן. נְיָר.
עֵינַיִם בְּצֶבַע נְיָר אָפֹר
מְקֻמָּט קִמְעָה, נִקְרָע בְּקַלּוּת. חִיּוּךְ

רָפֶה. לֹא בָּעֵינַיִם. שְׁנֵי קַוִּים
יוֹתֵר כֵּהִים, לְמַטָּה
בַּקְּצָווֹת קְצָת מִתְרוֹמְמִים.
זָוִית מְשֻׁנָּה, פֶּה

מְחַיֵּךְ, נָצוּר, לֹא פוֹצֶה, לֹא הֶגֶה, לֹא כְלוּם.
לֹא הֶבֶל, לֹא כְלוּם. פִּי נְיָר מְחַיֵּךְ.

הַפָּנִים
פְּנֵי נַעַר. אִם לְדַיֵּק, מִי
שֶׁהָיָה נַעַר, שֶׁהָיוּ לוֹ
פָּנִים.

פְּנֵי נַעַר אֶפְרִים, פְּנֵי נְיָר
מֻטָּלִים עַל שֻׁלְחָן מַבְרִיק.
בִּמְהֵרָה יַצְהִיבוּ
אֵי־שָׁם, בָּעֲרֵמָה.

214

PHOTOGRAPH

Eyes the color of a winter sky.
Ash. Cloud. Paper.
Eyes the color of gray paper
slightly wrinkled, easily torn. A weak

smile. Not in the eyes. Two darker
lines, lower down, turn up
a bit at the edges.
Strange angle, a sealed

smiling mouth, soundless, not opening, nothing.
No breath, nothing. A paper mouth smiling.

The face
is the face of a boy. More exactly, he
who was a boy, he who had
a face.

The gray face of a boy, a paper face
left lying on a polished table.
Very soon it will yellow
somewhere in the pile.

יום הזיכרון

הֵם עוֹמְדִים בֵּין הָאֲבָנִים
כְּמִי שֶׁאֵינֶנּוּ יוֹדֵעַ לְאָן.
הָאָבוֹת, פְּנֵיהֶם נְמוֹגוֹת, מוּתְּשֵׁי זְכִירָה
כְּעָנָף שָׁבוּר תָּלוּי מֵעֵץ. הַנָּשִׁים
בְּלֹא רַחֲמִים, עֵינֵיהֶן פְּקוּחוֹת כְּשֶׁל אָח.
אִמָּהוֹת מְרוֹקָנוֹת כְּמוֹ בָּלְעוּ תְּהוֹם.
עוֹמְדִים זָעִים כְּאִלּוּ בִּקְשׁוּ לְהָנִיחַ לְגוּפָם
וְלָצֵאת לְמָקוֹם אַחֵר.

הוֹ, אֶרֶץ יָפָה, רוֹדֶפֶת
מִסּוֹף הָעוֹלָם עַד סוֹף הָעוֹלָם
בְּשִׁטְחֵי הַצָּהֹב וְיָרֹק בְּצִלְלֵי עֲנָנִים אֵלּוּ בְּאֵלּוּ.
אֲפִלּוּ בְּקוֹץ וְדַרְדַּר תְּפַתִּי, בִּגְדִילָן וּבַרְקָן נָחוֹחַ
לָבוֹא בְּתוֹכֵךְ, לַחְדֹּר עָמֹק עָמֹק אֶל תּוֹכֵךְ
גּוּף בְּגוּף עַד־לֹא־יֵדַע.

אֵיזוֹ אַהֲבָה נוֹרָאָה שָׁנָה בְּשָׁנָה, זִכָּרוֹן שֶׁאֵינוֹ חָדֵל
שֶׁנּוֹכֵחַ תָּמִיד כְּמוֹ פֶּצַע נִפְתָּח וּפוֹרֵחַ שׁוּב וָשׁוּב
בָּאָבִיב הַמַּטְרִיף אֶת הַדַּעַת וּכְבָר נוֹטֶה
לְקַיִץ קָצוּר, לַמֶּרְחָבִים הַשְּׂרוּפִים בָּאוֹר שֶׁאֵין לָשֵׂאת
וְעַכְשָׁו הַבֹּשֶׂם הַזֶּה בָּאֲוִיר שֶׁנִּמְזַג בְּמִין רֵיחַ
עוֹלֶה מֵהָאֲדָמָה וּמֵהָאֲבָנִים שֶׁפְּנֵיהֶן הִלְבִּינוּ.
הוֹ, בֵּן.

SOLDIERS' MEMORIAL DAY

They stand among the stones
as though not knowing where to turn.
The fathers, their faces melting, memory-weary
like broken branches hanging from the tree. The wives
pity-less, their eyes as wide open as the owl's.
The mothers are emptied as if they've swallowed an abyss.
Others shudder as though wanting to shed their bodies
and flee to somewhere else.

Oh, beautiful country, pursuing
us from one end of the world to the other
in yellow and green fields in cloud shadows.
Even with thorn and thistle, with nettle and briar, you seduce
to enter you, to penetrate deep deep within you
body into body to no end.

What a terrible love, year after year, this ceaseless memory
always tearing open the wound until it blooms again and again
in this maddening spring becoming already
shorn summer, to the burnt expanses in the unbearable light
and now this aroma in the air mixes with the smell
rising from the ground and from the pallid stones.
Oh, my son.

הַהִיסְטוֹרְיָה

כְּמוֹ מַעֲרָבוֹן הִיא אוֹהֶבֶת הַרְבֵּה הֲרוּגִים.
קָרְבָּנוֹת, קָרְבָּנוֹת, הִיא תּוֹבַעַת, בִּלְעֲדֵיהֶם
כֵּיצַד אֲפָאֵר מְנַצְּחִים?
יֵשׁ מְנַצְּחִים? אַתָּה שׁוֹאֵל וּמַחֲרִישׁ.
מִי שֶׁשּׂוֹרֵד הוּא גִּבּוֹר. וּמִי שֶׁעָזַר לוֹ לִשְׂרֹד
שְׁמוֹ הָלַךְ עִם הָרוּחַ הַמֵּצֶן אֶת הַלַּהַט
שֶׁרוֹבֵץ עַל פְּנֵי שְׂדֵה-הַקְּרָב.
בּוּשָׁה? תְּמֵהָה הַהִיסְטוֹרְיָה, בּוּשָׁה? מֵעוֹלָם לֹא שָׁמַעְתִּי.
דִּין וְחֶשְׁבּוֹן? עֲזֹב, אֵיזֶה פָּתוֹס.
פְּנֵי הַהִיסְטוֹרְיָה קָדִימָה, אָחוֹרָה, לְאָן מַבָּטָהּ?
יֵשׁ שֶׁהִיא מִתְמַמֶּמֶת וּמְסַפֶּרֶת סִפּוּרֵי סַבְתָּא
עַל הָיָה הָיָה, עַל אָבוֹת וּבָנִים, עֲלִילוֹת נִפְלָאוֹת, כְּאִלּוּ הֵחֵל
דְּבַר-מָה וּמַמְשִׁיךְ וּמַמְשִׁיךְ –
דָּבָר לֹא קָרָה. בְּהֶבְזֵק זִכָּרוֹן קוֹפֵא שֶׁהָיָה וְנוֹכֵחַ.
הַדָּם הוּא אוֹתוֹ הַדָּם. הַבָּשָׂר אוֹתוֹ הַבָּשָׂר.
הַגֻּלְגֹּלֶת לֹא הִשְׁתַּנְּתָה, וְאִם – אָז בִּמְעַט
וּמִתּוֹךְ אַרְבּוֹת עֵינֶיהָ נִבֶּטֶת אוֹתָהּ אֲפֵלָה.
הִיא זוֹרֶקֶת שֵׁמוֹת שֶׁל כַּמָּה מְלָכִים, נַהֲגֵי מֵרוֹץ
כּוֹכְבֵי קוֹלְנוֹעַ אַלְמוֹתִיִּים. בְּנֵי אָדָם סְתָם
אֵינָם מְעַנְיְנִים אֶת הַהִיסְטוֹרְיָה, אַף שֶׁהֵם
מְזוֹנָהּ הַיּוֹמִי. אַהֲבָה? הִיא שׁוֹתֶקֶת.
הָאוֹהֲבִים מִצִּדָּם גַּם הֵם פּוֹנִים לָהּ עֹרֶף
כִּי מַה כָּל הַזְּמַנִּים לְעֻמַּת הָרֶגַע הַזֶּה
כַּאֲשֶׁר גּוּף וְעוֹד גּוּף נַעֲשִׂים גּוּף אֶחָד, כֻּלּוֹ נְשִׁימָה.
נְשִׁימָה? – הַהִיסְטוֹרְיָה שׁוֹאֶלֶת וְחֶרֶשׁ צוֹחֶקֶת צְחוֹק שֶׁל בַּדְיָה –
מָה אַתָּה סָח.

HISTORY

Like a good western, It loves its piles of dead.
Victims and more victims, It demands, without them
how will I glorify the Victors.
Are there victors? you ask, and fall silent.
He who survives is the hero. And he who helped him survive,
his name will be lost with the wind that cools the heat
crouching over the battle-field.
Shame? History asks in wonder. Never heard of it.
Accountability? Forget it, pathetic.
Facing forward, backward, where does History gaze?
There are those who say It feigns innocence, tells tall tales
of Once Upon a Time, of fathers and sons, of wondrous feats, as though
something began and goes on and on –
but nothing happened. In a flash, memory freezes what was.
The blood is the same blood. The flesh, the same flesh.
The skull hasn't changed, and if it has – then only a little,
the same darkness still peers out of the eye-sockets.
History bandies about the names of a few kings, race-car drivers,
immortal movie stars. Regular people
don't interest History, even though
they are its daily bread. Love? It falls silent.
The lovers, for their part, turn their backs on It; after all
what are eras and epochs in comparison to the single moment
a body and another body become one, all breath.
Breath? – History asks, quietly laughing its lying laugh –
What are you talking about?

אחר־כך

בַּאֲגַם הָאֵפֶר
מְרַצְּדוֹת חֶרֶשׁ
בְּרוּחַ מְכֵּה יָרֵחַ
עֵינֵי הָעֵצִים הָעִוְּרוֹת

אוֹ שֶׁמָּא אֵלּוּ
נְשִׁימוֹת, נְשִׁימוֹת מִזְּמַן
נִשְׁכָּחוֹת

שֶׁמָּא שְׁאָגוֹת, רְצוּצוֹת
עַד דַּק
כִּמְעַט יְלֵל־לֹא־קוֹל
כִּמְעַט אַדְוַת גַּלִּים.

AFTER

The trees' blind eyes
leap around silently
in the ash lake
in the moonstruck wind

or are these
the breaths, breaths from the then
forgotten

or maybe these are howls, crushed
into thin nothing
an almost soundless wailing
almost the waves' rippling.

אבל האור הזה

אֲבָל הָאוֹר הַזֶּה
הָאוֹר בֵּין־עַרְבַּיִם שֶׁל סְתָו
אוֹר רַךְ שֶׁאֵינוֹ רוֹמֵס אֶת הָעַיִן
מִסְתַּנֵּן דֶּרֶךְ עַלְוָה מַצְהִיבָה
אֲבָל הָאוֹר הַזֶּה
הָאוֹר הַסְּתָוִי הֶעָנֹג הַזֶּה
הָאוֹר הַסְּתָוִי הֶעָנֹג הַזְּהַבְהַב הַזֶּה
הַחוֹסֶה וְסוֹכֵךְ, הַנָּקִי מֵחֶמְלָה
הַשָּׁרוּי עַל הַכֹּל
הַבָּא מִשָּׁם וְהוֹלֵךְ לְשָׁם
אֲבָל הָאוֹר, עַכְשָׁו, בָּרֶגַע הַזֶּה
עוֹד כָּאן עַל הָאָרֶץ הַקָּשָׁה
הַקְּרוּעָה, לִבָּהּ כָּבֵד, הַשּׁוֹתָה
דַּם בָּנֶיהָ, עַל הָאָרֶץ הַפְּצוּעָה
הָאוֹר הַזֶּה הַנֶּאֱסָף אֶל לִבּוֹ

אֲבָל הָאָרֶץ הַגּוֹלָה לְלֵילָהּ

BUT THIS LIGHT

But this light
this dusk autumn light
this soft light untrampling of the eye
filters in through the yellowing foliage
but this light
this tender autumnal light
this tender and golden autumnal light
sheltering, free of pity
spreading over everything
coming from there and going there
this light, now, in this moment
still here on this hard land,
this torn land of heavy heart, drinking
the blood of her sons, this wounded land,
this light converging inward towards its heart

But the land wanders off into her exiled night

מדריך למשורר צעיר

אַל תִּבְגֹּד בָּרַעְיוֹן
שְׁמֹר אֱמוּנִים לַנָּטוּשׁ
הַסְכֵּת לַמַּנְגִּינָה
בְּאָזְנַיִם אֲטוּמוֹת
שְׁמַע בַּיָּדַיִם
הַקֵּשׁ אֶת הַקֶּצֶב
בְּלִי לְהָזִיז אֶצְבַּע
שְׁכַח אֶת הַלַּעַג וְאֶת הַבְּדִידוּת
שְׁכַח אֶת הָאֵשׁ, שְׁכַח אֶת הָאֵפֶר
אֶת לִבְּךָ שְׁכַח
כְּלָא אֶת קוֹלְךָ
שְׁכַח מִי אַתָּה
וְתוּכַל לְהַתְחִיל
בְּזֵעַת אַפֶּיךָ.

GUIDE FOR THE YOUNG POET

Don't betray the idea
Be faithful to the forsaken
Study the melody
with sealed ears
Listen with your hands
Tap out the rhythm
without moving a finger
Forget the scorn and the loneliness
Forget the fire, forget the ash
Forget your heart
Imprison your voice
Forget who you are
Now you can begin
by the sweat of your brow.

אלשיר

אַחֲרֵי שֶׁסִּיַּמְתָּ שִׁיר וְהַמִּלִּים מָצְאוּ אֶת מְקוֹמָן
אֵינָן לֹא קוֹלָנִיּוֹת מִדַּי וְלֹא חֲרִישִׁיּוֹת מִדַּי
אַתָּה חָשׁ כִּי פָּג כִּי אֵיזֶה לַחַץ, כִּי פָּרַקְתָּ עֹל
וְנוֹשֵׁם לָרְוָחָה.

לֹא תָמִיד.
לִפְעָמִים הַמִּלִּים קָמוֹת עָלֶיךָ
שָׁבוֹת וְנִכְנָסוֹת בְּךָ בְּלִי עֶדְנָה יְתֵרָה
גּוֹרְמוֹת לְךָ לִכְאֹב אֶת הַכְּאֵב שֶׁהִדְמַמְתָּ עַל הַנְּיָר
נִדְחָקוֹת, נִדְחָסוֹת, נֶאֱסָפוֹת אֶל עַצְמָן
הוֹפְכוֹת לְמֵעֵין חוֹר שָׁחֹר
בְּדִמְמַת מָוֶת.

כָּתַבְתָּ עָשָׁן? עָשָׁן מוֹחֵק עָשָׁן.
כָּתַבְתָּ אֵפֶר? אֵפֶר מְכַסֶּה עַל אֵפֶר.
כָּתַבְתָּ רַכֶּבֶת? רַכֶּבֶת נִכְנֶסֶת בְּרַכֶּבֶת
מְנַתֶּצֶת אוֹתָהּ בְּלִי קוֹל.

יֵשׁ דְּבָרִים שֶׁהַכְּתָב מְתַכֵּוֵּן תַּחְתָּם.
יֵשׁ שִׁיר שֶׁאֵינֶנּוּ שִׁיר.

NOTPOEM

After you've finished a poem and the words have found their place
speaking neither too noisily nor too quietly
you feel a kind of relief, having cast off the yoke
you breathe freely.

Not always.
Sometimes the words rise up
to return and assault you, without excessive tenderness
they cause you to feel again the pain you bled on the page
they push and press, crowd into themselves
become a type of black hole
in a death-like silence.

You wrote smoke? Smoke erases smoke.
You wrote ash? Ash covers ash.
You wrote train? Train crashes into train
shatters it soundlessly.

There are things under which writing shrinks.
There's a poem that's not a poem.

טַשְׁטֵשׁ עֲקֵבוֹתֶיךָ
בְּלֵבָן לֹא גְבוּל
טַשְׁטֵשׁ עֲקֵבוֹתֶיךָ
אַל תֵּעָצֵר עַל
יַד הָאֶבֶן, אַל
תּוֹתִיר סִימָנִים, רֵד
אֶל הָאֲפֵלָה, וַעֲלֵה
בַּעֲלָוָה, הֱיֵה בָּהּ
כְּמוֹ הָרוּחַ

שְׁכַח אֶת שִׁמְךָ
אֶת יָדֶיךָ
זְכֹר אֶת הַמַּיִם
נִרְגָּשִׁים סָבִיב הָאֶבֶן שֶׁהִשְׁלַכְתָּ
גַּלִּים גַּלִּים, אַחַר־כָּךְ
רְגוּעִים
כְּבַתְּחִלָּה

כִּמְעַט מֻפְשָׁט

אֵלֶּה הָרְשׁוּמִים מַרְאִים
אֶת תַּהֲלִיךְ הַיְצִירָה:
בְּרֵאשִׁית הַכֹּל
אַחַר־כָּךְ הַוִּתּוּר עַל פְּרָטִים רַבִּים
אֲחִיזָה בָּזֶה וּבָזֶה
תָּמִיד פָּחוֹת
תָּמִיד רֵיק יוֹתֵר
הוּא הַנּוֹתֵן

הֱיֵה כְּמוֹ הָרוּחַ
מְצַיֵּר בַּחוֹל וּמוֹחֶה

♦

Erase your traces
with borderless white
blur your footprints
don't stop
by the stone, don't
leave any signs, descend
into the darkness, then rise
in the leaves, be there
like the wind

Forget your name
your hands
remember the water
swirling excitedly around the stone you tossed in
wave after wave, then
calm again
as in the beginning

Almost abstract

These sketches show
the creation process:
In the beginning, everything
then the slow surrender of so many details
still clinging to this or that
always less
always emptier
that which gives most

Be like the wind
which draws in the sand, then erases

VIII

BELATED BEAUTY

יופי מאוחר

אוּלְטְרָמָרִין
עָמֹק-עָמֹק
וְאִם חָפֵץ הָאוֹר
נִגְלֶה סוֹדוֹ: סָגֹל.
עָבַרְתִּי עַל פָּנָיו
וְשַׁבְתִּי
עָבַרְתִּי עַל פָּנָיו
וְשַׁבְתִּי
– מַה, בְּגִילִי? –

עַכְשָׁו נִבָּט בִּי בְּחַדְרִי.

לַיְלָה כָּחֹל
אוֹפֵף אוֹתִי
וְאֶבֶן הָאֵשׁ
שֶׁל שֶׁמֶשׁ שׁוֹקַעַת-לֹא-שׁוֹקַעַת
בְּאֹפֶק נוֹדֵם.

מַרְכּוּס רוֹטְקוֹבִיץ' מִדְּבִינְסְק
מֵ-1914 בְּארה"ב
מַרְק רוֹתְקוֹ
צִיֵּר תְּחִלָּה אַחֶרֶת
פִיגוּרָטִיבִית, עִם קַוִּים לָרֹב
עַד שֶׁמָּצָא
כִּי הַפָּחוֹת הוּא הַיּוֹתֵר
יָדַע
כִּי אֵין מֻרְכָּב מֵהַפַּשְׁטוּת
וְכָל צִבְעֵי הַקֶּשֶׁת
וּמַה שֶּׁבֵּינֵיהֶם
הֵם הַחַיִּים.

BELATED BEAUTY

Deep-deep
ultramarine
with light-longing
its secret revealed: Purple.
I walked past it
returned
walked past it again
and returned
– at my age? –

Now, consider me in my room.

A blue night
surrounds me
and the fire stone
of a setting-not-setting sun
sits silent on the horizon.

Marcus Rotkovitch of Dvinsk
from 1914 in America
Marc Rothko
painted differently at the beginning,
figures, many lines,
until he discovered that
less is more
and knew
that nothing is more complex than simplicity
and all the colors of the spectrum
and what is between them
is life.

וּכְמוֹ הַסַּתָו בְּוֶרְמוֹנְט
אָסַף בְּטֶרֶם הֶאָסְפָם
צִבְעֵי שֶׁל אַרְבָּעִים דּוֹרוֹת
וְהִנִּיחָם שִׁכְבָה שִׁכְבָה
מִישׁוֹר עַל גַּב מִישׁוֹר
הַמְּאָזֵן נִשְׁמַת הַמְּאָנֵךְ
וּכְמוֹ עָלְוָה בְּרוּחַ עֶרֶב
רוֹחֲשִׁים כָּל הַקּוֹלוֹת
חֶרֶשׁ חֶרֶשׁ
קוֹשְׁרִים שִׂיחָה
מִתְלַהֲטִים כָּל הַצְּבָעִים
גּוֹנֵי גְוָנִים שֶׁל אֲדָמִים
שֶׁל צְהָבִּים, חוּמִים, כְּחָלִים
כְּתֻמִּים וִירֻקִּים –
אֵיזֶה הַלֵּל לְכָל הַחַי

שֶׁל מִי אֲשֶׁר פָּתַח וְרִידָיו
שָׁפַךְ אֶת כָּל צִבְעֵי גוּפוֹ
הָפַךְ לְצֵל לָבָן.

Like autumn in Vermont
he collected before they were gathered up
the colors of forty generations
lay them layer by layer
level over level
horizontal breathing the vertical
and like leafage in an evening breeze
all the voices softly
whispering whispering
stitching together a conversation
the colors aflame
hues upon hues of red
of yellows, browns and blues
oranges and greens –
what praise for all the living

for he who opened his veins
poured out all the colors of his body
and became a white shadow.

בדרך לטבעון
(נילי שחור)

זֶה קָסוּם, תִּשְׁמָעִי, אֵיזֶה קֶסֶם!
לֹא יוֹם וְלֹא לַיְלָה
שְׁלֹשָׁה בְּרוֹשִׁים
אוֹ אַרְבָּעָה
דְּמָעוֹת שֶׁחָשְׁכוּ
כִּמְעַט שֶׁכְחָה
אָבְדָנִים שֶׁהָיוּ
לְאָחוּ
חֲרָדוֹת לְכָרֵי דֶּשֶׁא
מַשֶּׁהוּ בָּהִיר
פֹּה וָשָׁם
מַשֶּׁהוּ סָגֹל
מַרְאוֹת שָׁמַיִם סְגֻלִּים
זְעִירוֹת, שְׁלוּלִיּוֹת שֶׁל אוֹר
הַצִּפֳּרִים קִפְּלוּ קוֹלוֹתֵיהֶן
נוֹף שֶׁמֵּעֵבֶר
הָרוּחַ נֶאֶסְפָה

זֶה טִבְעוֹן?
הֲגַּעְנוּ?
אַתְּ אִתִּי?

אַתְּ עוֹד אִתִּי?

236

ON THE ROAD TO TIVON
(after a painting by Nili Shachor)

It's magical, listen, it's magic!
Not day not night
cypress trees, three
maybe four
are tears that have darkened
almost forgetting
the ruin that has become
a meadow
fears become green pastures
something light
a touch of something purple
here and there
mirroring slender
purple skies, pools of light
the birds have folded away their voices
the landscape beyond which
the wind is gathered up

Is this Tivon?
Have we arrived?
Are you with me?

Are you still with me?

הַשְּׁלֵמוּת

אִי אֶפְשָׁר עִם הַשְּׁלֵמוּת הַזֹּאת.
הַשְּׁלֵמוּת מְשֻׁלֶּמֶת מִדַּי.
קָשָׁה כַּמָּוֶת.
מוֹנַעַת מִמְּךָ לִנְשֹׁם.
עוֹשָׂה אוֹתְךָ מְגֻחָךְ בַּפֶּה הַפָּעוּר.
אִי אֶפְשָׁר לֶאֱכֹל בִּשְׁלֵמוּת
לִשְׁתּוֹת בִּשְׁלֵמוּת
לֶאֱהֹב אַהֲבַת מָתֶם.
מֵעוֹלָם לֹא כָּתַבְתָּ דָּבָר מֻשְׁלָם.
זֶה מֵצִיק? – רַק אִם הַשְּׁלֵמוּת
נוֹשֶׁפֶת בָּעֹרֶף: הֱיֵה כְּמַלְאָךְ!
– מָה אַתְּ יוֹדַעַת עַל מַלְאָכִים
יֵשׁ מַלְאָכִים חַסְרֵי כָּנָף
יֵשׁ מַלְאָכִים צְמֵאִים כִּצְפָרִים בְּיוֹם שָׁרָב
יֵשׁ מַלְאָכִים מַזִּיעִים לְהַצִּילְךָ וּבוֹכִים
כְּשֶׁאֵינָם מַצְלִיחִים.
מָה אַתְּ יוֹדַעַת, סְגוּרָה בְּעַצְמֵךְ
אָנָּא, עִזְבִי, סְעִי לְסִין
שָׁם תִּתְפָּאֲרִי בְּרִבְבוֹת זִקּוּקִים
בִּדְמוּת שֶׁאֵין בָּהּ פְּגָם.
רְאִי כַּמָּה יָפֶה הַוֶּנוּס מִמִּילוֹ
כְּשֶׁרוּחַ קַלָּה מְלַטֶּפֶת אֶת זְרוֹעוֹתֶיהָ.

PERFECTION

It's impossible, this Perfection.
This Perfection is too perfect.
Hard as death.
Stops your breath.
Makes you look ridiculous, gape-mouthed as you are.
You can't eat in perfection
or drink in perfection
or love a perfect love.
You've never written anything perfect.
Does that bother you? – Only when Perfection
breathes down my neck, demanding: Be like an angel!
– But what does it know of angels
there are wingless angels
there are angels as parched as birds in a heat-wave
there are angels sweating to save you and weeping
when they fail.
What does Perfection know of this, closed up in itself
so please, leave, go to China,
there you can flaunt yourself in a thousand firecrackers
unblemished in nature.
Just look at how beautiful Venus de Milo is
when a light wind caresses her arms.

אולימפיאדה

חַיִּים אוֹ מָוֶת.
הַמְנַצֵּחַ שׂוֹרֵד.
הַמּוּבָס נֶעֱלָם.
שְׁמוֹ לֹא יִזָּכֵר.
הַמְנַצֵּחַ מֶלֶךְ
לְשָׁעָה אוֹ לְשָׁנָה
וְאוּלַי לָנֶצַח בִּדְמוּת
גָּבִיעַ בַּאֲרוֹן זְכוּכִית
לַנְּכָדִים וְלַנִּינִים לְהִתְפָּאֵר
אִם יִהְיוּ נְכָדִים וְנִינִים שֶׁיִּתְפָּאֲרוּ.
אֲבָל עַכְשָׁו, בָּרֶגַע הַזֶּה
הַלֵּב פּוֹעֵם כְּעֵדֶר סוּסִים שׁוֹעֵט בָּעֲרָבָה
בְּמֵאִית הַשְּׁנִיָּה הָיָה מָהִיר מִירִיבוֹ.
מְחִיאוֹת כַּפַּיִם כְּעַרְבּוּל אֶלֶף תֻּפִּים.
מֵאַיִן?
הֲרֵי הָעוֹלָם רֵיק, רֵיק, הַמְנַצֵּחַ –
אֵין בּוֹדֵד מִמֶּנּוּ – נִצָּב בְּרוּמוֹ
שֶׁאֵינֶנּוּ.

OLYMPICS

Life or death.
The winner lives on.
The loser vanishes.
His name will be forgotten.
The winner is king
for an hour or a year
and maybe forever in the shape
of a chalice in the glass-paned cabinet
for the grandchildren and their children to boast about
if there will be grandchildren and their children to boast.
But now, in this moment
the heart beats like a herd of horses stampeding across the plains
he was a hundredth of a second faster than his opponent.
Hands clap like the whirl of a thousand drums.
From where?
After all, the world is empty, empty, and the winner –
no one is more alone than him – stands at its zenith
that isn't.

על הזמן

1

אַתָּה שׁוֹאֵל אוֹתִי עַל הַזְּמַן?
הוּא לֹא חָבֵר שֶׁלִּי. לָמָּה לְדַבֵּר עַל הַזְּמַן?
כִּי אֵין לוֹ פַּרְצוּף? כִּי לְעוֹלָם לֹא יַבִּיט
עַיִן בְּעַיִן וּלְפֶתַע יָכֶה וּמִיָּד יִטְעַן
כִּי אֵין כָּמוֹהוּ לְרַפֵּא אֶת הַפֶּצַע?
לוֹחֵשׁ עַל אָזְנֶיךָ נֶחָמוֹת קְטַנּוֹת
וּבִמְחִי יָד מוֹחֵץ אֶת גּוּפְךָ
וּמַשְׁלִיךְ אוֹתְךָ לְאֵיזוֹ זָוִית שְׁכוּחָה?

2

הַבֵּן, הַבֵּן הַשּׁוֹאֵל "מַה פִּתְאֹם?" אַחֲרֵי
חִבּוּק הַפְּרִידָה אָז בִּנְמַל הַתְּעוּפָה הַזָּר –
זֶה, זֶה הַזְּמַן.
זֶה הַזְּמַן הָעוֹמֵד וְאֵינֶנּוּ זָז.
זֶה הַזְּמַן בְּלִי זְמַן.
אוֹי לְכָל הַחֲכָמִים הַמְּנַסִּים לוֹמַר דְּבָרִים
חֲכָמִים אוֹ שְׁנוּנִים.
וַי לְכָל הַחָכְמָה הַזֹּאת.

3

אֵיזֶה חֲלוֹם מָתוֹק לְמִי שֶׁאֵינֶנּוּ מַחֲזִיק מַעֲמָד
בַּמָּקוֹם שֶׁנִּמְצָא בּוֹ, קְצַר-רוּחַ, מְבַקֵּשׁ
לָצֵאת מֵעוֹרוֹ וְתוֹקֵעַ עֵינַיִם בִּמְחוֹג הַשְּׁנִיּוֹת
הָרָץ רָץ רָץ כְּמוֹ רוֹדֵף אֶת צִלּוֹ
רַק הָלְאָה, רַק הָלְאָה מִזֶּה
רַק הָלְאָה, תָּמִיד הָלְאָה
תָּמִיד, תָּמִיד
לַמָּקוֹם שֶׁמִּמֶּנּוּ בָּא.

ABOUT TIME

1

You ask me about Time?
He's no friend of mine. Why bother talking about him,
about faceless time? Because he never looks you
straight in the eye, then suddenly strikes and claims right after
there's no one like him to heal all wounds?
Because he whispers small consolations in your ear
then with his own hands crushes your body
and tosses you into some forgotten corner?

2

The son, the son asking "But what happened" right after
the goodbye embrace back then in the foreign airport –
that's Time.
That's Time that stands still and never moves.
That's timeless Time.
Alas and alack to all those wise men trying to speak
wise and clever words.
Oh woe, to all that wisdom.

3

What a sweet dream for he who cannot endure
here where he is, restless, wanting
to shed his skin, staring at the clock's second-hand
that runs and runs like one chasing his shadow
onward, always onward away from here
only onward, ever onward
always and ever onward
to the place it came from.

כל הסבל הזה

כָּל הַסֵּבֶל הַזֶּה
כָּל הַצַּעַר
כָּל הַסֵּבֶל וְהַצַּעַר הַזֶּה
לַשָּׁוְא
כָּל הָאִמָּהוֹת
מְכֻוָּצוֹת חֲשָׁשׁ
הָעֵינַיִם הַסְּתוּרוֹת
כָּל הַטֵּרוּף הַשָּׁפוּי הַזֶּה
לַשָּׁוְא לַשָּׁוְא
הָאָבוֹת, כָּל הָאָבוֹת הָאֵלֶּה
מַסְתִּירֵי לִבָּם
מַעֲמִידֵי פָנִים
לַשָּׁוְא
כָּל הָאָרֶץ הַזֹּאת
מְשֻׁגַּעַת דָּם
לַשָּׁוְא, לַשָּׁוְא
הַפָּנִים הַצְּעִירִים אֶפְרֵי עִתּוֹן
אוֹי פְּנֵי הַנְּעָרִים הַצִּבְעוֹנִיִּים
אוֹי עַל שֶׁצִּבְעָם דָּהָה
הַצְּחוֹק הַמֻּצְלָם, הַנְּעָרוֹת וְהַנָּשִׁים הַצְּעִירוֹת
הַחִבּוּקִים הַנְּשִׁיקוֹת
לַשָּׁוְא, לַשָּׁוְא
דָּם שׁוֹתֶה דָּם
הַחַיִּים הַפּוֹרְחִים הַכְּמוּשִׁים הָאֵלֶּה
אוֹי הַבָּשָׂר הַנִּשְׂרָף
לַשָּׁוְא
כָּל הָאֲבַדּוֹן הַזֶּה
כָּל הָאֲבַדּוֹן הָעִוֵּר הַזֶּה
אוֹי, אוֹי

ALL THIS SUFFERING

All this suffering
all the sorrow
all this suffering and sorrow
in vain
all the fear-clenched
mothers
their eyes disheveled
all this sane madness
in vain in vain
the fathers, all these fathers
hiding their hearts
pretending
in vain
all this blood-crazy
land
in vain, in vain
the young faces a newspaper-grey
oh the colorful faces of youth
oh their faded colors
their photographed laughter, the girls and the young women
the kisses and hugs
in vain, in vain
blood drinking blood
these withering blossoming lives
oh the burnt bodies
in vain
all this destruction
all this blind ruin
Oh, oh

יוֹסְל, יוֹסְל

(יוֹסְל ברגנר)

יוֹסְל יוֹסְל, אֵיפֹה אַתָּה?
שׁוּב מִסְתַּתֵּר בְּתַחֲנַת הָרַכֶּבֶת
שֶׁתְּקוּעָה כְּמוֹ מַסְמֵר בַּלֵּב?
שׁוּם זִיעַ שׁוּם נִיעַ.
רַק הָעוֹרְבִים בְּקוֹל צָרוּד
מְשַׁחֲרִים לַטֶּרֶף.
הַחוּם בָּלַע אֶת הָאָדֹם, אֶת הַצָּהֹב
מְעַט מֵהַסָּגֹל.
הַשָּׁחֹר בָּלַע אֶת הַכֹּל.
מַה תַּעֲשֶׂה עִם חָלָל לְרַגְלֶיךָ
וְעֵינֶיךָ פְּרוּעוֹת?
מַזָּל שֶׁזֶּה הוּא.
מַזָּל שֶׁאַתָּה וַאֲנִי
"הֲלוֹ יוֹסְל"
"טוֹיְבֶּער יָאשׁ"
עִם הַיָּם שֶׁמְּשִׁתַּעֲשֵׁעַ מֵאֲחוֹרֵי גַּבֵּנוּ
תַּחַת שָׁמַיִם מְשַׁעַמְמִים מֶרֹב תְּכֵלֶת וְכָחוֹל
לְבַסּוֹף עוֹמְדִים חֲבוּקִים.

YOSL, YOSL

(after a pencil drawing by Yosl Bergner)

Yosl oh Yosl, where are you?
Hiding again in the train station
that is stuck in your heart like a nail?
Nothing moves, all is frozen.
Only the hoarse-voiced ravens
set off for their prey.
The brown has swallowed the red, the yellow,
a bit of the purple.
Black has swallowed everything.
What will you do with that chasm at your feet
and your wild eyes?
How lucky it's him.
How lucky that it's you and me
"Hallo, Yosl"
"*Toy'ber yoash,* my deaf friend"
With the sea frolicking behind our backs
under a sky bored to tears with all that blue
finally we are in each other's arms.

ליל ירח (2)

אֲנִי יוֹדֵעַ כִּי אֵינוֹ
אֶלָּא חֲלוֹם
וְכַחֲלוֹם יָעוּף
אֲבָל הַתִּקְוָה הַקְּטַנָּה הַזֹּאת
הַתִּקְוָה הַקְּטַנָּה הַנּוֹאֶלֶת הַזֹּאת
שֶׁאֵינֶנָּה פּוֹסֶקֶת
כִּי בְּבוֹא הַיּוֹם נִפְגֹּשׁ
בַּצַּד הָאָפֵל שֶׁל הַיָּרֵחַ
כְּאֵב אֵינֶנּוּ מְכַפֵּר עַל
מַחֲשָׁבוֹת מֵרַע
וְעַכְשָׁו לַיְלָה וְאַתָּה חָסֵר
וּמָחָר יוֹם וְאַתָּה חָסֵר
חָכְמָתְךָ חֲסֵרָה, קוֹלְךָ אֵינֶנּוּ
אַהֲבָתְךָ בְּכִי לִפְנִים מִבְּכִי
אַךְ לֹא יִרְחַק הַיּוֹם וְאֶהְיֶה
מֵעֵבֶר לָזֶה, וַחֲלוֹם יִהְיֶה
חֲלוֹם מִשְׁתָּהֶה
וְאַתָּה וַאֲנִי
בַּצַּד הַשֵּׁנִי שֶׁל הַיָּרֵחַ
נִהְיֶה אַתְּךָ וְאִתִּי
וְאַתָּה אִתִּי
לְתָמִיד, לְתָמִיד
בְּנִי, בְּנִי

MOONLIT NIGHT (2)

I know it's nothing
but a dream
and as a dream will flee
but this small hope
this small foolish unceasing
hope
that one day we'll meet
on the dark side of the moon
pain does not appease
the darkest thoughts
now it's night and you are missing
tomorrow will be day and you'll be missing
your wisdom is missing, your voice missing
your love a weeping deeper than tears wept
but the day is not far off when I'll be
beyond this, and the dream
lingers
you and me
on the other side of the moon
we'll be with you and with me
you and me as one
forever
my son, my son

מצילה

שִׁירַת הַבֹּקֶר שֶׁל הַצּוּפִיּוֹת כְּמוֹ קָשְׁרוּ אֶת גְּרוֹנָן.
כַּלְבּוֹ שֶׁל הַשָּׁכֵן הָרָגִיל לִנְבֹּחַ עַל כָּל עוֹבֵר עַל פָּנָיו
אִלֵּם כְּמֵת. יְמִיִם הַחֲתוּלָה
נִצְרָד עַד אֵין לִשְׁמֹעַ. רַחַשׁ הָרוּחַ הִתְאַבֵּן.

הַשְּׁתִיקָה הַגּוֹרֶפֶת
הַשְּׁתִיקָה הַזּוֹלֶלֶת כָּאַרְבֶּה
הַמְכַלָּה הַבִּלְתִּי נִרְאֵית
מְכַלָּה אֶת הַכֹּל
מְכַלָּה מַה שֶׁהָיִיתִי
מְכַלָּה מַה שֶׁהָיָה
מְכַלָּה אֶת הַגִּלְבֹּעַ, מְכַלָּה אֶת הָעֵמֶק
אֶת הַשְּׁקִיעוֹת הַוְּרֻדּוֹת, תַּפּוּז הַבֹּקֶר
מְכַלָּה צוּפִיּוֹת, מְכַלָּה חֲתוּלָה
מְכַלָּה אֶת הַדֶּשֶׁא, אֶת הַכֶּלֶב הַלָּבָן
מְכַלָּה אֶת הַחַי וּמְכַלָּה אֶת הַמֵּת.

מָה הַדְּמוּת שֶׁעַכְשָׁו נִכְנֶסֶת לַחֶדֶר?
אֵיזֶה אוֹר מְסַנְוֵר חוֹדֵר דֶּרֶךְ הַדֶּלֶת הַפְּתוּחָה!
אֲנִי אוֹמֵר: גָּלִילָה? כֵּן, כֵּן, זֹאת גָּלִילָה.
שֵׁם כְּמוֹ מְצִלָּה.

250

CHIMES

The morning songs of the humming-birds sound as though their throats are
   tied.
The neighbor's dog that barks at every passer-by
is as mute as the dead. The cat's mewing
is so hoarse it's inaudible. The wind's rustling has turned to stone.

This sweeping silence
as gluttonous as the locusts
devouring the unseeable
devours everything
devours what I was
devours what I'll be
devours the mountain, the valley
devours the pink-hued sunsets, the morning orange
devours the hummingbird, the cat
devours the white dog, the grass
devours the living and the dead.

What is the figure that now enters the room?
What blinding light penetrates through the open door!
I say: Galila? Yes, yes, it's Galila.
A name like chimes.

ג'אקומטי: איש צועד
(ליטוגרפיה 57/200)

הוֹלֵךְ הוֹלֵךְ

לְאַט
לְאַט
לֹא
יֵרָאֶה

הִזְקִין
הִצְהִיב

יִבָּלַע
בַּשֶּׁטַח
הָרֵיק
בַּמִּדְבָּר הַמַּקִּיף

– אוֹמֵר קָטָן־אֱמוּנָה
וּמַחֲרִישׁ.

GIACOMETTI: WALKING MAN
(*Lithograph 57/200*)

He walks and walks

slowly
slowly
becoming
in
visible

he's grown old
has yellowed

will be
swallowed
up in the
empty
space
of the
surrounding desert

– says he of little faith
and falls silent.

הזקן והיופי

כָּל הַיֹּפִי הַזֶּה
אֵיזֶה יֹפִי
אֵיזֶה יֹפִי לַעֲמֹד מוּל
כָּל הַיֹּפִי הַזֶּה
כָּל-כָּךְ יָפֶה
גַּם בְּעֵינַיִם עֲצוּמוֹת
וְגַם בְּעֵינַיִם קְרוּעוֹת
כָּל הַיֹּפִי הַזֶּה
פַּס דַּק כָּתוֹם זָהֹב דַּק עוֹד יוֹתֵר דַּק שָׁחֹר
הוֹ אֵיזֶה אוֹר נִפְלָא
הוֹפֵךְ לְאֵפֶר
עֵינַי הָרוֹאוֹת
פָּחוֹת תָּמִיד פָּחוֹת
חַיִּים כָּאן
חַיִּים כָּאן וְעַכְשָׁו וְכָל זֶה
לִחְיוֹת
אֵיזֶה יֹפִי לִחְיוֹת
לַמְרוֹת כָּל
זֶה
כָּל הַיֹּפִי הַזֶּה
לַמְרוֹת לַמְרוֹת
מַה
כָּל
זֶה

אוֹמֵר הַיֹּפִי:

אֲנִי אֲנִי
אֶהְיֶה אֲשֶׁר אֶהְיֶה

THE OLD MAN AND BEAUTY

All this beauty
Such beauty
How beautiful to stand before
All this beauty
So beautiful
With eyes shut tight
Or even ripped open
All this beauty
A thin stripe of orange then gold even thinner then black thinner still
Oh what wondrous light
Becoming ash
My eyes seeing
Less always less
Of life here
Living here and now and all this
Life
What beauty it is living
Despite
Despite all
This
All this beauty
Despite despite
What is
All
This

Says Beauty:

I am I
I am that I am

היום האחרון בים הצפוני

פְּנֵי הַדְּבָרִים הֵם רַק פְּנֵי הַדְּבָרִים.
הַבָּתִּים עוֹמְדִים כְּמוֹ קְלִפּוֹת רֵיקוֹת.
הַנּוֹף נָמוֹג בַּעֲרָפֶל בְּהִיר־עַיִן.
אִם תִּתְעַטֵּף בּוֹ תֵּעָלֵם כָּלִיל.
"בְּגַן הָעֵדֶן," כָּךְ אָמְרוּ חַכְמֵי הַמֵּאָה
"בְּנֵי אֱנוֹשׁ כְּבָר נוֹלָדִים מֵתִים."
מִי עוֹד זוֹכֵר אֶת סַעֲרַת־אֶתְמוֹל
כְּשֶׁהִרְתִּיחָה אֶת הַיָּם כְּמוֹ יוֹרָה, הִשְׁלִיכָה
נַחְשׁוֹלָיו נֶגֶד חוֹמַת הַחוֹף. הַיּוֹם
הַיָּם עָצַר נְשִׁימוֹתָיו, רְאִי רָגוּעַ לְכִפַּת עָבִים.
רַק הַשִּׂמְחָה, גְּרוּטָה שֶׁל מִפְרָשִׂית
עוֹד מְנַסָּה לָשׁוּט, אֵי־שָׁם בָּאֹפֶק הַמְּפַקְפֵּק.

256

LAST DAY AT THE NORTH SEA

The surface of things is only the surface of things.
The houses stand like empty peelings.
The view melts in a light-eyed fog.
If you wrap yourself in it you'll vanish entirely.
"In paradise," the Mayan sages would say,
"Humans are born already dead."
Who even remembers yesterday's storm
that boiled the sea like a kettle, tossing
torrents against the shore's walls. Today
the sea holds its breath, placid mirror to domed clouds.
Only happiness, a broken-down sailboat,
still tries to sail on, somewhere there at the doubtful horizon.

שיר

אֲבָל עַכְשָׁו נִבְרָא יָרֹק
כִּי טוֹב, כִּי טוֹב.

וְנַחֲלִיאֵלִי מֵהֶנָּה בְּמוֹ זְנָבוֹ
בִּמְעִילוֹ הָאֲפַרְפַּר, אֲפֻדָּתוֹ הַצְּהֻבָּה
כִּי שׁוֹב חָזֹר וְשׁוֹב יַחֲזֹר
הַמְנַתֵּר עַל כְּלוֹנְסָאוֹת.

שְׁתֵּי לְטָאוֹת יְשַׁנָּן אֵינָן
נִצָּנוּץ שֶׁל שֶׁמֶשׁ, וּמִבְרַח –
שֶׁיִּתְבָּרֵךְ
עַל שֶׁבַח מַעֲשֵׂה יָדָיו.

עֵץ הַפֶּקָן עַכְשָׁו מֵשִׁיר
וּמְנַקֵּד אֶת הָאֲוִיר

וַעֲנָנִים מְשׁוֹבְבִים
נַפְשׁוֹ שֶׁל כָּחֹל נִדְהָם

וְשִׁיר מֵשִׁיב גַּם בְּשִׁבְרוֹ
לֵב אָדָם עַל אָדָם וְכֵן עַל לֹא.

POEM

But now green has been created
and it is good, it is good.

A wagtail in its grey coat and yellow vest
nods its tail in agreement
as the prancing bird on picket posts
has returned and will return yet again.

Two lizards are here-and-gone
sun glimmer, fugitive bliss –
May he be blessed
for his creations' glory.

Now the pecan tree sheds its leaves
green-verses punctuating the air

and mischievous clouds seduce
the soul of a stunned blue

and a poem brings back, also in its brokenness,
a heart to a heart, and to what is not.

IX

BUT WHAT WOULD WE DO

WITHOUT POEMS

אִי אֶפְשָׁר

אִי אֶפְשָׁר לוֹמַר שִׁירָה שׁוּב וָשׁוּב.
אֶלְזֶה לַסְקֶר-שִׁילֶר, הַמְּשׁוֹרֶרֶת הַמֻּפְלָאָה
אָמְרָה עַל אֶרֶץ יִשְׂרָאֵל שֶׁהִיא "כְּמוֹ עוּגָה
אֲבָל אִי אֶפְשָׁר לִחְיוֹת רַק מֵעוּגוֹת."
דְּבָרִים רַבִּים מִדַּי אֵינָם נֶחֱרָזִים עוֹד.
וְיֵשׁ שֶׁהַנֶּפֶשׁ נוֹקַעַת מִשֵּׁמַע הַ"כְּמוֹ"
וּמִמּוּזִיקָה הַגּוֹנֶבֶת אֶת הָאֹזֶן אַחֲרֵי כָּל הַהֲוָעָה.
יֵשׁ דְּבָרִים שֶׁאֵינָם מִסְתַּדְּרִים בְּקֶצֶב
וְקוֹפֵי הַקּוֹל מְקַפְּצִים בְּכָל מָקוֹם.

אַךְ מַה נַּעֲשֶׂה לְלֹא שִׁירִים?
הֲנִתְלֶה כִּנּוֹרוֹתֵינוּ
וְנִבְכֶּה? וּמַה נַּעֲשֶׂה עִם הַנְּשָׁמָה
מַה נַּעֲשֶׂה עִם רְעַב הַנְּשָׁמָה
שֶׁאִישׁ אֵינוֹ יוֹדֵעַ מִי הִיא וּמַה הִיא וְאֵיפֹה הִיא
מַה נַּעֲשֶׂה עִם הָרָעָב לַמִּלִּים הַנְּכוֹנוֹת, לַשֶּׁקֶט שֶׁבֵּין הַמִּלִּים
לַמִּלִּים שֶׁהֵן שֶׁקֶט?
מַה נַּעֲשֶׂה עִם הָרָעָב הַזֶּה שֶׁאֵין לְהַשְׂבִּיעוֹ?

ONE CANNOT

One cannot recite poetry over and over again.
The great poet Else Lasker-Schüler
said of the State of Israel that "it's like cake,
but one cannot live on cake."
Too many things don't rhyme any more.
And the spirit abhors the abundance of "like"s
and the somber music that steals the ear after every horror.
There are things that won't fit into any rhythm
and aping voices jump around everywhere.

But what would we do without poems?
Shall we hang up our lyres
and weep? What would we do with the soul,
with the soul's hunger
which no one knows who or what it is and where,
what would we do with the hunger for the right words, for the silence
    between words,
for the words that are silence?
What would we do with this hunger that will not be sated?

מונולוג של השירה

אֲנִי מִתְחַבְּאָה מִפְּנֵי עַצְמִי וְלוֹבֶשֶׁת פְּרוֹזָה.
שְׂמֵחָה בְּחֶלְקִי לִהְיוֹת לְלֹא תּוֹעֶלֶת
אֲנִי מְטַיֶּלֶת אִינְקוֹגְנִיטוֹ, נִטְמַעַת בֶּהָמוֹן
הַהוֹמֶה וְרוֹחֵשׁ עִם צְרִיחוֹת פִּרְסוֹמוֹת
וְהִשְׁתַּפְּכוּת טְרוּבָּדוּרִים.
נָעִים הַקּוֹל הַמָּתוּן, הַגָּמִישׁ, שֶׁל שׁוּרוֹת אֲרֻכּוֹת
אַחֲרֵי הִתְנַפְּלוּת אֶחָד גַּס־רוּחַ וְרֵיק שֶׁקָּרַע אֶת
הָעֲנָק מִצַּוָּארִי וְכָל הַחֲרוּזִים הִתְגַּלְגְּלוּ בַּטִּיט וּבָרֶפֶשׁ.
אָמַר מִי שֶׁאָמַר: לִבַּת הַשִּׁיר הִיא פְּרוֹזָה. וְאֵין אֱמוּנָה בְּלִי סָפֵק.
עֲלוּמָה בַּלִּבָּה (כָּל כְּבוֹדִי פְּנִימָה) אֲחַיֶּה אֶת הַחַי
כִּי שֶׁבַע פָּרוֹת רָזוֹת הַמִּלִּים בִּלְעָדַי.

POETRY'S SOLILOQUY

I hide from myself in the clothes of prose.
Happy to be useless me
I wander incognito, getting lost in the crowd
of teeming and screaming ads
and troubadorean effusions.
How pleasant is the moderate and flexible voice of long lines
after the attack of the rude and vapid one who ripped
the necklace from my neck and all my pearled rhymes rolled into the dirt and
    grime.
Someone once said: The heart of poetry is prose. And there's no such thing
    as faith without doubt.
Hidden at the core (all my glory inward), I live my life,
for words would ever be the seven thin cows without me.

אל הירח

יָרֵחַ, אִישׁ זָקֵן, מַה, שָׁכְחוּ שִׁמְךָ?
אָבַד עָלָיו כָּלַח? סַהַר, רַק סַהַר?
כָּל הָרֹךְ הָלַךְ.

אוֹמְרִים, אַתָּה רָזֶה
רָזֶה
מִיּוֹם
לְיוֹם
פּוֹחֵת

לֹא יִשָּׁאֵר מִמְּךָ גַּם פְּסִיק
יִקַּח אוֹתְךָ הָאֹפֶל.

תַּרְאֶה לָהֶם עַכְשָׁו
תַּרְאֶה שֶׁהוּא צַדָּק, זֶה שֶׁאָמַר
גַּם לְמַרְאֶה נוֹשָׁן יֵשׁ רֶגַע שֶׁל הֻלֶּדֶת.
הֲלֹא מָצְאוּ לְפֶתַע בְּגוּפְךָ הַמְּיֻבָּשׁ
מָקוֹר שֶׁל מַיִם! עוֹד תֶּחֱזֶה
שֶׁתִּתְכַּסֶּה בְּיֶרֶק כְּמוֹ
הַכּוֹכָב שֶׁלָּנוּ אַחֲרֵי הַיּוֹרֶה.

הֶבֶל יָרֹק תְּחִלָּה, כִּמְעַט חֲלוֹמִי
וְאַחַר כָּךְ אֲפִלּוּ
מִשְׁבַּץ פְּרָחִים.

הוֹ יָרֵחַ, גּוּיָּה מִתְגַּלְגֶּלֶת

266

TO THE MOON

Moon, Old Man, what, have they forgotten your name?
Are you obsolete? A crescent, just a crescent?
All softness gone.

They say you're skinny
skinnier
from day
to day
diminishing

there'll be nothing left of you not even a comma,
darkness carrying you away.

Show them now
show them he was right, he who said
even the antiquated has a moment of rebirth.
After all, they suddenly found on your dried-up body
a water source! You'll see
soon you'll be covered in green like
our planet after the first rain.
First a patch of green, almost dream-like
and then even
flower fields.

Oh Moon, you spinning corpse

לא בכל יום

לֹא בְּכָל יוֹם אַתָּה אִתִּי בִּנוֹכְחוּת עֵרָה.
אֲנִי עָסוּק בְּכָל מִינֵי דְבָרִים, טְפֵלִים וְלֹא טְפֵלִים.
הַרְבֵּה שָׁנִים חָלְפוּ מֵאָז רְאִיתִיךָ –
עֶשְׂרִים וָשֶׁבַע, בְּקֵרוּב עֶשְׂרִים וּשְׁמוֹנֶה
לְמַעְלָה מִשְּׁנוֹת דּוֹר.
לֹא בְּכָל יוֹם, אַךְ דֵּי שֶׁמַּשֶּׁהוּ, אֵיזוֹ זוּטָה, אֵיזֶה לֹא־כְלוּם
יַזְכִּיר אוֹתְךָ, וְלוּ מֵרָחוֹק, וְשׁוּב אַתָּה אִתִּי
יֵשׁ וְכָל כָּךְ אִתִּי עַד
שֶׁבְּכִי מְזַעֲזֵעַ אֶת כָּל גּוּפִי. תָּמִיד שָׁמַרְתִּי זֹאת בֵּינִי לְבֵינִי.
זֹאת זָקַנְתִּי שֶׁכָּךְ כּוֹתֵב.
חִבַּקְתִּי אוֹתְךָ שָׁם כְּשֶׁנִּפְרַדְנוּ בִּנְמַל הַתְּעוּפָה שֶׁל חֹרֶף
פְּרֵדָה שֶׁבִּבְשָׂרִי כְּמַכְוַת אֵשׁ. שָׁאַלְתָּ "לָמָה?"
כִּי מַשֶּׁהוּ נָכְרִי הִגְנִיב עַצְמוֹ בֵּינֵינוּ אַחֲרֵי הַמִּלְחָמָה הָאֲרוּרָה.
בָּאתָ שׁוֹנֶה אֵלֵינוּ מִשֶּׁהָיִיתָ קֹדֶם, וַאֲנִי מָתוּחַ וְלָחוּץ
וְלֹא יָכוֹל לְהִתְרַכֵּז וּמַצְפּוּנִי מֵצִיק שֶׁשְּׁנַת הַשַּׁבָּתוֹן
הָלְכָה לָרִיק.
עַד מָה אֲנִי מֵצַר, נֶחָם, עַד מָה אֲנִי נֶחָם שֶׁלֹּא הֵבַנְתִּי
מָה עָבַר עָלֶיךָ בִּלְעָדֵינוּ, וְנָהַגְתִּי בְּחָמְרָה.
אֲנִי זָקֵן, זָקֵן מְאֹד, אֵינִי קוֹבֵל, אֲבָל אַתָּה חָסֵר
אַתָּה חָסֵר לִי, חָסֵר חָסֵר חָסֵר לִי, בִּנְיָמִין שֶׁלִּי
בְּנִי הַצָּעִיר מוֹרָן.
חֶמְלָה עַצְמִית בְּזוּיָה. אַהֲבָתְךָ אוֹכֶלֶת אוֹתִי חַי.

NOT EVERY DAY

Not every day are you with me with full presence.
I'm busy with all kinds of things, insignificant and not.
Many years have passed since last I saw you –
twenty-seven, soon twenty-eight
more than forever.
Not every day, but it's enough for something, some nothing
to recall you, even from a distance, and then again you are
here, so much with me until
weeping shakes my whole body. I've always kept this to myself.
It is my old age writing this now.
I embraced you there when we parted at the winter airport,
a leave-taking seared into my flesh. You asked "why?"
for something foreign had wormed its way between us after that cursed war.
You returned to us different from what you had been before, but I was
tense, unable to concentrate, troubled by the sabbatical that had
come to nothing.
How sorry I am, how deeply repentant, for not understanding
what you went through without us, for responding severely.
I am old now, very old, I'm not complaining, but I miss you
I miss you, I miss and I miss you, my Benjamin,
my youngest son Moran.
Self pity is contemptible. But your love is eating me alive.

פָּאוּל שְׁטַיְנֶר, בַּשּׁוֹמֵר הַצָּעִיר, שִׁמְשׁוֹן, לֹא לִזְמַן רַב, הָיָה בְּלוֹנְדִינִי
בַּעַל עֵינַיִם כְּחֻלּוֹת, הָיָה לוֹ סֵבֶר "אֲרִי" מֻבְהָק.
הוּא הָיָה שׁוֹרֵד, הָיָה בּוֹ מַשֶּׁהוּ בָּהִיר, מַשֶּׁהוּ מֵאִיר
בַּעַל לֵב זָהָב, אוּלַי לִבּוֹ שֶׁהִגִּיהַּ הַחוּצָה. הָיָה מִתְחַמֵּק, אֲבָל אִמּוֹ
הָיְתָה אַלְמָנָה, לְבוּשָׁה שְׁחוֹרִים תָּמִיד, אִשָּׁה אֲצִילָה, גְּבֶרֶת שְׁטַיְנֶר
גַּם שִׁמְשׁוֹן הָיָה אָצִיל, הוּא לֹא רָצָה לְעָזְבָהּ.

גַּם אוֹתִי לֹא עָזַב עַד שֶׁעֲזַבְתִּי אֲנִי אוֹתוֹ וּבָאתִי לָאָרֶץ הַזֹּאת
בָּהּ זָקַנְתִּי וּבָהּ אֲנִי רוֹשֵׁם אֶת הַדְּבָרִים הָאֵלֶּה.

הוּא פָּרַשׂ חָסוּתוֹ עָלַי, שִׁמְשׁוֹן יְדִידִי.
הָיָה עָלָיו וְיָדַע דְּבָרִים שֶׁאֲנִי לֹא יָדַעְתִּי, נָבוֹן מִמֶּנִּי, לֹא הָיָה חוֹלְמָנִי.
בְּאַחַד הַיָּמִים, כְּבָר הָיִינוּ מִנְּדִים, הֵבִיא, הַשֵּׁד-יוֹדֵעַ-מֵאַיִן
אֶקְדּוֹחַ יָשָׁן וְתַחְמֹשֶׁת וְיָרִינוּ בְּמָקוֹם רֵיק מֵאָדָם,
וְחָרַכְתִּי אֶת יָדִי.
חֶשְׁבּוֹן שֶׁלָּמַדְנוּ שְׁנֵינוּ אֵצֶל מוֹרֶה פְּרָטִי
– לְבָתֵּי הַסֵּפֶר כְּבָר נֶאֱסְרָה כְּנִיסָתֵנוּ –
תָּפַשׂ הוּא בְּקַלּוּת, אֲנִי בְּקֹשִׁי.

בְּעֶרֶב יָמַי לוֹ אַךְ יָכֹלְתִּי לְהַעֲמִיד יָד לָאָדָם הַבָּהִיר הַזֶּה שֶׁנָּמוֹג בֶּעָשָׁן
וְאֵין לְאֵל יָדִי אֶלָּא מַצֵּבָה קַלָּה, וְהִיא כָּל מַה שֶּׁלִּי, יָד שֶׁל כְּתָב.

אֲנִי רוֹאֶה אוֹתְךָ, רֵעַ נְעוּרַי, אֲנִי שׁוֹמֵעַ אֶת צְחוֹקְךָ.

MEMORIAL

Paul Steiner, from the Youth Movement, known as Shimshon for awhile, was
blond, blue-eyed, had classic "Aryan" features.
He would have survived, he had that fair look, seemed always illuminated
as if his golden heart shone outward. He could have got away, but his mother
was a widow, always dressed in mourning black, a noble woman, Mrs. Steiner,
Shimshon was noble too, and he wouldn't leave her.

He didn't leave me either, until I left him and came to this country where
I've grown old and write down these things now.

He watched over me, my friend Shimshon.
He was joyful and knew things I didn't know, he was wiser than me, wasn't a
    dreamer.
Once, when we were all already outcasts, he brought, who knows from where,
an old pistol and ammunition and we fired a few rounds in an abandoned
    place
and I burnt my hand.
As for the mathematics we learned together with a private tutor
– the schools had already banned us –
he learned with ease while I struggled.

Now in my darkening days if only I could erect a memorial to that fair-haired
    boy who faded away in the smoke
but my hands can offer only this small monument, an inked epitaph.

I see you, beloved friend of my youth, I hear your laughter still.

גלויה משם: כמעט שיחה

הֵם בְּנֵי אָדָם.
- אֱמֶת.

מַרְאֵה הָעֵצִים שׁוֹנֶה מִשֶּׁהָיָה.
- צֶבַע הַשָּׁמַיִם שׁוֹנֶה.

"בְּנֵי אָדָם" - צְלִיל מוּזָר.
- רֵיחַ מוּזָר.

זֶהוּ זֶה.
מִי מְדַבֵּר עַל צֶדֶק.

- וְהַזְּעָקוֹת?

הַאִם מָוֶת - מָוֶת?

וְהַיְלָדִים?
מָה עַל הַיְלָדִים?

- יְפִי בִּלְתִּי נִתְפָּס לֶהָרִים, שָׁם, מֵעֵבֶר.

A POSTCARD FROM THERE: ALMOST A CONVERSATION

They're human beings.
– True.

The look of the trees is different from what it was.
– The color of the sky is different.

"Human beings" – sounds strange.
– There's a strange smell.

That's it.
Who's talking about justice.

– And the screams?

Is death – death?

And the children?
What of the children?

– An unimaginable beauty to the hills, there, beyond.

תצלום שחור-לבן, קיץ 1939

הִנֵּה הֵם כֻּלָּם, חַבְרֵי תְּנוּעַת הַנֹּעַר בְּסְלוֹבַקְיָה
הַמִּסְתַּכְּלִים שִׁבְעִים שָׁנָה הַיָּשֵׁר אֶל תּוֹךְ עֵינַי.
לֹא, לֹא כֻּלָּם, יֵשׁ צוֹחֲקִים זֶה אֶל זֶה, אֶחָד
עוֹסֵק בְּדֶגֶל קְטַנְטַן, וּבַחוּרָה אַחַת מִסְּבָּה
אֶת רֹאשָׁהּ. הַיַּעַר שֶׁבָּרֶקַע הֶאֱפִיר כֻּלּוֹ.
אֶת הַשֵּׁמוֹת אֲנִי זוֹכֵר רַק בְּחֶלְקָם.
לְמַעְלָה אַמְנוֹן, שִׁמְשׁוֹן, אַחַר כָּךְ אֵלִי, בָּהִיר מְאֹד,
וִיהוֹשֻׁעַ, חוֹלְמָנִי מְעַט, גֵּרְשׁוֹן, מִטְפַּחַת עַל רֹאשׁוֹ
כְּמוֹ סְפָרַדִּי אוֹ אִינְדְּיָאנִי, מָצוֹ הָרוֹצֶה לְהִסְתַּתֵּר
דּוּבְּקוֹ – חִיּוּךְ וּמִשְׁקָפַיִם.
לְמַטָּה, בַּשּׁוּרָה הָרִאשׁוֹנָה אַיָּה וְשִׂמְחָה.
מְעַט מֵעֲלֵיהֶן בָּאֶמְצַע מִיכָאֵל וְגַבְרִיאֵל, חַיִּים
חֶצְיוֹ נוֹעָז וְחֶצְיוֹ רָהוּי, וְגַם אֲנִי לְלֹא חַלְצָה.
אַף לֹא אֶחָד לֹא הִסְתַּלֵּק מִכָּאן. אַף לֹא אֶחָד.
אֲנַחְנוּ בְּטִיּוּל, בְּפֶסֶק-זְמַן, שְׂמֵחִים.
כָּל הֶעָתִיד לְפָנֵינוּ.

BLACK & WHITE PHOTOGRAPH, SUMMER 1939

Here they are, all of them, the Youth Movement members in Slovakia,
seventy years staring into my eyes.
No, not all of them – there are a few laughing to each other, one boy
is busy with a little flag, and one of the girls is turning her head
away. The forest in the background has turned entirely grey.
I remember only some of their names.
In the top row there's Amnon, Shimshon, then fair-haired Eli,
and Yehoshua, a bit of a dreamer, Gershon with a bandana on his head
like a Spaniard or Indian, there's Matso who wants to hide
and Dubko with his glasses and smile.
In the bottom row, Aya and Simcha,
a bit above them in the middle, Michael and Gavriel, Haim
half-bold, half-hesitant, and I'm there too, shirtless.
Not one got away. Not even a single one.
We are on a school trip, on a break, happy.
The entire future is before us.

חשבתי שלא אכתוב עוד גם לא שורה אחת על המוות
והוא היה חזק ממני

הַשָּׁעָה הָיְתָה שֵׁשׁ לִפְנוֹת עֶרֶב.
הָאֲוִיר הָיָה הָבִיל. הָיָה יוֹם לוֹהֵט.
הַבָּתִּים לְמַטָּה כְּמוֹ מִצְצַעֲפֵי עֲרָפֶל.
כְּעָנָן זַרְזִירִים כִּסּוּ אֶת מוֹרְדוֹת גִּבְעַת הַמּוֹרֶה
אַלְפֵי צְעִירִים, גַּם בְּנֵי חֲמִשִּׁים וּמַעְלָה, גַּם יְשִׁישִׁים.
חֲמִשָּׁה־עָשָׂר אוֹטוֹבּוּסִים עָמְדוּ בְּשׁוּרָה זֶה לְיַד זֶה
וּמֵאוֹת מְכוֹנִיּוֹת בְּשֵׁשׁ לִפְנוֹת עֶרֶב.
לֹא רָאִיתִי מְאוּם לְבַד מִצְּפִיפוּת שֶׁל גּוּפִים.
קְבוּצוֹת קְבוּצוֹת עָמְדוּ כְּמָתוֹת אֲדֻמּוֹת, חֲבוּקִים.
הָיוּ שֶׁגֻּבָּם הִתְכַּוֵּץ, הִרְפָּה, הִתְכַּוֵּץ, הִרְפָּה,
הָיוּ שֶׁרֶטֶט רָץ בָּם.
קוֹל עָמֹק סִלְסֵל נִגּוּנִים נוּגִים.
אִישׁ חוֹבֵשׁ־כִּפָּה הִנְמִיךְ אֶת קוֹלוֹ וְאָמַר לְאִשְׁתּוֹ:
"בַּחַיִּים שׁוּם דָּבָר אֵינוֹ שָׁלֵם בֶּאֱמֶת, שׁוּם דָּבָר."
נִשְׁמְעוּ מִלִּים לָרֹב, לִפְעָמִים נִקְטָעוּ.
הָיָה יוֹם לוֹהֵט, אֲבָל עַכְשָׁו נָשְׁבָה רוּחַ מְשִׁיבַת נֶפֶשׁ.
הַמִּלִּים עָלוּ וְצָנְחוּ לַקַּרְקַע כְּמוֹ קְלִפּוֹת רֵיקוֹת.
רִגְבֵי אֲדָמָה נְקָשִׁים, לֹא־מְתוּקִים, הִתְנַגְּשׁוּ
עִם קִיר הָעֵץ. בְּבַת אַחַת נָסְקָה יְבָבָה
וְהִתְגַּלְגְּלָה בְּמִין קוֹל מִשְׁנֶה שֶׁל חַיָּה.
אַחַר כָּךְ דְּמָמָה. מִישֶׁהוּ בִּקֵּשׁ מְחִילָה מֵהַמֵּת.
הַחֲשֵׁכָה יָרְדָה וְעוֹד עָמְדוּ שָׁם, לֹא יָדְעוּ לְהִנָּתֵק מֵהַמָּקוֹם
כְּמוֹ הַבְּרוֹשִׁים הַנּוֹתָרִים אַחֲרֵי הַמִּיתָה הָאִטִּית שֶׁפָּשְׁטָה בָּם.

I THOUGHT I WOULDN'T WRITE EVEN ONE MORE LINE ON DEATH BUT IT WAS STRONGER THAN ME

It was six o'clock, early evening.
The air was heavy. It had been a scorching day.
The houses below were shrouded in haze.
Like a cloud of starlings they covered the slopes
thousands of youngsters, middle-aged, the old too.
Fifteen buses stood in a row one next to the other
and hundreds of cars, it was six in the early evening.
I could see nothing but the crowdedness of bodies.
The red-bereted soldiers stood in small groups, wrapped in each others' arms.
There were those whose backs tensed up, relaxed, tensed again, relaxed,
and those through whom deep tremors passed.
A low voice trilled somber songs.
A religious man said softly to his wife:
"Nothing is really whole in life, nothing."
Innumerable words were spoken, some cut-off in the middle.
It was a scorching day, but then a cooling wind blew.
The words lifted and fell back to the ground like empty peelings.
Hard clods of earth, not sweet, hit
the plank of wood. All at once a keening rose
and whirled around in a strange animal-like voice.
Then, silence. Someone asked forgiveness of the dead.
Darkness fell, and still they stood there, not knowing how to leave,
like the cypress trees still standing even after a slow death has begun
to spread through them.

עברית, אהובתי

חַיִּים שְׁלֵמִים בְּיַחַד
חֲמִשִּׁים שָׁנִים? שִׁשִּׁים? כַּמָּה?

מֵעוֹלָם לֹא הָיִינוּ כְּאוֹתָהּ פְּקַעַת
שֶׁרֶק אִבְחַת הַחֶרֶב מַתִּירָה.
פָּנִיתִי לָךְ עֹרֶף.
פָּנִית לִי עֹרֶף
וּדְבֵקִים זֶה בָּזוֹ כַּמַּגְנֵט וְהַקֹּטֶב
כְּמוֹ הַיָּרֵחַ וְהַגֵּאוּת.

נָטִיתִי לִנְטִיּוֹתַיִךְ, קִבַּלְתִּי אֶת דִּין גְּזֵרוֹתַיִךְ
שָׁאַלְתִּי לְשָׁרָשַׁיִךְ
גִּמְגַּמְתִּי, דָּמַמְתִּי, בִּקַּשְׁתִּי, לָחַשְׁתִּי
וְאַתְּ מְכֻנֶּסֶת בְּעַצְמֵךְ וְלֹא רָאִית.
עַד שֶׁלְּפֶתַע נִפְתַּחַתְּ כִּשְׂדֵה בָּרוּחַ
עַד שֶׁבָּקַע קוֹלֵךְ מִגְּרוֹנִי.

278

HEBREW, MY LOVE

It's been a lifetime together.
Fifty years? Sixty? How many?

We were never like that coiled knot
only the slash of the sword could undo.
I turned my back on you.
You turned your back on me
though still we pulled toward each other like magnets to the pole
like the moon and the tides.

I conjugated at your will, I accepted your grammared sentences
I queried your roots,
I stuttered, became silent, I begged and whispered,
and you, turning inward, saw nothing.
Until suddenly, you opened up wide like a field in the wind
and your voice burst forth from my throat.

נוכח אישה בוכייה של פיקאסו

אֵשֶׁת יִסּוּרִים בְּכוֹבַע אָדֹם
שְׁבוּרָה כִּרְאִי
הַכְּאֵב צִיֵּר אֶת פָּנַיִךְ בְּיָרֹק וּבְצָהֹב
מִפִּיךְ שֶׁיָּרַד תְּהוֹמוֹת – אֲנִיָּה טְרוּפָה –
נֶעֶתֶקֶת צְעָקָה אִלֶּמֶת כֻּלָּבֶן
נֶגֶד הַשֶּׁקֶר נֶגֶד הַהֶרֶג
נֶגֶד הָעָוֶל שֶׁלַּמָּוֶת
וּדְמָעוֹת כְּבֵדוֹת כָּאֶבֶן
אֵינָן מִתְחַשְּׁבוֹת בְּיָדַיִךְ
נוֹפְלוֹת עַל אַדְמַת תַּלְאוּבוֹת סְחוּטָה
שׁוֹאֲלוֹת אֶת הַשָּׁחוֹר.
כְּלוּם לֹא יָדַעַתְּ שֶׁהַיֹּפִי מְכַסֶּה
עַל הַמִּפְלֶצֶת שֶׁבּוֹ, וְעֵינַיִךְ
כּוֹכָבִים כְּבוּיִים?

280

BEFORE PICASSO'S WEEPING WOMAN

Tortured woman in a red hat
shattered like a mirror
pain has painted your face in yellow and green
from your mouth sunk to the ocean's depths – ravaged ship –
a scream mute as whiteness rises
against the lies against the killing
against death's injustice
and tears heavy as stone
heedless of your hands
fall to the scorched, depleted earth
seeking blackness.
Did you know nothing of how beauty hides
the monster within it, and your eyes
are extinguished stars?

בזקנתי

יָמַי לְאַט נוֹשְׁרִים מִמֶּנִּי כְּמוֹ מֵעֵץ מַשִּׁילֵךְ.
הַמִּלִּים סוֹגְרוֹת עָלַי וְהֵן אִלְּמוֹת.
הַמִּלִּים הָאִלְּמוֹת מִתְחַנְּנוֹת בְּאֶלְמָן:
פְּתַח לָנוּ שַׁעַר בְּעֵת נְעִילַת שַׁעַר, הֱיֵה לָנוּ לְפֶה.

אֵיךְ אֶהְיֶה לָהֶן לְפֶה
וְכָל חַיַּי הָיוּ חִפּוּשׂ מִלִּים חַיּוֹת
וִימֵי נְעוּרַי צָפִים וְעוֹלִים
כִּי אֲנִי עָנִיתִי מְאֹד, כִּי הָאִלֵּם
הוּא הֵד הַקּוֹלוֹת שֶׁמֵּעֵבֶר.

אֲנִי יוֹשֵׁב לִפְנֵי הַשַּׁעַר
רֹאשׁוֹ שֶׁל שׁוֹמֵר הַשַּׁעַר כֻּלּוֹ הַקְּרִיחַ
גַּבּוֹ כָּפוּף וְכוֹאֵב, עֵינָיו כָּהוּ
אָזְנָיו כָּבְדוּ עַד מְאֹד.
הוּא מְלַמְלֵם אֶל תּוֹךְ זְקַנְקַנּוֹ הַמְדֻבְלָל
"אֲשֶׁר לָשִׁיר, אֲשֶׁר לָשִׁיר."

IN MY OLD AGE

My days slowly fall from me as from an autumn tree.
The words close in on me and they are mute.
The mute words in their muteness beg:
Open for us a gate at the hour of the gate's closing, be for us a mouth.

But how will I be for them a mouth
when my whole life has been a search for living words
and my youthful days surface, rise up,
for I was greatly afflicted, and the muteness
is the echo of voices from beyond.

I sit before the gate.
The gatekeeper's head is bald
his back is bent and aching, his eyes are dim
his ears barely hear.
He is murmuring into his scraggly beard
"Poems are happiness, happiness."

תמיהה

אַחֲרֵי כָּל מַה שֶּׁהָיָה
אִם אַתָּה עוֹד מְסֻגָּל לִשְׁמֹעַ אֶת הַשִּׁחְרוּר
אֶת הָעֶפְרוֹנִי הַמְצַיֵּץ הַשְׁכֵּם בַּבֹּקֶר וְהַבַּלְבּוּל וְהַצּוּפִית
אַל תִּתְמַהּ שֶׁשִּׂמְחָה הִיא לִרְאוֹת עֲנָנִים נִשָּׂאִים בָּרוּחַ
לִשְׁתּוֹת אֶת קָפֶה הַבֹּקֶר, לָדַעַת לְבַצֵּעַ אֶת כָּל צָרְכֵי הַגּוּף
לָלֶכֶת בַּשְּׁבִילִים בְּלִי מַקֵּל
וְלִרְאוֹת אֶת הַצְּבָעִים לוֹהֲטִים אַחֲרֵי הַשְּׁקִיעָה.

בֶּן אָדָם מְסֻגָּל לָשֵׂאת כִּמְעַט הַכֹּל
וְאִישׁ אֵינוֹ יָכוֹל לָדַעַת מָתַי וְהֵיכָן
תַּכְנִיעַ אוֹתוֹ הַשִּׂמְחָה.

WONDER

If after everything that has happened
you can still hear the blackbird,
the tufted lark at dawn, the bulbul and the honey-bird –
don't be surprised that happiness is watching the clouds being wind-carried
    away,
is drinking morning coffee, being able to execute all the body's needs
is walking along the paths without a cane
and seeing the burning colors of sunset.

A human being can bear almost everything
and no one knows when and where
happiness will overcome him.

X

LAST ONES

עוֹלָם מֻפְלָא

אֲפִלּוּ תִּמְצָא אֶלֶף סִבּוֹת לְהִתְנַגֵּד – הָעוֹלָם מֻפְלָא.
תֹּאמַר: נוֹלָדִים כְּדֵי לָמוּת – אֵיזֶה זָדוֹן!
אֲבָל עַד אָז – הָעוֹלָם מֻפְלָא.
מֻפְלָא בַּמֶּה שֶׁהוּא מְגַלֶּה וּבַמֶּה שֶׁהוּא מַסְתִּיר.
מֻפְלָא בְּבָרְאוֹ יוֹם אַחַר יוֹם וּמֻפְלָא בְּקָטְלוֹ לַיְלָה אַחַר לַיְלָה
בְּהַפְצִיעַ הַחַמָּה אֶת הָעוֹר הַקָּרִיר, הַדַּק שֶׁל הַשַּׁחַר
וּבִשְׁקִיעָתָהּ בְּכָל צִבְעֵי הַקֶּשֶׁת.
מֻפְלָא שֶׁאַתָּה מֵקִיץ בַּבֹּקֶר חַי וּמֻפְלָא שֶׁגּוּפְךָ
הִגִּיעַ לְגִיל מֻפְלָג כָּזֶה.
מֻפְלָא שֶׁשְּׁנֵי הַטּוֹרֵף נִנְעָצוֹת בְּדִיּוּק בִּבְשַׂר הַנִּטְרָף
וּבְרָכָה וּקְלָלָה חוֹבְקוֹת זוֹ אֶת זוֹ.
וְהַיּוֹרֶה, כְּבָר בְּרֵאשִׁית סֶפְּטֶמְבֶּר, כְּחוֹמָהּ שֶׁל אֲוִיר – לֹא מֻפְלָא?
וְרָאִיתָ אֶת פָּרַת מֹשֶׁה רַבֵּנוּ (פָּרָה מֻפְלָאָה, אֵין לְהַכְחִישׁ)
אֵיךְ טִפְּסָה עַד קְצֵה הֶעָצָב (כְּאִלּוּ הִדְבִּיקָה אֶת פִּסְגַּת
אַל קַפִּיטָן בְּיוֹסָמִיטִי אוֹ אֶת הַקִּיר הַצְּפוֹנִי שֶׁל הָאַיְגֶּר
בָּאַלְפִּים הַבֶּרְנָאִים) וְלֹא אִבְּדָה גַּם לֹא נְקֻדָּה אַחַת מִגָּבַהּ?
הֲלֹא מֻפְלָא הוּא שֶׁגּוּשֵׁי אֵשׁ וְגוּשֵׁי קֶרַח מִלְּפָנֵי טְרִילְיוֹן שָׁנִים
מְצִיצִים עָלֶיךָ כְּעֵינֵי שַׂחְקָנִים דֶּרֶךְ חוֹר בְּמָסַךְ הַבָּמָה
נְצַנוּצִים נְצַנוּצִים?
וּמֻפְלָא, מֻפְלָא שֶׁמִּתּוֹךְ הָאֲדָמָה בּוֹקְעִים גִּבְעוֹלִים יְרֻקִּים זְעִירִים
שֶׁסּוֹפָם הַלֶּחֶם שֶׁאַתָּה וַאֲנִי אוֹכְלִים

עַל חֻדּוֹ שֶׁל סַכִּין.

A WONDROUS WORLD

Even if you find a thousand reasons to protest – the world is wondrous.
Say: We are born to die – what wickedness!
But until then – what a wondrous world.
Wondrous in what is reveals and in what it conceals.
Wondrous in its creation day after day and wondrous in its destruction night
    after night,
in the sun breaking through the chilled, thin skin of dawn
and in its setting in all the rainbow colors.
Wondrous that you wake up alive in the morning and wondrous that your
    body
has reached this illustrious age.
Wondrous that the teeth of the predator fasten precisely on the flesh of his
    prey
and blessing and curse embrace each other.
And the first rain, already in early September, like a wall of air – isn't that
    wondrous?
And you've seen how the ladybug (a wondrous lady, there's no denying)
climbed to the top of the hyacinth (as though she ascended the peak
of El Capitan in Yosemite or the northern wall of the Eiger
in the Bernese Alps) and didn't lose even a single spot from off her back.
Isn't it wondrous how clumps of fire and ice from a trillion years ago
peek at you like the eyes of actors through a hole in the backstage curtain
sparkling and sparkling?
And wondrous, wondrous that from out of the earth burst slender green
    stalks
that in the end will be bread you and I eat

on the edge of a knife.

לִידִידִי

אָמַרְתָּ, אֲנִי רוֹצֶה לִחְיוֹת עוֹד אַרְבָּעִים שָׁנָה.
אָמַרְתִּי, לָמָּה לֹא? אֶחְיֶה גַּם אֲנִי. אַתָּה
בֶּן 79, אֲנִי מִתְקָרֵב לְ-90. לָמָּה לְהִפָּרֵד?
הֲרֵינוּ יְדִידִים, וּמַה לֹא עוֹשֶׂה יָדִיד לְיָדִיד?
אֲבָל נִחְיֶה בְּפִזּוּר נֶפֶשׁ, לֹא נִתְמַקֵּד בִּכְלוּם –
הֲלֹא כָּל נְקֻדָּה הִיא מָוֶת.
נִתְפַּזֵּר בֶּעָלִים, בִּתְנוּעָה וּבְרֶגַע, בְּכַנְפֵי צִפֳּרִים
בַּיֵּבֶשׁ וּבַגֶּשֶׁם, נָשׁוּט קַלֵּי דַּעַת עִם הָעֲנָנִים, בְּעִקָּר
עִם אֵלֶּה הַלְּבַנְבַּנִּים, הַשְּׁקוּפִים.
כִּמְעַט שֶׁכַחְנוּ אֶת מַכְאוֹבֵינוּ וְזוֹכְרִים אֶת שְׁעוֹת הַשִּׂמְחָה.
נֵשֵׁב עִם הָרוּחַ, נָזִיז חֻלְיוֹת, נְכַסֶּה כָּלִיל אֶת זֵכֶר הַזְּוָעָה.
נִטְבֹּל בַּיָּם, נִתֵּן אֶת עֵינֵינוּ בְּכָל הָרָאוּי לָתֵת בּוֹ עֵינַיִם
נֹאהַב כְּפִי שֶׁמֵּעוֹלָם לֹא אָהַבְנוּ, נֹאכַל אֵצֶל רוֹטֶנְבֶּרְג, כִּי
שִׁבְּחוּ בְּפִי כֹל, נִשְׁתֶּה יַיִן סְט. אֱמִילְיוֹן פְּרֶמְיֶיר קְרִי, 1924
אוֹ לְפִי בְּחִירָתְךָ, נַעֲשֶׂה חַיִּים, כְּמוֹ שֶׁאוֹמְרִים, מְשֻׁגָּעִים
לָמָּה לֹא?
הֲלֹא יֵשׁ גַּם דְּבָרִים נִפְלָאִים בָּעוֹלָם הַזֶּה
אָז לָמָּה אַחֵר?

TO MY FRIEND

You said, I want to live another forty years.
I said, why not? I'll live too. You're
79, I'm nearing 90. Why part?
After all we're friends, and what won't friends do for each other?
But we'll live absent-mindedly, we won't focus on a thing –
as every point is death.
We'll scatter ourselves among the leaves, in motion and tranquility, in birds'
wings, in dryness and rain, we'll sail light-headed with the clouds, above all
those whitish, transparent ones.
We've almost forgotten our pains and remembered our hours of joy.
We'll blow with the wind, we'll move our bones, we'll obscure all memory of
    horror.
We'll swim in the sea, we'll gaze at whatever is worthy of being gazed at
we'll love like we've never loved, we'll dine at Rotenberg's, as
he's praised by all, we'll drink St. Emilion Premier Cru, 1924
or as you choose, we'll have, as they say, a crazy time
why not?
After all, there are still wonderful things in this world
so why any other?

העורבים רוצים

הָעוֹרְבִים רוֹצִים לְהַצְמִיחַ
נוֹצוֹת לְבָנוֹת.
הֲיַעֲלֶה בְּיָדָם?

הַשִּׁירָה מְבַקֶּשֶׁת
לְהוֹרִיד מֵעַצְמָהּ שִׁירָה.
הֲיַעֲלֶה בְּיָדָהּ?

הַפֶּה הַמְעֻקָּם מְבַקֵּשׁ
לַחְסֹם אֶת הַזְּעָקָה.
הֲיַעֲלֶה בְּיָדוֹ?

הַזִּכָּרוֹן מְבַקֵּשׁ לִהְיוֹת
תּוֹלַעַת גֶּשֶׁם וּלְהֵעָלֵם בָּאֲדָמָה.
הֲיַעֲלֶה בְּיָדוֹ?

הַמַּעֲנֶה רוֹצֶה
לְהִקָּרֵא קָרְבָּן.
הֲיַעֲלֶה בְּיָדוֹ?

הַלֵּב עוֹרֵג לִהְיוֹת מִשְׁכַּן הַבְּהִירוּת
הָאַהֲבָה לִשְׁכֹּחַ אֶת חֶשְׁכַת הַבְּכִי.
הֲיַעֲלֶה בְּיָדָם?

THE CROWS WANT

The crows want to grow
white feathers.
Will they manage to?

Poetry wants
to shed from itself poetry.
Will it manage to?

The crooked mouth wants
to block the shout.
Will it manage to?

Memory wants to be
a rain-worm and disappear into the earth.
Will it manage to?

The torturer wants
to be called a victim.
Will he manage to?

The heart longs to be the dwelling-place of clarity,
love to forget the gloom of weeping.
Will they manage to?

ברויגל: הציידים בשלג

שָׁמַיִם יְרֻקִּים-אֲפֹרִים כְּמוֹ קֶרַח.
"מָגֵן כְּנֶגֶד מִי שֶׁמְּבַקֵּשׁ אֶת עֶזְרָתָם."
הַצַּיָּדִים חוֹזְרִים חֲפוּיֵי רֹאשׁ.
שְׁלָלָם שׁוּעָל חָלוּל.
גַּם הַכְּלָבִים הוֹלְכִים בְּרֹאשׁ מֻרְכָּן.
הַחֲנֻיּוֹת כְּבֵדוֹת מִדַּי.
הַמּוֹרָד בַּשֶּׁלֶג הֶעָמֹק תָּלוּל מִדַּי.
הָאֵשׁ הַמְבֹעֶרֶת פּוֹנָה עֹרֶף.
שְׁלֹשֶׁת הַצַּיָּדִים רֵיקִים כַּצֵּל.
הָרִים לְבָנִים מְשֻׁנִּים. שְׂדוֹת שֶׁלֶג.
אֵיזֶה כְּפָר כִּמְעַט לֹא-נִרְאֶה.
אֵיזוֹ עֲגָלָה זְעִירָה עִם סוּס.
מַחֲלִיקִים קְטַנְטַנִּים עַל פְּנֵי הַקֶּרַח.
עוֹרְבִים בְּתוֹךְ עֵצִים קַרְחִים.
אִשָּׁה, עַל רֹאשָׁהּ אֲגֻדַּת זְרָדִים.
שְׁתֵּי נָשִׁים וּמִזְחֶלֶת.
מַבָּט לֹא נִשְׁלָח.
אִישׁ חֶלְקוֹ מֻסְתָּר עִם מַקְלֵעַ.
עֲקַעֲק, גּוּף כְּמוֹ חֵץ וָקֶשֶׁת, חוֹתֵר לִשְׁבֹּר אֶת
קִיר הָאֲוִיר הַקָּפוּא.

אֵיךְ לְהִמָּלֵט מֵהַנּוֹף הָאִלֵּם הַזֶּה
אֵיךְ מִכְּפוֹר הַבְּדִידוּת שֶׁל כִּשָּׁלוֹן.

BRUEGHEL: THE HUNTERS IN THE SNOW

A sky grey-green as ice.
"A silver shield against those seeking its aid."
The hunters return, covered heads bowed.
Their catch a hollow fox.
Also the dogs walk with lowered heads.
The spears are too heavy.
The slope is too steep in the deep snow.
The burning fire has turned its back on them.
Three hunters as empty as shadows.
Jagged white hills. Snow fields.
An all-but-invisible village.
A small carriage and horse.
Tiny skaters on the ice.
Ravens in the bald trees.
A woman, a bundle of twigs on her head.
Two women with a sled.
Looking nowhere.
A half-hidden man with a rifle.
A magpie, body like a bow and arrow, trying to break through
the wall of frozen air.

How are we to flee from this mute landscape,
from this frozen loneliness of failure.

מָוֶת בְּוֶנֶצְיָה? תָּאֵי עוֹפֶרֶת? גֶּשֶׁר הָאֲנָחוֹת? מִזְמַן עָבְרוּ מִן הָעוֹלָם.
הַגּוֹנְדוֹלוֹת כַּאֲרוֹנוֹת־קְבוּרָה שָׁטִים? רַק בְּיָמִים קוֹדְרִים שֶׁל חֹרֶף.
וֶנֶצְיָה שׁוֹקַעַת? תַּעֲלֵם? מִי מְנַבֵּא שְׁחֹרוֹת לְיֹפִי חַי, אֵין כְּמוֹתוֹ?
וֶנֶצְיָה בִּיזַנְטִית, גּוֹתִית, רֶנֶסַנְסִית, הִיא בָּרוֹקִית, קְצָת הַשְׂפָעָה
שֶׁל הַמִּזְרָח.

פַּעֲמוֹנֵי הַצָּהֳרַיִם, אֵלֶּה אַחַר אֵלֶּה – הָעִיר כֻּלָּהּ דִּנְדּוּן –
הִשִּׁיטוּ אֶת וֶנֶצְיָה אֶל הָאֳנִיָּה וּבָהּ בְּנֵי בֵּיתִי.
הֵם נִפְנְפוּ מִן הַסִּפּוּן, אֲנִי אֲלֵיהֶם מֵהַחוֹף, מִקֵּץ שָׁעָה קַלָּה כֻּלָּנוּ שׁוּב בְּיַחַד.

כְּבוֹד הָאַרְיֵה בִּקֵּשׁ לָרֶדֶת מִמְּרוֹם עַמּוּדוֹ וְלַחֲלֹק עִמָּנוּ אֶת שִׂמְחָתֵנוּ
אֲבָל חָכַךְ בְּדַעְתּוֹ, שֶׁלֹּא נָאֶה לִנְהֹג כָּךְ בִּסְמַלָּה שֶׁל עִיר, וְהוּא וִתֵּר.
לְעֻמָּתוֹ הֵחֵל אַרְמוֹן הַדּוֹגִ'ים בִּמְלֹא כְּבֹדוֹ
לִרְקֹד קַלּוֹת עַל עַמּוּדָיו הַדַּקִּיקִים
וְהַקְּשָׁתוֹת, תּוֹמְכָיו, לֹא גִּלּוּ הִתְנַגְּדוּת.
אִישׁ מִלְּבַדֵּנוּ לֹא שָׂם לֵב לְכָךְ.

הִמְשַׁכְנוּ וְהִגַּעְנוּ חֲמִשְׁתֵּנוּ (אֵינִי זוֹכֵר עוֹד אֵיךְ) אֶל הַפִּיאָצָה הַקְּטַנָּה
בְּאֵר בְּטַבּוּרָהּ וּלְצִדָּהּ הָאַכְסַנְיָה שֶׁלָּנוּ.
הָאַרְבָּעָה עוֹד שְׁכוּרִים מִן הַמַּסָּע וּמֵהָעִיר הָעֲשׂוּיָה מֵחֹמֶר
שֶׁחֲלוֹמוֹת עֲשׂוּיִים מִמֶּנּוּ, הִבִּיטוּ בִּי, אֲנִי בָּהֶם, צָחַקְנוּ.
יוֹם שֶׁכֻּלּוֹ שִׂמְחָה.
הָיִינוּ שׁוּב בְּיַחַד, כָּל הַחֲמִשָּׁה.

A MEETING IN VENICE

Death in Venice? Leaden Chambers? The Bridge of Sighs? All long gone
   from the world.
The gondolas as floating burial caskets? Only in the gloomy days of winter.
Venice is sinking? Will disappear? Who is prophecizing doom for
   unparalleled, living beauty?
Venice the Byzantine, Gothic, Renaissance, Baroque, with a touch
of the East.

The bells of noon, one after another – the entire City tolling –
set Venice asea, toward the ship that carried my family.
They waved at me from the deck, I at them from the shore, a short while later
   we were all together again.

The Honorable Lion wanted to descend from his pillar heights to share in our
   joy
but reconsidered, thinking it unseemly to behave thus with the City's symbol.
In contrast, the Doge's Palace, in all its splendor, started
dancing lightly on its slender pillars,
its supporting arches offering no resistance.
Only we noticed.

We continued on our way and arrived all five of us (I don't remember how)
at the little Piazza with a well at its navel and our inn at its edges.
The four of them still drunk from their journey and from the City made of
such stuff as dreams are made of, looked at me, I at them, and we all laughed.
A day abounding with happiness.
We were together again, all five of us.

Immersed in its dream Venice sails on bright waves toward the ship. The

שְׁקוּעָה בַּחֲלוֹמָהּ שָׁטָה וְנָצְיָה צְלוּלַת גַּלִּים לִקְרַאת הָאֳנִיָּה.
קַמְרוֹנֵי סַן מַארְקוֹ קוֹרְנִים מִתּוֹךְ הַמַּיִם.
CASA D'ORO, תַּחְרָה שֶׁל אֶבֶן, זָהָבָּה יוֹתֵר.
בַּרְטוֹלוֹמֵאוֹ קוֹלִיאוֹנִי, פָּרָשׁ גֵּאֶה, אֵינוֹ עוֹזֵב אֶת קַמְפּוֹ סַן גְּ'וֹבַנִי אֶ פָּאוֹלוֹ. אֵינִי שׁוֹמֵעַ,
אַךְ בְּטוֹרוֹ דֶל אוֹרְלוֹגְיוֹ אֲנִי רוֹאֶה אֶת הַפַּטִישִׁים יוֹרְדִים בִּידֵי שְׁנֵי גַּבְרְתָנִים עַל זוּג
הַפַּעֲמוֹן
בִּשְׁתֵּים־עֶשְׂרֵה עַל הַדַּקָּה. הָאֳנִיָּה עוֹגֶנֶת.
רִאשׁוֹן יוֹרֵד בְּרִיצָה אֶל זְרוֹעוֹתַי בְּנִי הַקָּטָן —
מִי דִּבֵּר כָּאן עַל מָוֶת?

domes of San Marco shine from the water.

Casa D'Oro, stone lace, is more golden still.

Bartolomeo Colleoni, noble horseman, never leaves the Campo San
Giovanni

e Paolo. I can't hear, but in Torre dell'Orologio I can still see

the hammers in the hands of two gentleman falling on the bell's husk

at exactly noon. The boat anchors.

First to rush off the boat and into my arms is my youngest son –

who spoke here a word on death?

אברהם

זָבַחְתִּי.
בְּלִבִּי
זָבַחְתִּי.
דָּמִי בְּדְמֵי הָהָר
שְׁתוּקִים כָּאֶבֶן.
הַיּוֹם כָּבָה.
אֲנִי
לֹא אָב.
אָב בְּלִי בֵּן לֹא אָב.
רָחָם. רָחָם
מִן הַמָּקוֹם הַזֶּה
אֵין
שִׁיבָה.

300

AVRAHAM

I slaughtered.
In my heart
I slaughtered.
My blood in the mountain's blood
is as silent as stone.
Day is done.
I am
no *av*
no father.
Father with no son is no Av.
Raham. Raham
from this place
there is no
returning.

אב

כְּמוֹ שֵׁנָה בְּלִי עַפְעַפַּיִם
כְּמוֹ קוֹל בְּלִי צְלִיל
אֶצְבָּעוֹת בְּלִי יָד
אָב שֶׁבְּנוֹ אָבַד

מִתְאַלֵּם לְאַט.

FATHER

Like a lidless sleep
like a soundless voice
fingers with no hand
the father of a lost son

slowly becomes mute.

בלי שם

כְּמוֹ עַלְוָה מְשֻׁלֶּכֶת בָּרוּחַ.
כְּמוֹ קְרָעִים שֶׁל נוֹף.
כְּמוֹ יְבָבַת לַיְלָה.
כְּמוֹ עֶרְווֹנוֹ הָאָדֹם שֶׁל הַסַּהַר.
כְּמוֹ תְּהוֹם אַרְבַּע לִפְנוֹת בֹּקֶר.

לֹא כְּמוֹ

UNTITLED

Like leaves driven in the wind.
Like tattered remnants of a scene.
Like a night's sobbing.
Like the moon's red blindness.
Like the abyss of four in the morning.

Not like

נטוש

נָטַשְׁתִּי.

הָרַכֶּבֶת נָסְעָה וְנָסְעָה וְנָסְעָה.

הִיא גָּמְעָה אֲרָצוֹת בְּטַאק טַאק טַאק.

הָיְתָה מְלֵאָה נְבוּאַת לֵב.

לֹא נִשְׁאֲרוּ מִמֶּנִּי אֶלָּא פָּנַי וְגוּפִי.

פָּנַי הִתְקַשּׁוּ וְרָזוּ.

כַּמָּה שִׁלֵּם אָבִי כְּדֵי לִנְטֹשׁ אוֹתִי

מֵרֹב אַהֲבָה לִנְטֹשׁ אוֹתִי.

לָקְחוּ אֶת בֵּיתוֹ.

לָקְחוּ אֶת כְּבוֹדוֹ אֶת תְּמִימוּתוֹ.

אִמִּי וַאֲחוֹתִי בָּכוּ. הַתִּקְוָה הָפְכָה מְגֻחֶכֶת.

הַשָּׁמַיִם הִשְׁתַּנּוּ.

מֵרֹב אוֹר רָאוּ עֵינַי שָׁחוֹר.

הַקַּרְקַע בָּעֲרָה מִתַּחַת לָרַגְלַיִם.

הַשֵּׁנָה נִמְלְטָה מִמֶּנִּי, בִּקְשָׁה לַחֲזֹר הַבַּיְתָה.

אֵיזֶה צְחוֹק. הֵם לֹא יָדְעוּ מָה

הֵם לֹא יָדְעוּ כְּלוּם לֹא יָדְעוּ

לֹא יָכְלוּ לָדַעַת שָׁנָה וְחָדְשַׁיִם וְלֹא יָכְלוּ

לֹא לָדַעַת וְלֹא כְּלוּם מַשֶּׁהוּ גִּמְגֵּם בִּי

שִׁבְעִים שָׁנָה גִּמְגֵּם בִּי מַה זֶּה עוֹזֵר

הָרִיק הוּא רִיק אִלְמָלֵא הָיָה רִיק

הָיָה מִתְמַלֵּא בַּמֶּה הָיָה מִתְמַלֵּא

בַּמֶּה? בִּדְמָעוֹת?

ABANDONED

I was abandoned.
The train traveled on and on and on.
It swallowed up countries one two three.
It was full of foreboding.
Nothing was left of me but my body and my face.
My face hardened and grew thin.
How much did my father pay to abandon me
from an abundance of love abandoning me.
They took his home.
They took his honor his innocence.
My mother and sister wept. Hope became absurd
the skies changed.
From so much light my eyes saw darkness.
The ground underfoot burned.
Sleep fled from me, begged to go home.
What a joke. They didn't know what
they didn't know nothing they didn't know
couldn't know a year and two months and they couldn't
not know anything something stuttered in me
seventy years stuttered in me what good does it do
this emptiness is emptiness if it weren't emptiness
it would fill up with what would it fill up
with what? With tears?

הוא

הוא תּוֹקֵף אוֹתִי.
כָּל הַזְּמַן הוּא תּוֹקֵף אוֹתִי.
הוּא אֵינוֹ מַנִּיחַ לִי.
גַּם לֹא בַּלַּיְלָה.
הוּא מִתְיַשֵּׁב עַל לוּחַ לִבִּי.
אֲנִי חוֹלֵם עָלָיו.
הָיִיתִי זוֹרֵק אוֹתוֹ, מְחַסֵּל אוֹתוֹ
הָיִיתִי שׁוֹבֵר לוֹ אֶת הָרֹאשׁ.
אַחַר־כָּךְ הוּא מִתְחַנֵּף כְּמוֹ חָתוּל:
שַׁלְוָה, שָׁלוֹם נִצְחִי, הוּא לוֹחֵשׁ, דְּאִיָּה קַלִּילָה
לְאֶרֶץ־אֵין־גְּבוּלוֹת.
לֹא עוֹד אֶחָד, לְבַד.
אוּלַי. אוּלַי כָּךְ. אוּלַי אֶפְשָׁר שֶׁכָּךְ.
אֵינֶנִּי רוֹצֶה לַחְשֹׁב עָלָיו.
אֲבָל אֲנִי חוֹשֵׁב.
אִי אֶפְשָׁר לָדַעַת אֵיךְ הוּא בֶּאֱמֶת.
לְהִתְיַדֵּד אִתּוֹ?
הוּא מַפְרִיעַ לִי בְּעוֹדִי קוֹרֵא סֵפֶר.
אֲנִי יוֹשֵׁב לִפְנֵי הַבַּיִת וּמַאֲזִין לְצוּפִית
וְהִנֵּה, הוּא מוֹפִיעַ.
רַק בִּכְתָבַי עָלָיו הוּא זוֹנֵחַ אוֹתִי.
אַתָּה שׁוֹאֵל אֵיךְ קוֹרְאִים לוֹ?
הוּא.

זֶה שְׁמוֹ. הוּא הוּא.
כַּמָּה יָפוֹת הַנַּסְטוּרְצִיּוֹת וְהַגּוּרִיּוֹת
בָּאוֹר הָרַךְ.

308

HE

He attacks me.
He attacks me all the time.
He won't leave me alone.
Not even at night.
He sits on the tablet of my heart.
I dream of him.
I would toss him away, finish him off
break open his head.
Afterwards he comes purring and placating like a cat:
Tranquility, eternal peace, he whispers, an easy flight
to the land-with-no-borders.
Not one more, alone.
Maybe. Maybe this way. Maybe it's possible this way.
I don't want to think about him.
But I do.
There's no knowing what he's really like.
Should I befriend him?
He bothers me while I'm reading a book.
I sit by my house, listening to the honey-sucker bird
and there he appears.
Only when I write about him does he leave me be.
You ask what his name is?
He.

That's his name. He is he.
How beautiful are the nasturtiums and the buttercups
in the gentle light.

אִם תְּתָאֵר לְעַצְמְךָ לֹא
לִהְיוֹת קַיָּם (אַתָּה מְסֻגָּל? וּבְעֶצֶם, לְשֵׁם מָה?), לֹא
לְהַרְגִּישׁ נִרְדָּף, לֹא לְפַחֵד, לֹא
לִהְיוֹת גַּלְמוּד, לֹא
לָחוּשׁ קִנְאָה, זִכָּרוֹן לֹא
לִקְשֹׁר בִּכְאֵב, לֹא
לַחְשֹׁב עַל מַה שֶׁאָבַד, בִּכְלָל לֹא
לַחְשֹׁב, לֹא טוֹבוֹת וְלֹא
רָעוֹת, לֹא לְהַעֲלוֹת עַל הַדַּעַת שְׁגִיּוֹת שֶׁשָּׁגִיתָ, לֹא
כִּשְׁלוֹנוֹת, לֹא הַכְרָעוֹת מֻטְעוֹת וְלֹא
לְהַרְהֵר שׁוּב וָשׁוּב בְּחֹסֶר הַבּוּשָׁה, לֹא
לְאַבֵּד עֶשְׁתּוֹנוֹת בִּגְלַל אִי-צֶדֶק אוֹ עָוֶל, לֹא
לִרְצוֹת, לֹא לְבַקֵּשׁ דָּבָר, לֹא
לִכְסֹף, לֹא לָחוּשׁ חֶסְרוֹן כָּלְשֶׁהוּ – אוֹ אָז
(תָּאֵר לְעַצְמְךָ) עָשׂוּי לִהְיוֹת הַלֹּא כְּלוּם
מְקוֹם נֶפֶשׁ חָבִיב אוֹ לֹא
לִהְיוֹת.

IF

If you imagine not
existing (can you? and actually, what for?), not
feeling persecuted, not being afraid, not
being alone, not
feeling jealousy, memory not
being tied to pain, not
thinking about what's been lost, not
thinking at all, not good things not
bad, not pondering mistakes you've made, not
failures, not wrong decisions and not
thinking again and again on the shamelessness, not
losing your mind because of an injustice or wrongdoing, not
wanting, not wanting a thing, not
desiring, not feeling lack of any sort – or then
(just imagine) the nothing may be
a pleasant place to rest or not
to be.

אם בתי

אֵיךְ רַק הַיּוֹם מִקֵּץ שִׁשִּׁים שָׁנָה, בְּקָרוֹב־בְּקָרוֹב שִׁשִּׁים וְשָׁלֹשׁ
יָצָאת מֵהַמִּסְגֶּרֶת שֶׁעַל שֻׁלְחָנִי
וְהֶעֱרַתְּ אוֹתִי לְנוֹרְאוֹת מוֹתֵךְ
אֵם בִּתִּי, כָּל־כָּךְ אִלֶּמֶת.
אֵיךְ הִתְנַפֵּל מִן הַמַּאֲרָב הַנָּבָל הַזָּקֵן
חָמַד אֶת גּוּפֵךְ הַצָּעִיר, הַצָּמֵא לְשִׂמְחָה
וְשָׁפַךְ עָלָיו אֵשׁ, אֵשׁ, אֵשׁ
וְלֹא מָצָאת מוֹצָא מִבֵּין הַשְּׁבָרִים
לְכוּדָה כְּמוֹ צִפּוֹר־יַעַר בִּשְׂרֵפַת יַעַר
הִצְטָרַפְתְּ לַאֲחוֹתִי, הִצְטָרַפְתְּ לְהוֹרַי.
לְאָן חִלְחֲלָה הַזְּוָעָה
לְאֵיזֶה מְעָרוֹת מֹחִי, קִפְלֵי לִבִּי
שֶׁשָּׁם יָשְׁבָה בַּמִּסְתּוֹר כָּל הַשָּׁנִים הָאֵלֶּה
בִּי שֶׁנִּשְׁאַרְתִּי חַי

THE MOTHER OF MY DAUGHTER

How is it that only today sixty, almost sixty-three, years later
you stepped out of the frame on my desk
and woke me to the horrors of your death,
mother of my daughter, ever silent.
How he attacked you from the ambush, that old villain
coveting your young body thirsty for joy
and poured on it fire, fire, fire
and you found no way out from among the broken pieces
trapped like a forest-bird in a forest fire
you joined my sister, you joined my parents.
Where did that terror penetrate
to what caverns of my brain, folds of my heart
where did it sit in hiding all these years
in me who lived

איזו שמחה

אֵיזוֹ שִׂמְחָה! נִין נוֹלַד לָנוּ – וְאֵיזֶה נִין!
גָּדוֹל כְּמוֹ שָׁתִיל שֶׁל סֶקְווֹיָה, רֹאשׁ כְּיָרֵחַ שֶׁהִתְאַחֵד עִם הַשֶּׁמֶשׁ.
עֵינַיִם כָּחֹל עָמֹק, אָמַרְתִּי, עִם שֶׁמֶץ חוּם. כְּמוֹ יַהֲלוֹמִים כֵּהִים שֶׁל
אֵשׁ כְּחֻלָּה, אָמַרְתְּ. עִשְׂבֵי הַדֶּשֶׁא הֵחֵלּוּ לִרְקֹד, יַרְגְּזִים, קִיכְלִים וּבַלְבּוּלִים
פָּתְחוּ בְּמַקְהֵלָה, דּוּכִיפַת הִגִּיבָה בְּהֶן-הֵן שֶׁל רֹאשָׁה
הַכֶּלֶב הַלָּבָן הֵרִים אֶת קְצוֹת פִּיו, הֲרֵי הוּא מְחַיֵּךְ! וְהֶחָתוּלָה הַפַּרְסִית
בְּתִסְפֹּרֶת קַיִץ עָשְׂתָה פַּרְצוּף שֶׁל שְׁאֵלָה: לְשִׂמְחָה מַה זֹּה עוֹשָׂה?
לֹא יָדַעְתִּי שֶׁהִיא בְּקִיאָה בַּמְּקוֹרוֹת.
פְּנֵי הַבְּרִיּוֹת הִתְבַּהֲרוּ פִּתְאֹם, כְּאִלּוּ לֹא הָיָה עוֹד לָמָה לִדְאֹג
לֹא נִשְׁמְעָה אֲפִלּוּ לֹא סִירֶנָה אַחַת בַּכְּבִישׁ הַקָּרוֹב, הַמְּכוֹנִיּוֹת גָּלְשׁוּ
כְּמוֹ שָׂחוּ בְּמַיִם וְגַם הַשָּׁמַיִם שָׁטוּ בְּשַׁלְוָה מֵאַיֵּי הַמְּאֻשָּׁרִים
לְאַיֵּי הַמְּאֻשָּׁרִים, הַבְּרוֹשׁ הַכָּחֹל קַד קִדּוֹת קַלּוֹת בָּרוּחַ וּבִרְאִי הָאֲוִיר הִשְׁתַּקְּפוּ רַבְסַבָּא
מְחַבֵּק רַבְסַבְתָּא וְנוֹשֵׁק עַל פִּיהָ כְּבֶן עֶשְׂרִים.

WHAT JOY

What joy! A great-grandson is born unto us – and what a great grandson!
Large as a sequoia tree, head like a moon that married the sun.
Deep blue eyes, I said, with a touch of brown. Like dark diamonds of
blue fire, you said. The blades of grass have begun to dance, the bulbuls
and warblers have all broken into song, a hoopoe has answered
with the nod-nod-nodding of her
head, the white dog has turned up the edges of his mouth, he's
smiling! And the Persian cat in a summer haircut has a querying expression:
"And this mirth, what doth it accomplish?"
I didn't know she was learned in the Jewish sources!
The faces of all living creatures have suddenly brightened, as though
there's nothing more to worry about not even a single wailing siren
can be heard from the nearby road, the cars flow as though swimming in
water and the skies also sail peacefully from the Isles of the Blessed to the
Isles of the Blessed, the araucaria tree bows gently in the wind and in the air's
mirror one can see a great-grandfather embracing a great-grandmother
and kissing her on the mouth as though he were a boy of twenty.

בְּהַפְצִיעַ הַשֶּׁמֶשׁ מֵעַל גִּבְעַת הַמּוֹרֶה
וְהַגִּלְבֹּעַ מִתְעַרְטֵל מֵעַרְפִּלֵּי בֹּקֶר כְּאִלּוּ הָיָה הַיָּה אַנָאפּוּרְנָה
וְהָעֵמֶק מִתְגַּלֶּה בְּבַת אַחַת בְּכָל יָפְיוֹ הָאֲבִיבִי
וַאֲנִי יוֹשֵׁב וּמַקְשִׁיב לַשָּׁקוֹן מֵהַפַּרְטִיטָה הַשְּׁנִיָּה שֶׁל בַּאךְ
וְשַׁעַר אַחַר שַׁעַר נִפְתָּח וְאֵין שׁוֹמֵר נוֹרָא מִקּוֹדְמוֹ בַּפֶּתַח
וּלְאַט אֲנִי מַשִּׁיל מִמֶּנִּי אֶת יִצְרֵי הָרַע וְאֶת אַכְזְרִיּוֹתַי הָאֱנוֹשִׁית
וְתוֹפֶסֶת אֶת מְקוֹמָם מֵעֵין חֶמְלָה, חֶמְלָה עַל כָּל הַקַּיָּם
וְרָצִיתִי לוֹמַר: גַּם עַל הַלֹּא קַיָּם, כִּי הֲרֵי כֻּלָּנוּ נִדּוֹנִים.
וּלְפֶתַע נִרְאָה לִי צִבְעָן שֶׁל הַחֲטָמִיּוֹת הַשָּׁנָה אָדֹם
שֶׁעוֹד לֹא רָאִיתִי כָּמוֹהוּ.

הוֹ, כָּל הָאֲרָצוֹת שֶׁזָּכִיתִי לִרְאוֹת מִמַּעֲרָב עַד מִזְרָח
הַכִּכָּרוֹת הַקְּטַנּוֹת הַמַּמְתִּיקוֹת סוֹד, הַפִּנּוֹת הָאַלְמוֹת
שֶׁאֵינָן מְגַלּוֹת מִי בָּא מֵעֶבְרָן, הַגְּשָׁרִים, קְטַנִּים כִּגְדוֹלִים
וְהַמַּיִם הַזּוֹרְמִים אִטִּיִּים כַּנֶּצַח וּזְרִיזִים כִּמְשַׂחֲקֵי מַחֲבוֹאִים
אוֹ שׁוֹצְפִים בְּבוֹאָם מֵהֶהָרִים הָרְחוֹקִים, מֵהַהִימָלָיָה אוֹ מֵהַטַּטְרָה.
וְהִנֵּה הַמִּלְחָמוֹת הַקַּיָּמוֹת תָּמִיד הִשְׁתִּיקוּ אֶת עַצְמָן כָּלִיל
לִכְבוֹד שִׁיר זֶה שֶׁהוּא שִׁיר תּוֹדָה
תּוֹדָה עַל שֶׁאָהַבְתִּי נֶעֱנְתָה בְּאַהֲבָה וְלֹא נִשְׁאַרְתִּי לְבַדִּי בְּזִקְנָתִי
תּוֹדָה עַל שֶׁלֹּא כָּל הַפָּנִים שֶׁעוֹבְרוֹת עַל פְּנֵי עֵינֶיהֶן בּוֹהוֹת
תּוֹדָה שֶׁכָּךְ וְתוֹדָה שֶׁעוֹד הָיִיתִי מְסֻגָּל לוֹמַר כָּל זֹאת.
אֵין בִּרְצוֹנִי לְהִפָּרֵד. בְּרוּכִים הַבָּאִים אַחֲרַי.

WITH DAY BREAKING

With day breaking in sunlight over the hills
and the Gilboa mountain rising from morning mists as if it were the
   Annapurna
and the valley revealing itself all at once in its full spring beauty
and me sitting here and listening to the chaconne from Bach's second partita
and gate after gate opening with no guard worse than his predecessor at the
   entrance
slowly I shed all ill-will and human cruelties
a kind of compassion taking their place – compassion for all that exists
and, I wanted to say, also for what doesn't, for we are all sentenced.
Suddenly, the color of the hibiscus flower this year is a red
I've never seen before.

Oh, all the lands I've seen from west to east
the little piazzas sweet with their secrets, the silent corners
never revealing who is on the other side, the bridges, small and large alike
the waters flowing as slowly as eternity, as fast as in a game of hide-and-seek
or streaming torrential from the distant mountains, the Himalayas or Tatras.
And then there are the wars existing always that have quieted themselves
entirely in honor of this song which is a song of thanks and praise,
thanks that my love was answered with love and I wasn't left alone in my old
   age
thanks that not every face passing by has staring eyes
thanks for that and thanks I'm still able to say all this.
I don't want to say good-bye. Welcome to all
who come after me.

נוסח בקט

אַתָּה כּוֹתֵב?

לֹא. אֲנִי לֹא.

אָז מִי כּוֹתֵב?

מִנַּיִן לִי?

אָז מִי אִם לֹא אַתָּה?

לָמָּה אֲנִי?

יֵשׁ עוֹד מִישֶׁהוּ בַּחֶדֶר?

אֵינֶנִּי רוֹאֶה.

מָתַי כֵּן?

כֵּן, מָתַי?

אֱמֹר אַתָּה.

בִּזְמַן שֶׁעוֹד הָיִינוּ בְּנֵי אָדָם.

וּמַה אֲנַחְנוּ עַכְשָׁו?

כֵּן, מַה.

אַחַר כָּל הַ־

אַתָּה רוֹצֶה מַה?

שִׂמְחָה, לִגְרֹם שִׂמְחָה.

הוֹ, כֵּן, שִׂמְחָה.

שֶׁיִּשְׂמְחוּ קְצָת.

עַל מַה?

עַל מַה שֶׁאַתָּה כּוֹתֵב.

אֵינְךָ שׁוֹמֵעַ?

מַה?

אֶת הַהִתְאַלְּמוּת.

שׁוֹמְעִים הִתְאַלְּמוּת?

מִי שֶׁמַּקְשִׁיב, שׁוֹמֵעַ.

אֵיזוֹ הִתְאַלְּמוּת?

שֶׁל הַמִּלִּים. הַמִּלִּים הַדּוֹמְמוֹת.

מִי יָכוֹל הָיָה לָדַעַת

כֵּן.

320

AFTER BECKETT

Do you write?

No. Not me.

Then who writes?

How would I know?

Then who if not you?

Why me?

Is there anyone else in the room?

I can't see.

When yes?

Yes, when?

You tell me.

When we were still human beings.

And what are we now?

Yes, what.

After all the

You want what?

Happiness, to bring happiness.

Oh, yes, happiness.

That they might be a little happy.

About what?

About what you've written.

Can't you hear?

What?

The becoming mute.

You can hear something becoming mute?

The one who listens, hears.

What is becoming mute?

The words. The silent words.

Who could have known

Yes.

מַה מִלִּים יְכוֹלוֹת לְחוֹלֵל.

כֵּן. מִי.

הַקַּיִץ הוֹלֵךְ וְדוֹעֵךְ.

בָּרוּךְ הַשֵּׁם.

אַתָּה עוֹד בַּלֹּא שֶׁלְּךָ?

לֹא.

מְאָחָר. צָרִיךְ לוֹמַר שָׁלוֹם.

מִסְתַּבֵּר.

אֲבָל חֹשֶׁךְ.

יֵשׁ בְּרֵרָה?

What words can make happen.

Yes. Who.

The summer is fading.

Thank god.

You are still in your no?

No.

It's late. We have to say good-bye.

Seems so.

But the darkness.

Is there any choice?

NOTES

The untitled epigraph poem is from Ruebner's tenth poetry collection כמעט שיחה (*Almost a Conversation*, 2011).

Biblical citations in these notes are from the Jewish Publication Society (JPS) translation unless otherwise indicated.

I / TESTIMONY

The poems in this section are from Ruebner's first two collections, האש באבן (*The Fire in the Stone*, 1957) and שירים למצוא עת (*Poems Seeking Time*, 1961), with the exception of "This Night," taken from Ruebner's 1970 collection אין להשיב (*Unreturnable*).

TESTIMONY

LINE 3: The word here rendered as "parched" – צחיח – is a hapax legomenon in the Hebrew Bible, appearing only in Ezekiel 24:7–8. In these two verses, the word is collocated both times with the word "rock" – צחיח סלע.

[LIKE AN ECHOLESS VOICE]

LINE 8: Genesis 28:12: "And [Jacob] dreamed, and behold a ladder set up on the earth, and the top of it reached to heaven; and behold the angels of God ascending and descending on it."

AMONG THESE MOUNTAINS

LINE 6: The Hebrew word *tav*/תו, rendered here as "mark," appears a single time in the Hebrew Bible, in Ezekiel 9:4.

LINE 7: The line echoes the verse פתח לנו בעת נעילת שער כי פנה יום/*petach lanu sha'ar, be'et ne'ilat sha'ar, ki fanah yom* ("open for us a gate, at the hour the gate is sealed, for the day has turned") – from the Yom Kippur liturgy. The verse is sung during the *ne'ilah* service, the final service of the fast day.

OBLIVION

LINES 1–4: Cf. Ezekiel 37:1–5. LINE 6: The imperative "Arise" is in the plural form.

MY LITTLE SISTER

Cf. The Song of Songs.

VOICES

Cf. Genesis 22:1–14, the story of the *Akedah,* the Binding of Isaac.

[JUST THE DAYS AND THE DOVES]

LINE 6 literally reads as "just the tears and the shells." Changes in lexis were inserted to recreate the strong rhythms and music of the Hebrew.

THIS NIGHT

This poem is built on the structure of the Four Questions from the Haggadah, the liturgy for the Passover seder. In the Haggadah, the four-part answer to the leader's question "What makes this night different from all other nights?" repeats the formulaic response of "...on all other nights, we [did something]; this night we [do something different] ...." The Four Questions are traditionally recited by the youngest person at the Passover feast.

CHILDREN

LINES 3–4: Cf. Genesis 28:10–12.

LINE 6: Cf. Hosea 10:8; Isaiah 32:13.

FATHER AND INFANT

LINE 19: Cf. Genesis 2:23.

MY SISTER

SECTION 2, LINE 7: The reference to "unblessed lips" (שפתיים בלי קדוש/ *sefatayim beli kiddush*) alludes to the ceremonial blessing over the wine recited on the Sabbath and holidays, and to the blessing over wine recited under the bridal canopy at the traditional marriage ceremony.

OLD KING DAVID

First published in the 1961 collection *Poems Seeking Time,* this poem was significantly revised by Ruebner for his 2005 anthology *Traces of Days: New & Selected Poems.* It is the revised version which is used here. For the biblical episode referenced, see 1 Kings 1:1–4.

FINAL LINE: King David is commonly credited with composing the 150 poems and prayers that together constitute the Book of Psalms.

II / AS LONG AS

The poems in this section are all from Ruebner's book כל עוד (*As Long As*, 1967).

SOMEONE WILL SAY

LINE 6: For "image of a memory," *tzelem zikharon*/צלם זיכרון, see Genesis 1:27: "And God created man in his own image, in the image of God [*tzelem elohim*/צלם אלוהים] created He him....."

SHE WAS

LINE 4: The "dining hall" reference is to the communal eating arrangement once the norm in kibbutz life.

LINE 14: For "like darkness over the deep" see Genesis 1:2.

FROM THE SHADOW IN MY EYES

LINES 6 AND 11: For "Who is she who rises" see Song of Songs 3:6 and 8:5.

LINE 7: For "I lift my eyes to the hills" see Psalm 121:1.

THE SWORD

The title and final line of the poem together evoke the turning sword (החרב המתהפכת) placed outside the Garden of Eden to prevent entry. Cf. Genesis 3:24: "[God] drove the man out, and stationed east of the Garden of Eden the cherubim and the fiery ever-turning sword, to guard the way to the Tree of Life" (New Jewish Publication Society translation).

LINE 5: The Hebrew phrase *asher ahavta*/ אשר אהבת, rendered here as "that you loved," evokes God's words to Abraham when instructing him to sacrifice his son Isaac on the hilltop. See Genesis 22:2: "Take now thy son, thine only son, whom thou lovest [אשר אהבת]...."

DISTANCE YOURSELF, DON'T

The "you" in the poem is female.

AWAKENING (2)

In Ruebner's collection *As Long As*, two separate poems are titled "Awakening"; the first appears on page 8 of that collection, and the second on page 53. To avoid confusion, I've added a number "2" to the second "Awakening" poem.

[AS LONG AS]

This eponymous poem stands as the epigraph poem to Ruebner's 1967 collection.

LINE 8: For "and it is good," *ki tov*/ כי טוב, see Genesis 1:3–4. The *ki tov* formula is repeated six times in the creation process; see also Genesis 1:10, 12, 18, 21, 25. The biblical tone of the poem is also accentuated by the construction of the words immediately following "and it was good": אומר לאמור ("to say").

III / THE BATTLES OF THE NIGHT LEFT BEHIND

"The Mother's Face in the Palm of Her Hands" is from the 1967 collection כל עוד (*As Long As*). "This City" and "Summer" are from אין להשיב (*Unreturnable*, 1970), and "1983" and "Farewell from a Friend" are from ואל מקומו שואף (*And Hasteneth to His Place*, 1990). The remaining poems in this section are all from the collection שמש חצות (*Midnight Sun*, 1977).

THIS CITY [JERUSALEM]

The word "Jerusalem" does not appear in the Hebrew original; it was added here to elicit the immediate recognition of "this city" as Jerusalem, in keeping with the Hebrew reader's experience. The 1970 version of this poem included an additional opening section, omitted from the 2005 *New & Selected* collection. It is the later version of the poem that is given here.

SECTION 1: *BOUND ON HER BOULDERS*

The word "city" in Hebrew is gendered female

LINES 1–2: The words *olah*/עולה and *tamid*/תמיד closing these two lines and standing juxtaposed to each other are both technical biblical terms relating to daily sacrifices. Ruebner is intertwining them and punning on their different usages. Cf. for example Exodus 29:42 and Numbers 28:31, *olat tamid*/עולת תמיד (the daily burnt offering); Leviticus 6:6, *esh tamid*/אש תמיד (a perpetual fire shall be kept burning) and Exodus 27:20, *liha'alot ner tamid*/להע־לות נר תמיד (for the kindling of lamps continually).

LINE 3: The single Hebrew adjective used to describe the city, *homiyah*/הומיה, means noisy or bustling. However, a second denotation of the word is "longing," and the line clearly alludes to the Israeli national anthem "Hatikvah" which describes the Jewish soul as *homiyah*/הומיה – yearning, for 2,000 years, to return to Zion.

SECTION 2: *STONES WANT TO FLOW*

LINE 11: "He who sleeps and his heart is awake" – Cf. Song of Songs 5:2: "I sleep but my heart is awake. Listen! My lover is knocking" (New International Version translation). In the biblical verse, the speaking voice is female.

SECTION 4: *OPEN AND QUIET SKIES*

LINES 2–3: These two lines are a single line in the Hebrew original, encompassed in the phrase *achuzat elohim*/אלוהים אחוזת. This phrase – rendered here first as "God's treasured possession," then as "God-possessed" – evokes two separate meanings in Hebrew: God's estate or mansion (from the noun *achuzah*/אחוזה), and "in the grip of God" (from the root א ח ז, meaning "to clutch or hold fiercely").

RONDANINI PIETÀ

The reference here is to the unfinished marble sculpture Michelangelo worked on from the 1550s until the last days of his life. The sculpture is housed in the Castello Sforzesco in Milan, though it stood for many years in the Palazzo Rondanini in Rome, from which it took its name. In the sculpture, a standing Mary is grasping the dead body of Jesus as it seems to slip toward the ground. In his memoir Ruebner quotes the following passage by art critic Lutz Heusinger describing the sculpture thus: "The intermingling of mother and son becomes more and more complete, until one cannot know who is holding whom; is the mother holding the lean corpse of her son or is the son holding up the falling woman. Both of them are in great need of help; both stand before the world and the Creator as supplication and lament." See *A Short Long Life*, 104.

Ruebner included an earlier and longer version of this poem in his 1967 collection *As Long As*.

1983

SECTION 1: The final stanza of this section appears on a plaque on a statue by Israeli sculptor Shoshanah Heiman (1923–2009), in memory of Ruebner's lost youngest son, Moran. The statue stands near the Kibbutz Merchavia dining hall. The final line of this alludes, through the Hebrew phrase *lo ukal*/אוכל לא, to the unconsumed burning bush. Cf. Exodus 3:2.

SECTION 3 alludes to the prayer recited each morning by observant Jews: "Blessed are You O Lord who has given the rooster the understanding to distinguish between night and day."

FAREWELL FROM A FRIEND

Hebrew poet Dan Pagis was Ruebner's closest poetic colleague and life-long friend. Pagis passed away in 1983, after a battle with cancer. Ruebner writes that "it wouldn't be the absolute truth to say I continue talking to Dan...but neither would it be a lie. The dead are not mute if we aren't deaf." *A Short Long Life*, 121.

LINE 11: See Proverbs 18:21.

LINE 16: Moreh Hill overlooks the Jezreel Valley and Ruebner's home in Kibbutz Merchavia. For a biblical reference to the hill, see Judges 7:1.

IV / A GRAVEN AND A MOLTEN IMAGE

With the exception of "Memory of a Woman in the Egyptian Wing" (which is from *Midnight Sun*), all the poems in this section are from Ruebner's 1982 collection פסל ומסכה (*Pesel U'masekha*), here rendered as *A Graven and A Molten Image*. The collocation of *pesel*/פסל (idol, statue, graven image) and *masekhah*/מסכה (a molten image) is used four times in the Hebrew Bible, each time in the prohibition of idolatry. See Deuteronomy 27:15, Judges 17:3–4, Nahum 1:14. Ruebner's entire collection *Pesel U'masekhah* is composed of ekphrastic poems.

A list of the artworks with which each poem is in conversation appears at the end of the Hebrew collection *Pesel U'masekhah*. These attributions have been attached here to the English and Hebrew poetic texts where necessary for identification; the attributions, when used, are as Ruebner noted them.

WHY

Ruebner states that he wrote this poem on the poetry of Dan Pagis. Ruebner credits Pagis – who was imprisoned as a child in a Ukranian concentration camp before fleeing and making his way to Palestine – with writing "poetry of unparalleled power" on the Holocaust.

THE YOUTH

FINAL STANZA: The reference is to the Athenian King Aegeus and his son Theseus. As the tale is told, when Theseus returned from slaying the Minotaur, he forgot to change his ship's black sail to a triumphant white one, as instructed. His father, keeping anxious watch from the high cliffs for his son's return, saw the black sail and, thinking his son dead, plunged into the sea. The sea is thereafter named for him – the Aegean.

THE SMILE

LINE 12: In "Death is what the wakeful see, but in sleep – ," Ruebner is alluding to a fragment of Heraclitus.

A PAINTING AND A CONVERSATION

LINE 1: The terms "lesser light" and "greater light" allude to the Genesis creation story. Cf. Genesis 1:16: "And God made the two great lights: the greater light to rule the day, and the lesser light to rule the night; and the stars."

HORSE AND HIS RIDER

The full and formal identification of the painting behind this poem is "Equestrian Portrait of Guidoriccio da Fogliano," Palazzo Pubblico, Sienna. Also cf. Jeremiah 51:21: "And with thee will I shatter the horse and his rider, and with thee will I shatter the chariot and him that rideth therein."

ANGELUS NOVUS

The angel in this Klee watercolor, painted in 1920, was famously described by Walter Benjamin in his 1940 essay "Theses on the Philosophy of History":

... [the] Angelus Novus shows an angel looking as though he is about to move away from something he is fixedly contemplating. His eyes are staring, his mouth is open, his wings are spread. This is how one pictures the angel of history. His face is turned toward the past. Where we perceive a chain of events, he sees one single catastrophe which keeps piling wreckage upon wreckage and hurls it in front of his feet. The angel would like to stay, awaken the dead, and make whole what has been smashed. But a storm is blowing from Paradise; it has got caught in his wings with such violence that the angel can no longer close them. The storm irresistibly propels him into the future to which his back is turned, while the pile of debris before him grows skyward. This storm is what we call progress.

Benjamin owned the painting, which then came into the possession of Gershom Scholem. The painting now hangs in The Israel Museum in Jerusalem.

THE MEMORY

LINE 16: For "Come, little bride, light as a cloud..." cf. Song of Songs 4:8. Ruebner's original line has קלה (qalah: "light" as in "weight," "ease," or "little one," female) as a homophonic exchange for כלה (kallah: "bride"). The Hebrew reader will hear "bride" even as the visual marker is "light one."

V / POSTCARDS FROM

All the poems in this section are from שירים מאוחרים (*Latter Day Poems*, 1999).

FAR AWAY

The Hebrew word for soul, *neshama*/נשמה, is gendered female.

A POSTCARD FROM PRESSBURG-BRATISLAVA

Ruebner was born and raised in Pressburg-Bratislava, Slovakia. The city was annexed to neighboring Austria by Nazi Germany in 1938. The deracination of the Jewish population of Pressburg-Bratislava – approximately 15,000 people – began in 1941, with thousands of Jews sent to ghettos in other parts of Slovakia, and culminated in mid-1942 with the deportation of hundreds of Jews to the Auschwitz-Birkenau and Majdanek death camps.

A POSTCARD FROM SHASTIN: AUTUMN FIRES

Ruebner's mother was from Shastin, and Ruebner and his sister would spend a month every summer at his grandparents' house there. In his memoir Ruebner writes that it is Shastin "...that comes to me most often. The sky there, and time too, were wider and slower." Ruebner's detailed descriptions of Shastin – his grandparents' home, the houses and people, the nature of the days there – occupy pages in the memoir. See *A Short Long Life*, 35–39. As the laws and edicts against the Jews became increasingly more severe, Ruebner's parents and sister moved from Pressburg to the grandparents' house in Shastin in the summer of 1941, hoping to enjoy greater freedom there. It is from Shastin that they were deported to Auschwitz in June 1942.

A POSTCARD FROM BUDAPEST

LINE 8: "the tears of things" is from Virgil, *lacrimae rerum* in the original Latin. See *The Aeneid* Book I, line 464. Interestingly, the line appears at the beginning of an early example of ekphrastic verse, where Aeneas describes a mural depicting scenes from the Trojan War.

A POSTCARD FROM TEL AVIV

LINE 14: Hebrew writer S.Y. Agnon wrote the following of Jaffa, the ancient port city abutting on modern-day Tel Aviv: "Jaffa, belle of the seas, ancient city. Japheth, son of Noah, built it and gave her his name. But of all the Greek beauty of Japheth, all that remains is what human beings can't remove from her...." (translated by Barbara Harshav).

LINES 16–19: Legend has it that an outcropping of rocks near the port of Jaffa is where Greek Andromeda was chained (as punishment for her mother's boasting of Andromeda's great beauty). The Medusa-slaying Perseus rescued and wed her.

LINES 27–29: Ruebner is alluding to T.S. Eliot's "The Love Song of J. Alfred Prufrock": "I grow old … I grow old … / I shall wear the bottom of my trousers rolled" and "I have heard the mermaids singing, each to each. // I do not think that they will sing to me."

A POSTCARD FROM THE HEBRON REGION

LINE 2: Tradition has it that all the biblical patriarchs and matriarchs, with the exception of Rachel (who is buried near Bethlehem), are buried in the Cave of Machpelah ("cave of the doubled tomb") in Hebron, also known as Cave of the Patriarchs. Cf. Genesis 23:7–20, which describes Abraham's purchase of the site in order to bury his recently deceased wife Sarah there. The site is sacred to Jews and Muslims alike. In 1994, Jewish settler Baruch Goldstein went on a shooting spree at the site, resulting in the death of 29 Muslims, who were at prayer. Since then, Jewish and Muslim entrance into and worship in the cave has been strictly separated, regulated, and heavily guarded.

LINE 12: The phrase "stiff-necked" (קשה עורף), meaning stubborn, is used six times in the Bible as an epithet describing the Israelites. Cf. for example Exodus 33, verses 3 and 5.

FINAL LINE: Cf. Genesis 1:28: "And God said to them, Be fruitful, and multiply, and replenish the earth … ."

A POSTCARD FROM VIENNA

LINE 5: In his memoir, Ruebner notes that Vienna, home of the most illustrious European composers, writers and painters, was the first city where Jews were forced to scrub the pavements with toothbrushes. It was there, he writes, where Jews encountered humiliations greater than in any German city. See *A Short Long Life*, 123.

VI / HOW DO WE END THAT WHICH IS HAS NO END

The poems "Victim, Again," "Still Afraid?," "Footnotes to the Book of Job" and "One Plague and Another" are from כמעט שיחה (*Almost a Conversation*, 2002). The poems "Voices (2)" and "Audrey's Birds" are from יופי מאוחר (*Belated Beauty*, 2009). The poems "Man with a House," "It's Been Years" and "Question" are from שירים סותרים (*Contradictory Poems*, 2011).

The poems from *Almost a Conversation* in particular reflect the period when

the Israeli-Palestinian peace talks broke down entirely, and the second inti-
fadah began (October 2000 and onward).

VICTIM, AGAIN

LINE 11: Khan Younis is a Palestinian city and refugee camp in the south-
ern part of the Gaza Strip. The refugee camp was established in 1948 and
initially held 35,000 refugees, mostly from the Be'er Sheva area. The num-
ber of refugees (including descendants) registered with UNRWA is currently
72,000. Before and also after the 2005 unilateral Israeli disengagement from
the Gaza Strip, Khan Younis has been the site of frequent raids by the IDF
(Israel Defense Forces); ensuing battles in the densely populated area have
resulted in the deaths of children and other innocent civilians.

VOICES (2)

In the original Hebrew, this poem is titled "Voices." The number "2" was
added in order to distinguish this poem from an earlier poem by Ruebner,
bearing the identical title. See pages 16–17.

FINAL LINE: "The blood of a child" is an allusion to Hayim Nachman Bi-
alik's iconic poem "On the Slaughter" ("על השחיטה"), which was written
in response to the Kishinev Pogroms of 1903. The well-known lines which
Ruebner is referencing are:

And cursed is he who says "Avenge!"
Such revenge, vengeance for the blood of a small child,
Satan has not yet created.

STILL AFRAID?

LINE 4: Literally, "mark with a cross."

LINE 21: The Hebrew term for an Orthodox Jew, hared/חרד (or, more com-
monly, haredi), also means "fearful." Both denotations are resonant in this
line.

AUDREY'S BIRDS

The artist Audrey Bergner (b. 1927), wife to artist Yosl Bergner (b. 1920), was
born and raised in Australia, lived for many years in Europe, and has lived
in Israel for over fifty years. Both Audrey and Yosl have been lifelong friends
with Ruebner. The painting which this poems speaks to hangs above Rueb-
ner's dining table.

IT'S BEEN YEARS

LINE 11: The Hebrew original חבלי־חבלים, here rendered as "roped ago-
ny," plays on the strong sound similarity between chevel (rope) and cheivel

(agony). The possessive term חבלי (agony of) is most commonly used in the collocation חבלי־לידה (birth throes) and חבלי־משיח (pre-Messianic tribulations).

LINE 16: "How, oh how" – איכה – alludes to The Book of Lamentations, known in Hebrew simply as איכה after the text's first word. Cf. Lamentations 1:1.

FOOTNOTES TO THE BOOK OF JOB:

SECTION 12: Inger Christensen (1935–2009), Danish poet, novelist and essayist, was the most prominent poetic experimentalist of her generation.

SECTION 13: For the final line of the poem, cf. Job 1:21 and 2:9.

ONE PLAGUE AND ANOTHER

The ten poems in this series each refer to one of the Ten Plagues visited on Egypt (Exodus, chapters 7–12). As this series relies heavily on word similarities and end-rhymes, certain words have been added or changed in the English renderings in order to evoke similar sound patterns.

"The Blue above is bleached deep through"

FINAL LINE: Cf. the story of Cain and Abel, particularly Genesis 4:8–10.

"Lice have conquered you, Land of the Deer"

The phrase "the Land of the Deer" is a biblical appellation for the Land of Israel, accentuating its beauty and glory. See Daniel 11:16.

"Sweet-swarming is Hebrew on a foreign tongue"

The poem opens with the word arev/ערב – meaning "pleasant" or "sweet," as in a sweet voice (cf. Song of Songs 2:14). The same three root letters, ayin, resh, bet (ע ר ב), combine to make the word arov/ערוב, the fourth plague, a swarm of wild beasts. The line accentuates the sound similarity between the two words.

LINE 3: The line alludes to the Samaritans' belief that Mount Gerizim is the sacred and blessed site, as opposed to the neighboring Mount Eval (both mountains overlook the Palestinian city of Nablus, the biblical Shechem). Cf. Deuteronomy 27. The biblical chapter instructs the Israelites to follow the law upon entering the land, and lists the sins for which a person will be cursed.

"The Heart is Parched. The dirty blood shines."

LINE 2: The Hebrew original is "you [female]), me, you [male]." The second "you" was changed here to "he" to evoke the gendered address.

LINE 3: "God, Full of Compassion" (*El male rachamim*/אל מלא רחמים) are the opening words of the Hebrew prayer for the dead.

"Loathsome, what has happened, is happening, so much"

In the Hebrew original, the opening word of the poem, *harbeh*/הרבה, meaning "many" or "so much," has a strong sound similarity with the the Hebrew word for locusts – *arbeh*/ארבה – which appears in the third line of the poem and is the eighth plague in the Exodus story. In a similar fashion, the word "loathsome" opens the English version in order to evoke and anticipate the first syllable sound of the word "locusts" that appears two lines later.

FINAL LINE: The word "sin" was added to recreate the rhyme in the original.

"Oh Let the Darkness cover our eyes!"

LINE 3: Cf. Deuteronomy 21:7: "Our hands have not shed this blood" ("ידינו לא שפכו את הדם הזה"). Ruebner changes the *lo*/לא ("no" or "not") of the biblical verse into *halo*/הלא meaning, "indeed [it is]" or "is it not the case?"

VII / HISTORY

All the poems in this section, with the exception of the final one, are from Ruebner's collection כמעט שיחה (*Almost a Conversation*, 2002).

[MY FATHER WAS MURDERED]

In this poem, Ruebner references well-known Hebrew and Israeli scholars and writers, all of whom were close friends and colleagues. The references include: LUDWIG STRAUSS (German/Israeli scholar and writer, 1892–1953), LEA GOLDBERG (Hebrew poet, 1911–1970), YAAKOV (YANKELEH) SHABTAI (Israeli novelist and playwright, 1934–1981), DAN PAGIS (Israeli poet and Holocaust survivor, 1930–1986), ERNST NATAN (German/Israeli composer and lecturer, returned to Germany and died there), WERNER KRAFT (German/Israeli scholar and writer, 1896–1991), OZER RABIN (Israeli poet, 1921–1999) and YEHOSHUA LAKNER (Slovakian/Israeli composer, relocated to Switzerland and died there, 1924–2003).

Of Ludwig Strauss and Werner Kraft, Ruebner writes, "I owe them my poetic and spiritual existence" (59). The two German writers, immigrants like Ruebner (though of an older generation), became his mentors and, by Ruebner's own account, exercised the most lasting influence on his poetry. He states also that he believes it was their influence which contributed to the distinctiveness of his poetry and its difference from the canonic Hebrew poetry of his day. "Without these two," writes Ruebner, with expansive gratitude, "my life would have been immeasurably poorer" (*A Short Long Life,* 63).

Ruebner became friends with Lea Goldberg in the late 1940s, and it was Goldberg who published his first Hebrew poem (in 1950). After Goldberg's early death in 1970, her mother appointed Ruebner the literary executor of Goldberg's work.

Yaakov Shabtai lived on Merchavia, Ruebner's kibbutz, from 1957–1967.

Yehoshua Lakner was a childhood friend of Ruebner, born and raised in the same village. Lakner was also one of the eight youths who traveled with Ruebner to Palestine in 1941.

Additional names in the poem are: Ada, Ruebner's first wife, killed in a car accident in 1950; Moran, his youngest son, lost during a trip to South America in 1983; Eva is a reference to Eva Strauss, wife of Ludwig, and daughter of Martin Buber; Aya is Aya Goldstein, Ruebner's childhood sweetheart and one of the eight youths with whom he traveled overland to Palestine in 1941; Natan is Natan Sufrin, a photographer-friend.

MY FATHER

LINE 24: Shavei Tzion (literally "Returnees to Zion") is a moshav (a communal village) in the north of Israel, on the coastal road between Acre and Nahariya. It was founded in 1938 by German immigrants who arrived during the Fifth Aliyah (1929–1939).

BUT THIS LIGHT

LINES 13–16: The Hebrew word for "land," *aretz/*ארץ, is gendered female.

GUIDE FOR THE YOUNG POET

FINAL LINE: Cf. Genesis 3:19: "By the sweat of your brow shall you get bread to eat, until you return to the ground, for from it you were taken; for dust you are and to dust you shall return." (New Jewish Publication Society translation).

[ERASE YOUR TRACES]

This poem is from Ruebner's 1982 collection *A Graven and A Molten Image.* In his memoir, where he quotes this poem in full, Ruebner's states that he wrote this poem after viewing a series of Picasso's drawings of a bull, in which the details of the bull become fewer and fewer from draft to draft, until only a few lines are left.

FINAL LINE: The Hebrew word for "erase," מוחה, root letters מ ח ה, means also "to protest."

VIII / BELATED BEAUTY

All the poems in this section are from the collection יופי מאוחר (*Belated Beauty*, 2009).

PERFECTION

LINES 12 and 17: These lines are addressed directly to "Perfection" with the second person female pronoun את (*at*) in the Hebrew original. I've changed this to a third-person form in the English in order to avoid confusion with the previous "you," a male אתה (*atah*) in the poem.

MOONLIT NIGHT (2)

The "2" was added to the title to distinguish this poem from an earlier poem with the intentical title (see pages 212–13).

YOSL, YOSL

LINE 15: *toy'ber yoash* is Yiddish for "you deaf fellow."

CHIMES

LAST LINE: The tri-syllabic Hebrew word for chimes, *mitsilah*/מצילה, has a rhythm similar to "Galila," the name of Ruebner's wife of 60 years.

GIACOMETTI: WALKING MAN

This thirteen-line poem in the original Hebrew is a seventeen-line poem in its English rendering. The radical departure from the original line number is due to the inflected nature of Hebrew (whereby prepositions, articles and modals are added to the root word), in comparison to the non-inflection of English. As a result, the English line renderings were significantly longer than the original Hebrew. In order to preserve the text's visual representation of the Walking Man's sparsity and leanness, lines were added.

A reproduction of Giacometti's lithograph appears side by side with the poetic text in *Belated Beauty*. Ruebner owns the lithograph and it hangs above one of his desks.

THE OLD MAN AND BEAUTY

FINAL LINE: Cf. Exodus 3:13–14: "And Moses said to God: 'And when I come to the Israelites and say to them: The God of your fathers has sent me to you, and they ask me: What is His name? What shall I say to them?' And God said to Moses: 'I am that I am' [אהיה אשר אהיה]...." (New Jewish Publication Society translation). The enigmatic answer is also translated as "I am who I am" and "I will be who I will be"; the exact meaning of these words is the subject of vigorous debate among bible scholars.

POEM

LINE 2: For "and it is good" – cf. the Creation story, Genesis 1:1–31. The phrase "and God saw that it was good" – *ki tov* – is repeated six times during the creation week.

IX / BUT WHAT WOULD WE DO WITHOUT POEMS

All the poems in this section are from Ruebner's collection שירים סותרים (*Contradictory Poems*, 2011).

ONE CANNOT

LINE 2: Else Lasker-Schüler (1869–1945) was a German Jewish poet who lived the last years of her life in Jerusalem.

LINES 11–12: Cf. Psalms 137:1–3: "By the rivers of Babylon there we sat down and wept when we thought of Zion. There on the poplars we hung up our lyres, for our captors asked us there for songs." (New Jewish Publication Society translation).

POETRY'S SOLILOQUY

LINE 8: The phrase rendered here as "beaded rhymes" is simply *charuzim/* חרוזים – in the Hebrew original. The word *charuzim* means both rhymes and beads.

LINE 11: "all my glory inward" – cf. Psalms 45:14. The phrase is often used in the context of female modesty; the Hebrew word for poetry – *shirah*/שירה – is gendered female.

FINAL LINE: The reference in the final line is to the seven thin cows of Pharaoh's dream. Cf. Genesis 41:17–31. Joseph interprets these seven thin cows as seven years of famine which will follow seven years of plenty in the Land of Egypt.

NOT EVERY DAY

LINE 13: That "cursed war" is a reference is to the First Lebanon War (1982).

LINE 20: The allusion is to Benjamin, Joseph's brother and the youngest of Jacob's twelve sons. Cf. Genesis 35:18 and 42:38.

I THOUGHT I WOULDN'T WRITE EVEN ONE MORE LINE ON DEATH

LINE 16: Literally, "soul-restoring wind." For the phrase *meishiv nefesh*/מֵשִׁיב נֶפֶשׁ (soul-restoring), cf. Psalm 19:8.

LINE 18: "Hard clods of earth, not sweet" is an allusion to the blessing made for the dead, "May the clods of his dust be sweet" – *yimtiqu lo rigvei afaro*/ יִמְתְּקוּ לוֹ רִגְבֵי עֲפָרוֹ – meaning "May he rest in peace." The source of the blessing is believed to be Job 21:32–33: "For he is borne to the grave, and watch is kept over his tomb. The clods of the valley are sweet unto him ...."

LINE 21: Jewish burial practices dictate that the men of the *Chevra Kadisha* (literally "Holy Society," those responsible for preparing the dead for burial) ask forgiveness of the deceased at the gravesite for any offense or dishonor they may have unknowingly caused while bathing, preparing and burying the body.

HEBREW, MY LOVE

Ruebner's earliest writings were all in German, his native language. Ruebner continued to write in German for the first twelve years that he lived in Palestine/Israel (1941–1953). Strauss and Kraft both encouraged Ruebner to write in Hebrew, which he began to do in 1953, the year he married his second wife, Galila (who did not read German). Ruebner's first Hebrew poetry collection was published in 1957.

BEFORE PICASSO'S WEEPING WOMAN

The image in this painting, and in an entire series of "weeping women" paintings, is Dora Maar (1907–1997), Picasso's mistress-muse for many years. Dora Maar was a renowned photographer and talented painter in her own right, identified with the Surrealist movement. Picasso wrote, "For me, she is the weeping woman. For years I've painted her in tortured forms, not through sadism, and not with pleasure either; just obeying a vision that forced itself on me. It was the deep reality, not the superficial one. Dora, for me, was always a weeping woman ...." "The Weeping Woman" hangs in the Tate Gallery in Liverpool.

Coincidentally, this collection of Ruebner translations was completed at the Dora Maar House in Ménerbes, Provence – the house Picasso gave to Dora Maar at the end of their relationship. Dora Maar lived the last decades of her life in this house, in a reclusive state.

IN MY OLD AGE

Line 4: "the gate's closing" – *ne'ilat hasha'ar*/נעילת השער – contains an allusion to the end of Yom Kippur (the Day of Atonement) when the gates of heaven close and one may no longer pray to be inscribed and sealed in the Book of Life. The concluding prayer of the day is called *ne'ilah* – literally, closing.

Line 8: Ruebner uses the exact words from Psalms 116:10: "I trusted even when I spoke: 'I am greatly afflicted.'"

X / LAST ONES

All the poems in this section are from Ruebner's 2013 collection entitled אחרונים (*Last Ones*).

A WONDROUS WORLD:

LINE 13: The phrase for "ladybug" in Hebrew is *parat moshe rabeinu*/פרת משה רבינו – literally, "the cow-of-our-rabbi-moshe." Hence this line reads literally: "and the cow-of-our-rabbi-moshe (a wondrous cow, there's no denying)."

LINE 14: The *chatzav*/חצב flower referenced in the Hebrew is, actually, a squill; however, the name in English does not evoke the same familiarity and recognition that the Hebrew does. Hence, I've changed it to a hyacinth (which also offers some resemblance to the *chatzav* in sound).

THE CROWS WANT

LINE 16: The word here rendered as "dwelling place," *mishkan*/משכן, carries religious signification. Cf. Exodus 25:7–9 where God instructs the wandering Israelites to construct a *mishkan*, a sanctuary or dwelling place for the divine presence in the desert.

AVRAHAM

Avraham is the Hebrew name of Abraham, the biblical patriarch. The name is seemingly composed of two parts: *av* (father) and *raham*. The etymology and meaning of the word *raham* are unclear, though the biblical verse telling of Abraham's divine name-change (from Abram) connects the name to "a mutltitude of nations." See Genesis 17:5: "Thy name shall be Abraham; for the father of a multitude of nations have I made thee."

LINE 1: The opening and repeated word *zavachti*/זבחתי, here rendered as "I slaughtered," evokes ritual slaughter, as in a sacrifice. The poem is in dialogue with the story of the Binding of Isaac (Genesis 22:1–19). The verb *zavach*/

זבח does not appear in the biblical telling, though the word *mizbeach*/מזבח, altar, composed of the same three root letters – ז ב ח – does.

BRUEGHEL: THE HUNTERS IN THE SNOW

LINE 2 is from Kafka's short story "The Bucket Rider." A reproduction of this painting hangs over one of Ruebner's work-desks.

WHAT JOY

The thirteen lines of the Hebrew original have expanded to sixteen lines in the English due to the length of the original lines. A choice was made not to use run-over lines in order to convey the rapid flow and visual density of the original. Line-breaks have been respected wherever possible.

LINE 7: For "And this mirth, what doth it accomplish?" see Ecclesiastes 2:2.

WITH DAY BREAKING

This poem was published in *Ha'aretz* newspaper in the spring of 2012; it is also the signature poem in Ruebner's last book, *Last Ones* (Spring 2013).

LINE 1: Literally, "…over Moreh Hill." Givat Hamoreh overlooks the Jezreel Valley and Ruebner's home in Kibbutz Merchavia. For a biblical reference to the hill, see Judges 7:1.

LINE 2: For Mount Gilboa, see 1 Samuel 31:8 and 2 Samuel 1:21.

CODA: "AFTER BECKETT"

This poem, penned in the late summer of 2013, has not been published in Hebrew. Ruebner asked that it be included in this English collection.

CHRONOLOGY OF TUVIA RUEBNER

1924 JANUARY 30: Tuvia Ruebner is born in Pressburg-Bratislava, Slovakia, first child of Manfred Moritz (b. 1885) and Elisabet (b. 1899) Ruebner.

1929 APRIL 23: Sister Alice, nicknamed Litzi, is born.

1933 JANUARY 30: Adolph Hitler becomes Chancellor of Germany.

1937 Ruebner has his bar mitzvah in the Neologist Synagogue of Pressburg-Bratislava.

1938 MARCH 12/13: Nazi troops invade and annex Austria.

NOVEMBER 9/10: Kristallnacht, "The Night of Broken Glass."

1939 MARCH 15/16: Nazi troops seize Czechoslovakia (Jewish pop. 350,000).

APRIL 19: Slovakia passes its own version of the Nuremberg Laws. Together with all the Jews of his region, Ruebner is banned from school. He has completed 9th grade. He begins working as an electrician's apprentice, though this too is forbidden.

1941 APRIL 28: Ruebner leaves Slovakia, together with eight other youths, traveling eastward and overland to reach Mandate Palestine. Together with his youth movement group he is placed on Kibbutz Merchavia, in the Jezreel Valley, where he works as a shepherd and studies.

In the same summer, Ruebner's parents and little sister move to the grandparents' home in Shashtin, where they stay, hoping to evade some of the harsher edicts being imposed on Jews.

1942 JANUARY 15: Eighteen-year-old Ruebner receives the final letter from his parents.

JANUARY 20: Wannsee Conference in Berlin is held to coordinate the "Final Solution." Mass killings of Jews using Zyklon B begin at Auschwitz-Birkenau.

MARCH 24: The deportation of Slovak Jews to Auschwitz begins.

JUNE 6: Ruebner's parents and sister Litzi are deported from Shastin to Auschwitz on Transport 46. The grandparents are sent on a transport a month later.

1944 Marriage to Ada Klein from Kosice, Slovakia (1924–1950) at Kibbutz Merchavia.

JUNE 6: D-Day: Allied landings in Normandy on the coast of northern France.

SUMMER: Auschwitz-Birkenau records its highest-ever daily number of persons gassed and burned at just over 9,000. Six huge pits are used to burn bodies, as the number exceeds the capacity of the crematories.

1945 APRIL 30: Hitler commits suicide in his Berlin bunker.

MAY 7: Unconditional German surrender to the Allies.

1948 Israeli War of Independence (Palestinian *Nakba*) erupts. Ruebner is stationed for a short while in the evacuated Palestinian village of Sepphoris, near Nazareth.

1949 AUGUST 4: Daughter Miriam (Miriyami) is born.

1950 FEBRUARY: Ada and Tuvia are involved in a bus accident. Ada is killed; Tuvia is seriously injured. He spends three months in the hospital recuperating.

1951 Ruebner starts working as kibbutz librarian and teacher.

1953 Marriage to Galila Jizreeli, a pianist of Kibbutz Ein Harod. Ruebner starts composing poetry in Hebrew.

1955 Ruebner is awarded The Anne Frank Award for his translations of Agnon.

1956 APRIL 27: Son Idan is born.

1957 *The Fire in the Stone* – Ruebner's first poetry collection – published.

1960 OCTOBER 5: Son Moran is born.

1961 *Poems Seeking Time* is published.

1963–66 Ruebner works as the General Director of the Jewish Agency in Zurich.

1966 Begins teaching at Oranim College in Kiryat Tivon (Haifa).

1967 JUNE: The Six Day War between Israel and Syria, Egypt and Jordan. The West Bank and Gaza Strip are occupied; as of 2014, the West Bank remains occupied and under Israeli military rule.

As Long As is published.

1970 *Unreturnable* is published.

1973 OCTOBER: The Yom Kippur War.

1977 *Midnight Sun* is published.

1972 Begins teaching at Tel Aviv and Haifa Universities, in their Comparative Literature departments.

Daughter Miriyami leaves Israel and settles in Iceland, where she lives until today.

1974 Becomes a professor at Haifa University, where he remains until retirement in 1993.

1977 Son Idan leaves for Nepal, where he begins his training to become a Buddhist monk. Idan lives in Nepal until today.

1981 Ruebner is awarded the D. Steinberg Prize (Zurich).

1982 *A Graven and A Molten Image* is published.

SUMMER: The First Lebanon War. Ruebner's son Moran is called up as a reservist.

1983 Son Moran visits his parents in the US, where Ruebner is spending a sabbatical at Harvard. Moran continues from there to South America. After a few letters, all traces of him are lost.

1990 *And He Hasteneth to His Place* is published.

1992 Ruebner travels to India and Nepal.

1994 Ruebner is awarded the Christian Wagner Prize (Germany).

1995–2000 Four collections of Ruebner's poetry in German translation are published in Germany to great acclaim.

1999 Ruebner is awarded the Jeanette Schocken Prize (Germany) and the Paul Celan Translation Prize.

Latter Day Poems is published.

2000 OCTOBER: The Second Intifadah (Palestinian uprising) erupts. Waves of violence sweep through the Occupied Territories and Israel.

2002 *Almost a Conversation* is published.

2004 *Nasty Children's Rhymes and More* is published.

2005 *Traces of Days: New & Selected Poems* is published.

2006 Ruebner is awarded the Prime Minister's Prize for Hebrew Writers.

2007 *Everything that Came After* is published (poems and photographs). Ruebner is awarded the Jerusalem Prize.

2008 Ruebner is awarded The Israel Prize (the most prestigious Israeli prize) for his contribution to Israeli arts & letters, and the Theodor Kramer Prize (Austria).

2009 *Belated Beauty* is published.

2011 *Contradictory Poems* is published.

2012 Ruebner is awarded the Konrad-Adenauer Prize (Austria).

2013 Ruebner's 15th poetry collection, entitled *Last Ones*, is published.

BOOKS BY TUVIA RUEBNER

POETRY

The Fire in the Stone [האש באבן] 1957
Poems Seeking Time [שירים למצוא עת] 1961
As Long As [כל עוד] 1967
Poems by Tuvia Ruebner [שירים] 1970
Unreturnable [אין להשיב] 1970
Midnight Sun [שמש חצות] 1977
A Graven and A Molten Image [פסל ומסכה] 1982
And Hasteneth to His Place [ואל מקומו שואף] 1990
Latter Day Poems [שירים מאוחרים] 1999
Almost a Conversation [כמעט שיחה] 2002
Nasty Children's Rhymes and More [חרוזי ילדים קלוקלים ואחרים] 2004
Traces of Days: New & Selected Poems 1957–2005 [עקבות ימים: מבחר שירים] 2005
Belated Beauty [יופי מאוחר] 2009
Contradictory Poems [שירים סותרים] 2011
Last Ones [אחרונים] 2013

AUTOBIOGRAPHY

A Short Long Life [חיים ארוכים קצרים] 2006
   Published first in German (titled *Ein langes kurzes Leben*, fourteen editions to date) and then in Hebrew.

PHOTOGRAPHY

Everything that Came After [כל מה שאחר כך] 2007
This Too My Eyes Have Seen [גם זו ראו עיני] – with poems 2008

CRITICAL MONOGRAPH

Lea Goldberg 1980

POETRY COLLECTIONS IN GERMAN

Wüstenginster, translated by Efrat Gal-Ed and Christoph Meckel 1990
Granatapfel 1995
Rauchvögel 1957–1997, vol. 1 1998

Stein will Fliessen 1999
Zypressenlicht 1957–1999, vol. 2 2000
Wer hält diese Eile aus 2007
Spätes Lob der Schönheit 2010
Lichtschatten 2011
In Vorbereitung: Wunderbarer Wahn 2013

SELECTED TRANSLATIONS

FROM HEBREW INTO GERMAN

Im Wald und in der Stadt [ביער ובעיר] by S.J. Agnon (in *Schalom: Erzählungen aus Israel*) 1964

Der Treueschwur: Erzählung [שבועת אמונים] by S.J. Agnon 1965

Schira: Roman [שירה] by S.J. Agnon 1998

Der Vorabend: Erzählung [עם כניסת היום] by S.J. Agnon 2004

Erdichteter Mensch: Gedichte Hebräisch/Deutsch [איש בדוי] by Dan Pagis 1993

FROM GERMAN INTO HEBREW:

Fragments by Friedrich Schlegel 1982
Chapters by Goethe 1984
Essays by Aryeh Ludwig Strauss 1984
Man and Poetry by Aryeh Ludwig Strauss. (With Yedidya Peles) 1985
An Introduction to Aesthetics by Jean Paul 1985
Poems by Christoph Meckel. (With Asher Reich) 2002
Black-winged Angel by Milan Richter 2005

SELECTED EDITED COLLECTIONS

IN HEBREW:

Hebrew Studies in Literature by Aryeh Ludwig Strauss 1959
Poems by Lea Goldberg 1970
Remains of Life by Lea Goldberg (a posthumous collection) 1971
The Collected Poems of Lea Goldberg (Three volumes) 1973
The Writings of Lea Goldberg (Five volumes) 1972–79
Plays by Lea Goldberg 1979
On the Aesthetic Education of Man in a Series of Letters by Friedrich Schiller. Translated from German by Shimshon Eilat 1986

The Surrealist Manifesto by André Breton 1986

On Modern Art by Paul Klee. Translated from German by Shlomo
Tanay 1987

Something Will Be: Selected Poems of Paul Celan. Translated by Ben-Zion
Orgad 1987

Plotinus's Aesthetics 1987

Conversations with Kafka by Gustav Janouch 1988

From Lessing to Kafka by Werner Kraft 1988

On Dramatic Poetry by John Dryden. Translated from English by David
Eren 1988

Baudelaire by Walter Benjamin. Translated from German by David Eren 1989

The Duende Game and Its Principles by Frederico García Lorca. Translated
from Spanish, annotated and introduced by Renee Litvin 1989

The Devil in the Artists' Quarter by Eliezer Steinman 1992

IN GERMAN:

Briefwechsel Martin Buber-Ludwig Strauss, 1913–1953; edited by Tuvia Ruebner
and Dafna Mach 1990

Gesammelte Werke in vier Bänden / Ludwig Strauss; edited by Tuvia Ruebner
and Hans Otto Horch 1998–2001

INDEX OF POEM TITLES

BOOKS BY RACHEL TZVIA BACK

POETRY

Litany 1995

Azimuth 2001

The Buffalo Poems 2003

On Ruins & Return: Poems 1999–2005 2007

A Messenger Comes (Elegies) 2012

TRANSLATIONS

Lea Goldberg: Selected Poetry & Drama (play translation by T. Carmi) 2005

Night, Morning: Selected Poems of Hamutal Bar-Yosef 2008

With an Iron Pen: Twenty Years of Hebrew Protest Poetry 2009

CRITICAL WORK

Led by Language: the Poetry & Poetics of Susan Howe 2002